Numbered Voices

How Opinion Polling Has Shaped American Politics

Susan Herbst

THE UNIVERSITY OF CHICAGO PRESS *Chicago & London*

The University of Chicago Press, Chicago 60637
The University of Chicago Press, Ltd., London
© 1993 by The University of Chicago
All rights reserved. Published 1993
Paperback edition 1995
Printed in the United States of America
02 01 00 99 98 97 96 95   5 4 3 2

ISBN (cloth): 0-226-32742-6
ISBN (paper): 0-226-32743-4

Library of Congress Cataloging-in-Publication Data

Herbst, Susan
    Numbered Voices: how opinion polling has shaped American politics /
Susan Herbst
        p.   cm.—(American politics and political economy series)
    Includes bibliographical references and index.
    ISBN 0-226-32742-6 (alk. paper)
        1. Public opinion—United States.   2. Public opinion—United
States—History.   3. Public opinion polls.   4. Public opinion polls—
History.   5. Political participation—United States.   6. Political
participation—United States—History.   I. Title.   II. Series:
American politics and political economy.
HN90.P8H47   1993
303.3'8'0973—dc20   92-14256
                                                                          CIP

Numbered Voices

AMERICAN POLITICS AND POLITICAL ECONOMY SERIES

Edited by Benjamin I. Page

For Doug

CONTENTS

PREFACE

THIS PROJECT BEGAN as a study in the communication of political authority. As a student of political science, and then of mass communication, I became increasingly interested in the ways that individuals and institutions gain influence through discourse. While considering an area for empirical research on this topic, I was drawn to one of the most prominent, authoritative voices in American politics—public opinion. In a mass democracy such as ours, the vox populi commands wide respect among leaders and citizens alike, so the way public preferences are expressed and assessed is particularly interesting to those who study power.

With the development of the sample survey in the 1930s, public opinion became a popular, exciting focus of study both inside and outside the academy. Since those early years, researchers refined their techniques for drawing random samples of the population, standardized their interviewing practices, and began to employ computers for efficient data analysis. These days, academic institutions, market research suppliers, political consultants, professional pollsters, and others use survey research methodology to probe the attitudes of the American public. In the course of the typical presidential election campaign, for example, polls are referred to incessantly on the evening news and in the pages of major newspapers. During those months, politicians, citizens, and journalists monitor the polls closely, but also decry the authority ascribed to survey results. Despite these habitual complaints, however, polls have attained a very secure place in the American political process. Few candidates run for office, express their views on current issues, or change campaign strategy without consulting opinion polls.

This book is not an analysis of public attitudes themselves, but an inquiry into the history and meaning of public opinion. Although opinion polls are now commonplace, we rarely reflect on the nature of the data they supply, how they came to gain authority, or why they play such a large role in public discourse. In this study, I try to address these issues, but also explore the changing character of public opinion expression and measurement over time. Since public opinion is such a complex phenomenon, I have used a wide range of theories and concepts from sociology, political science, philosophy, and communications. By taking an interdisciplinary approach to the history of public opinion, I hope to demonstrate that the study of public sentiment is not solely the domain of survey researchers.

The first two chapters of this book set out the theoretical underpinnings for my discussion of polling in American politics. Those readers who are more interested in political history than social theory may want to skip these early chapters, and begin with the chronicle of public opinion expression and measurement in chapter 3.

I began to write about public opinion while at the Annenberg School for Communications at the University of Southern California. Although the goal and the nature of the project have changed substantially since that time, several people at USC helped me to clarify my ideas. I am particularly grateful to Elihu Katz and Bob Meadow, who encouraged me to pursue theoretical and historical issues in public opinion. Peter Clarke and Susan Evans showed me how to think creatively about research design, and gave me an enormous amount of intellectual and emotional support.

During the course of this study, scores of former U.S. congressmen and journalists patiently responded to my questions about public opinion expression in the 1930s and 1940s. Without their help, writing about this period would have been virtually impossible.

At Northwestern, I benefited from the advice and criticism of many colleagues, students, and friends. Peter Miller gave me valuable suggestions as I wrote about contemporary polling, and Dan Merkle and Sarah Maza provided numerous useful citations. Peter, Kathy Galvin, and David Zarefsky helped me to secure funds for much needed research assistance in the summer of 1990, and Stacey Suyat helped to collect data from nineteenth century newspapers. I'd also like to thank Pat McGrath, who typed the bibliography.

Ben Page, the editor of this series, was enthusiastic about the project and appreciated its interdisciplinary tone. He and John

Tryneski at the University of Chicago Press both gave me sound advice which improved the structure and the argument of the book. Dan Hallin's critique of the manuscript was also very useful to me as I revised. Salena Fuller Krug edited the final copy.

Jim Beniger and I spent countless lunches and hours on the phone talking about public opinion. His fascination with social theory is contagious, and he inspired me to do historical work. For his continued intellectual camaraderie, and his friendship, I am grateful.

I am deeply indebted to my parents, for their encouragement and guidance during the rough periods. Finally, I dedicate this book to my husband, Doug Hughes, and thank him for his constructive criticism and loving support.

The following publishers have granted permission to use material in chapters 5 and 8, that originally appeared in their journals: "Classical Democracy, Polls, and Public Opinion: Theoretical Frameworks for Studying the Public Sentiment," *Communication Theory* 1, no. 3 (August, 1991), reprinted by permission of Guilford Publications; and "Public Opinion Measurement Strategies in the 1930s and 1940s: Retrospective Views of Journalists," *Journalism Quarterly* 67, no. 4 (Winter, 1990), reproduced with permission of the Association for Education in Journalism and Mass Communication.

Figure 3.3 is reproduced from *Coffee: The Epic of a Commodity* by Heinrich Eduard Jacob. Copyright 1934 by Ernst Rowohlt Verlag. English translation copyright 1935 by The Viking Press. Used by permission of Viking Penguin, a division of Penguin Books USA Inc.

INTRODUCTION

America has shown more boldness in trusting public opinion, in recognizing and giving effect to it, than has yet been shown elsewhere. Towering over Presidents and State governors, over Congress and State legislatures, over conventions and the vast machinery of party, public opinion stands out, in the United States, as the great source of power, the master of servants who tremble before it.

James Bryce
The American Commonwealth, 1891

[Americans] carry a trader's habits over into the business of politics. They like order, without which affairs do not prosper, and they set an especial value on regularity of mores, which are the foundation of a good business; they prefer the good sense which creates fortunes to the genius which often dissipates them; their minds, accustomed to definite calculations, are frightened by general ideas; and they hold practice in greater honor than theory.

Alexis de Tocqueville
Democracy in America, 1850

SINCE THE EARLIEST DAYS of the republic, Americans have placed great value upon two seemingly unrelated processes—public opinion expression and calculation. Both Bryce and Tocqueville remarked on these components of American culture, but neither could have predicted the ways that opinion expression and quantification would be linked in the late twentieth century. For instance, the modern public opinion poll or "sample survey" is now an essential part of politics: Those who compete for political office, the journalists who report on their campaigns, and the voters who must choose among aspirants, all pay close attention to numbers that supposedly describe public opinion.

Yet the opinion poll is not the only instance of quantification in the realm of politics. The appraisal of crowd size at political rallies, predictions about election turnout or voter returns, results of straw polls, sales figures for political paraphernalia (e.g., buttons, T-shirts, bumper stickers), and other such estimates all represent the intersection of two dominant ideological forces in American public life—science and democracy. Quantitative techniques for expressing and measuring public opinion are attractive because of their "objective" and seemingly decisive nature, as well as their ability to account for a multitude of individual opinions. Political leaders, pollsters, journalists, interest groups, and members of the public have been increasingly drawn to these methods of estimating public opinion because numerical data tend to communicate authority: The data provide, in theory, an undistorted portrait of the common man's convictions. Although academics and the occasional journalist question the validity of quantitative public opinion figures, there is little question that they carry great weight in political discourse.

This book describes and analyzes the rise of quantification in American politics. Of particular interest, however, is the measurement and expression of public opinion. One fundamental question animates this inquiry: How have numbers been used to describe the public mood, and why have quantitative discourses gained such widespread respect in the United States? Since the rise of quantification in politics is not the province of any one academic discipline, the question can only be addressed by using a variety of perspectives, from a variety of disciplines. As a result, this study employs analytic tools from the social sciences and also from philosophy and history.

The question of how numbers came to play such a significant role in politics is the starting point for my investigation, yet the book is organized around two central themes. The first of these themes concerns the linkage of democracy and rationality. Each chapter explicitly or implicitly addresses the connection between these two key elements of public life in the United States. Opinion polls, and other such quantitative descriptions of the American mood, are pervasive because they seem unprejudiced by ideology *and* are designed to communicate the general will.

The second theme concerns the use we make of numbers. Quantitative descriptions of popular opinion serve two very distinct, though intertwined, functions: We quantify in order to act in the most efficient manner possible, but also to communicate authority in public debate. Numbers are used to accomplish immediate and sometimes very private goals, but they are also widely used for their symbolic power. At times we count opinions in order to gain knowledge about public preferences. At other times, however, we use such data to communicate popularity or legitimacy. This study describes the relationship between these twin functions of numbers—instrumental and symbolic—throughout American political history.

In addition to these themes, a series of concepts, drawn from several academic fields, will illuminate the roles quantification has played in political history. One of these is rationality, a term first used by philosophers, but eventually employed by social theorists as well. The various conceptualizations of rationality, from Weber's fatalistic vision through Foucault's more complex one, help to explain the rise of statistics in the political sphere. Two other concepts critical to this study are power and social control. Both are classic concerns of social theorists and social scientists interested in human behavior, and both are extremely useful in the study of political action and expression.

I should emphasize that this book is about action, expression, and the relationship between the two. Too often scholars analyze one phenomenon or the other, avoiding the fact that behavior and discourse are interdependent. As a variety of contemporary philosophers and rhetoricians have argued, expression is a type of action. To ignore discourse is to gain an incomplete understanding of social and political life. This study attends to the ways people behave in the political sphere, but also to the ways they think about and talk about their actions.

Although much in politics has become quantified or at least quantifiable, the most obvious place to begin an exploration of the topic is in the arena of public opinion. Public opinion is our focus because it is undoubtedly at the heart of the democratic process, and because the general will has been quantified so readily throughout American history. Contemporary journalists, politicians, interest group leaders, and citizens complain often and loudly about the deluge of opinion polls and the attention they receive in the public forum. Yet we are simply witnessing the latest episode in a chronicle of public opinion quantification that began long ago. One goal of this book, therefore, is to place the current discussion of opinion quantification in its proper historical context. This book is divided into eight chapters. The first two chapters are largely theoretical, presenting the concepts and frameworks I will use in subsequent chapters. Chapter 1 briefly traces the history of quantification and then introduces the perspectives of two theorists—Max Weber and Michel Foucault—in order to identify trends in this history. The first chapter highlights the instrumental use of numbers, treating quantification as a case of rationalization. Chapter 2 focuses on the symbolic use of numbers, drawing from theories in sociology, anthropology, political science, and philosophy. Of particular interest in this chapter are the ways that numbers are used as part of a larger political ritual process. Taken together, these two early chapters provide the requisite tools for analyzing the texture of public opinion expression in American political history.

While chapters 1 and 2 concern the instrumental and symbolic uses of numbers, chapter 3 focuses exclusively on public opinion. In chapter 3 I concentrate on the history of public opinion—the techniques for expressing it, those used to measure it, and the changing definition of the concept itself. This historical overview of techniques—from the salons of eighteenth century Paris to the opinion polls of today—demonstrates how opinion measurement and the meaning ascribed to public opinion evolved together. One cannot understand modern techniques of public opinion expression or assessment, quantitative or qualitative, without understanding the progression of techniques over time. In chapter 3 I also take up a difficult definitional problem in democratic theory—the meaning of "public opinion." I argue that the definition of public opinion changes along with historical circumstances, but also with the development of new techniques for communicating opinion.

Chapters 4 and 5 are empirical studies in the quantification of public opinion. Both chapters examine critical periods in the development of the public sentiment, sets of measurement and expression practices, and the instrumental and symbolic uses of numbers. In chapter 4 I explore the history of straw polls, the ancestors of modern public opinion polls. Straw polls were used from the election of 1824 through 1936, when the *Literary Digest* wrongly predicted that Alf Landon would defeat Franklin Roosevelt in the U.S. presidential race. These polls were often employed by partisan newspaper journalists and politicians to delegitimate opposition candidates and parties during elections, and to exaggerate their own chances of victory.

Chapter 5 follows chapter 4 chronologically, analyzing the nature of public opinion quantification after 1936. This chapter reports on a study of U.S. congressmen and prominent American journalists who worked during the 1930s and 1940s. How did these two groups, both of whom needed to understand the nature of public opinion, assess the popular sentiment during a period when few people trusted the new opinion poll? Chapter 5 examines the types of techniques, both quantitative and qualitative, that congressmen and journalists utilized in order to understand the opinions of their constituents and readers.

Chapter 6 is devoted to a brief discussion of contemporary polling and survey research. Since the early days of opinion research, a number of parties—interest groups, broadcast media, political consultants, national party organizations, and others—have become interested in purchasing and collecting public opinion data. Their preoccupation with polling is the focus of chapter 6, where I also review recent developments in survey research methodology. Although all of the issues I discuss in this chapter have already received serious attention from public opinion researchers, this section completes the chronology of public opinion research begun in chapter 3.

In chapter 7 I take up another type of opinion quantification— the assessment of crowd size at political rallies. These estimates, which have always been part of American political discourse, have been largely ignored by historians of public opinion. Yet debates over crowd size provide a rich arena for inquiry into the nature of opinion quantification in America. The parties who counted crowds at rallies, the nature of their agendas, and the changing character of this practice are all addressed in chapter 7.

In the final chapter I discuss the implications of increasing quantification for public opinion expression in America. Does the practice of counting opinions and bodies enhance democratic processes, or does it hinder lively debate and political participation? And do numerical descriptions of public opinion help to clarify issues of concern in the public forum, or do these data leave us even more confused about the motivations and positions of parties and leaders?

Quantification and calculation have undeniably improved many aspects of our lives: We have erected a sophisticated technological infrastructure in order to communicate with each other, discovered treatments for a wide variety of human ailments, and learned an enormous amount about the natural environment we inhabit. Quantitative measurement tools have also been extremely useful to social scientists searching for more rigorous ways to understand human behavior. Yet whether or not quantification has improved the quality of political debate and discourse in America poses a unique and difficult set of questions. Some of these questions concern the numbers themselves—how they are arrived at, and who controls the communication of these data. But ultimately, questions about numbers in politics are questions about the nature and future of American democracy itself.

CHAPTER ONE

Quantification and Rationality

ORMALIZED TABULATION of political opinions began in the city-states of ancient Greece, where elections were viewed as central components of the democratic process.[1] Yet it was not until the eighteenth and nineteenth centuries that quantification became a significant element of political discourse in the West. Beginning in the eighteenth century, statesmen realized that numbers could help them to assess the needs and opinions of the populace and to make predictions about the future. If we are to understand the roles numbers have played in political life, however, we must start with the larger history of quantification.

This chapter traces the ascent of quantification in social and political life, and considers this history as a case study of increasing rationalization. The use of numbers in political discourse, and in other spheres, reflects the authority of instrumental reason in our lives: Quantifying phenomena seems to be the most efficient means to so many ends. A goal of this first chapter is to put quantification in its proper historical context, but also to assemble a set of useful theoretical "tools." These tools will become a critical part of my inquiry in subsequent chapters, as I begin to focus on quantitative dialogues in American politics.

The rise of quantification and statistics is important for our purposes because it directly informs the study of political communication in the nineteenth and twentieth centuries. After outlining this history, I introduce the sociological theory of Max Weber, who wrote extensively about the roles of calculation and rationality in social life. Weber's work illuminates how increasing quantification is part of a larger historical trend toward both intellectual and structural systematization.

The final section of this chapter focuses on the work of Michel Foucault, who, like Weber, had a great interest in the multiple functions of rationality. Although Weber and Foucault shared many perspectives on instrumental thinking and routinization, they concentrated on different levels of analysis: Weber was drawn to the study of human behavior in organizations and institutions, while Foucault theorized about the role of rationality in discourse. Foucault expanded Weber's theory, acknowledging the importance of rationalization and demonstrating how the concepts of power and knowledge enhance the study of instrumental reason. After considering some of the theorists' central insights, I'll conclude by discussing the application of these ideas to the history of public opinion expression and measurement.

The Rise of Statistics

Quantification has a long history, and numerous scholars have carefully documented the development of arithmetic and statistics in Western Europe and the United States.[2] The details of this history are well beyond the scope of this book, yet a brief review of this literature provides a context for the ensuing discussion of numbers in politics. What follows, then, is a synopsis of the history of quantification, emphasizing important milestones in the rise of statistical thinking.[3]

The appeal of quantification in the past is easy for us to understand, since the benefits we derive from counting are so conspicuous in our own lives. Counting demands uniformity of measurement, and uniformity often leads to efficiency. Patricia Cline Cohen has argued that numbers were valuable to American colonists because they permitted a variety of comparisons. By enumerating, one could compare distances between locales, the weights of various commodities, or the climates in different regions.[4] Many forms of quantification make the world seem less chaotic. By calculating how much people purchase during a particular season, the patterns of the tides, or the rate of mortality, one creates the illusion of an orderly environment.

Although enumeration itself has a very long history, the practice of applying numbers to social problems and topics has its roots in the late seventeenth century. In Great Britain, a variety of individuals tabulated statistics about the population—birth and death rates in London, for example. William Petty, an academic and former student of Thomas Hobbes, argued that government policy could be informed by the careful application of numbers to social affairs. He coined the phrase "political arithmetic," advocating the use of calculation to understand the nature of social life in England.[5] In France during these years, the collection of social statistics was not performed by academics or by curious political observers. Studies of this sort were executed primarily by the monarchy, which did not publicize the results of its population surveys.[6]

It seems that the accumulation of social data should have commenced much earlier, but there are reasons why the practice became attractive in the seventeenth century. Many historians believe that the growth of the insurance industry, the expansion of foreign trade, and a widespread concern over the number of deaths during the Great Plague of 1665 each contributed to the escalating interest in social statistics across Europe.[7]

Among the most thorough practitioners of political arithmetic was John Sinclair, who produced a twenty-one volume work titled *The Statistical Account of Scotland* during an eight-year period beginning in 1791. Sinclair asked clergymen throughout Scotland to report on a large number of items, from the number of parishioners and their occupations to the types of disease commonly found in their regions. He also asked a few opinion questions, such as "Are the people [in your parish] fond of a military life?" and "Are the people [disposed] to humane and generous actions; to protect and relieve the shipwrecked?" Sinclair believed "statistics" to be "an inquiry into the state of a country, for the purpose of ascertaining the quantum of happiness enjoyed by its inhabitants, and the means of its future improvement."[8]

In subsequent years Sinclair's study served as a model for scores of political elites, who sought to improve the state of their nations through quantification. As Theodore Porter points out, the "statists" of the nineteenth century were liberals who associated calculation with progressive social reform. These men found the stability of birth, death, and marriage rates impressive, since regularity could make human activity easier to understand and predict.[9] In the mid-nineteenth century, a Belgian named Adolphe Quetelet applied the "law of large numbers" to the study of society, in search of regular patterns of activity. One of his goals was to copy

76. What may be the number of perfons born in other diftricts or parifhes in Scotland ?

77. What may be the number of the nobility and their families ?

78. —————————————————— gentry ?

79. —————————————————— clergy ?

80. —————————————————— lawyers, and writers or attornies ?

81. What may be the number of phyficians, furgeons, and apothecaries ?

82. —————————————————— the eftablifhed church ?

83. —————————————————— feceders ?

84. —————————————————— epifcopalians ?

85. —————————————————— Roman catholics ?

86. Is the population of the parifh materially different from what it was 5, 10, or 25 years ago ? and to what caufes is the alteration attributed ?

87. What is the proportion between the annual births and the whole population ?

88. What is the proportion between the annual marriages and the whole population ?

89. What is the proportion between the annual deaths and the whole population ?

90. What is the proportion between the batchelors and the married men, widowers included ?

91. How many children does each marriage at an average produce ?

92. What may be the caufes of depopulation ?

93. Are there any deftructive epidemical diftempers ?

94. Have any died from want ?

95. Have any murders or fuicides been committed ?

96. Have many emigrated from the parifh ?

97. Have any been banifhed from it ?

98. Have any been obliged to leave the parifh for want of employment ?

99. Are there any uninhabited houfes ?

100. What may be the number of inhabited houfes, and the number of perfons at an average to each inhabited houfe ?

III. QUESTIONS *refpecting the* PRODUCTIONS *of the* PARISH.

101. What kinds of vegetables, plants, and trees, does the parifh produce ?

102. What kinds of animals ?

103. What at an average is fuppofed to be the number of cattle, fheep, horfes, hogs, and goats, in the diftrict ?

104. Is there any map of the parifh ? and has the number of acres in it been afcertained ?

105. How

FIGURE 1.1 A page from John Sinclair's *Statistical Account of Scotland*, published in 1798. The questionnaire, which was mailed to clergymen, contained 160 questions.

the natural sciences, with their precision and authority. As Porter notes, Quetelet's ideas about a "social physics" were fairly influential. He persuaded many scientists to focus their study on aggregate statistical data, and not on the behavior of individuals, in order to understand social phenomena.[10]

Although there was a decline in the amount of social research conducted in Great Britain after the mid-nineteenth century,[11] the social sciences were beginning to take shape in American academies. A great number of American students interested in politics, economics, and social behavior traveled to Europe to receive proper scientific training, and returned to establish research programs in the United States. It was during the late nineteenth century that William Graham Sumner and Lester Frank Ward worked to create a science of sociology, with positivism as its foundation.[12] In fact, quantitative data were key to the establishment of the social sciences. As Dorothy Ross points out in her history of the social sciences, "Instrumental positivism decreed that the statistical study of aggregate behavior would itself define the field of social inquiry."[13]

Quantifying Political Opinions in America

Bureaucrats, academics, and statesmen counted people and properties for centuries, but began to count their opinions much later. Early straw polls first appeared in the 1820s, and taking note of attendance at political rallies accelerated during the nineteenth century. Both of these forms of quantification, which have been largely overlooked by political historians, will be taken up in later chapters. Another form of opinion quantification, which has received more serious scholarly attention, is the sample survey or modern public opinion poll.[14]

Jean Converse, in her history of survey research, argues that the first modern opinion polls—which appeared in the 1930s—had three ancestors: the British studies of social conditions, early psychological studies of attitudes, and marketing research. Although polling was conducted during the Great Depression and the Second World War, universities did not establish centers for survey research until after the war. Converse describes the difficulties faced by early researchers, who often lacked funds for major survey endeavors and sought legitimacy within skeptical university communities. Yet over the past few decades, survey methodology has become eminently respectable as a tool for understanding social, political, and economic behavior. In the last twenty years, researchers have developed more sophisticated sampling techniques, have effectively used computers to draw representative samples of the population, and have paid increasing attention to questionnaire design.

Quantitative surveys, both scientific and unscientific, are now a pervasive component of public discourse: We regularly find poll results in the pages of our daily paper or weekly news magazine, and these same data are frequently reported on the nightly news. For example, Albert Gollin points out that one of the many organizations currently polling, *The New York Times*/CBS News team, conducted a total of 312 polls between 1975 and 1986. [15] Several hundred news organizations publish Gallup, Roper, and Harris polls, and many major newspapers have their own survey research capabilities. In addition to the enormous amount of polling conducted by media organizations and academic survey research centers, the U.S. government conducts a large number of surveys and uses a great deal of survey research data. [16]

Polling is only one form of opinion quantification in politics, but it is a critical one. We will return to the phenomenon of polling throughout this book, since it is a predominant form of numerical public expression in contemporary American politics. For now, though, it is necessary to explore the philosophical roots of this trend toward increasing quantification.

Numbers and Rationality

Although historians have carefully documented the rise of quantification and statistics, sociologists view these developments as evidence of a larger trend toward instrumental thinking. Counting people, calculating mortality rates, and systematically assessing the living conditions of the populace all evince a desire to routinize processes of observation. As time progresses, some scholars argue, social action tends toward increasing systematization or "rationalization." [17] Individuals and organizations create more and more standard operating procedures for accomplishing goals, because these procedures are thought to enable a degree of control: If one can routinize a set of practices in order to complete a task, he or she experiences a sense of mastery over that task. In this section, I explore the work of the German sociologist Max Weber (1864–1920), who wrote extensively about the historical process of rationalization. After a short explication of his theory and the debates surrounding it, I will reflect on how these ideas inform the study of quantification in politics.

From the mid-nineteenth century through the early decades of the twentieth, German sociologists and historians were working in the area of developmental history. Karl Lamprecht, Werner Sombart, and others were attempting to uncover "laws," or at least unilinear theories, to describe the development of Western economic and political systems.[18] Weber also worked in this tradition, combining detailed empirical study with philosophical insights inherited from other German social theorists—Kant, Hegel, and Toennies.[19] As Reinhard Bendix has pointed out, however, Weber was not only interested in political economy. He was deeply concerned about the impact of modernization on spirituality, ethics, and freedom:

> [Weber] left no doubt that his profound personal commitment to the cause of reason and freedom had guided his choice of subject matter; and his research left no doubt that reason and freedom in the Western world were in jeopardy. Weber was a contemporary of Freud, whose lifework consisted in safeguarding man's reason after comprehending in full measure the depth of man's irrationality. Similarly, Weber sought to safeguard the great legacy of the Enlightenment after fully exploring the historical preconditions of that legacy.[20]

The range of Weber's research endeavors was tremendous. He studied Eastern and Western religions, music, bureaucracy, law, party politics, agriculture, economics, and other spheres of social action in order to understand the development of rationality. Weber is most famous for his controversial book on the roots of Western capitalism, published in 1904 and titled *The Protestant Ethic and the Spirit of Capitalism*. Here he argued that goal-directed economic action and the calculated search for wealth evolved from religious doctrines associated with Calvinism. Weber's argument is much too complex to be summarized here, and academic debate about the thesis has generated numerous volumes.[21] Yet the central themes of the book—the influence of ideas upon human conduct and the role of instrumental reason—were ideas Weber struggled with ceaselessly until his death. Our focus here is on the rise of instrumental reason, since it provides one explanation for the increasing authority of quantitative discourse.

Embedded in Weber's numerous case studies are several arguments about rationality, articulated on two levels of analysis—the individual, micro level and the macrohistorical level. Individuals working alone, or within large organizations and institutions, often engage in instrumental reasoning. Weber called this type of means/end rationality—where one sets goals and figures out the most effective methods for attaining those goals—*formal rationality*. Central to the idea of formal rationality is the calculability of the action entailed: When one is absorbed in formally rational thinking, he or she is interested in the most efficient means for accomplishing a particular task. The type of task is irrelevant, however, since one can use means/end rationality to get children ready for school or to design a national political campaign. Although Weber did not explicitly articulate his theory of rationality,[22] pieces of the theory are scattered throughout his last, unfinished work, *Economy and Society*. In a section on rationality in economic markets, Weber defines formal rationality in terms of calculability:

> A system of economic activity will be called "formally" rational according to the degree in which the provision for needs, which is essential to every rational economy, is capable of being expressed in numerical calculable terms, and is so expressed. In the first instance, it is quite independent of the technical form these calculations take, particularly whether estimates are expressed in money or in kind. The concept is thus unambiguous, at least in the sense that expression in money term[s] yields the highest degree of formal calculability.[23]

Formal rationality does not always guide individual cognitive processes, however. Weber believed that formal rationality is dialectically opposed to another sort of thinking he called *substantive rationality*.[24] While formally rational action demands rigorous calculation, substantively rational action focuses on the value of the goals themselves, not the means for achieving them. If one acts in a manner consistent with a deeply held set of convictions or values, one is engaging in substantive rational thinking. The degree of substantive rationality exercised by an individual or organization, like its formal counterpart, can only be determined if the end goal or value is explicit. As Rogers Brubaker explains:

> From the point of view of a given *belief*, an action is rational if it is consistent with the belief, and irrational if it is not. A judgment of rationality or irrationality, in this case, is a judgment about the logical relation—or lack thereof—between action and belief. To return to Weber's example, a religious way of life is rational from the point of view of a belief in the existence of God or an afterlife or in the possibility of salvation through good works, but it is irrational from the point of view of the unbeliever, i.e. from the point of view of the belief that there is no God, no afterlife, and no possibility of salvation through good works. [25]

For Weber, these two types of rationality are in constant conflict with each other. When one decides to pursue a goal and achieve it through calculated procedures, he or she is taking a decidedly value-neutral stance, which often disregards values such as equality, love, or friendship. In a well-known passage in *Economy and Society* about the rise of capitalism, Weber writes about the conflict between brotherly love (substantive rationality) and profit-driven behavior (formal rationality):

> There is no possibility, in practice or even in principle, of any caritative [benevolent] regulation of relationships arising between the holder of a savings and loan bank mortgage and the mortgagee who has obtained a loan from the bank, or between a holder of a federal bond and a citizen taxpayer. Nor can any caritative regulation arise in the relationships between stockholders and factory workers, between tobacco importers and foreign plantation workers, or between industrialists and the miners who have dug from the earth the raw materials used in the plants owned by the industrialists. The growing impersonality of the economy on the basis of association in the market place follows its own rules, disobedience to which entails economic failure and, in the long run, economic ruin. [26]

It is important to note here that formal and substantive rationality are *ideal types*. Both constructs were created for the express purpose of theory building. It is likely that in the course of empirical study, one would encounter actions and behaviors which seem to combine (to some extent) the two types of rationality.

Although rationality on the individual level was critical to Weber's thinking about social action, he also argued that formally rational thinking and planning accelerated with the passage of time. Weber called this historical process, in which individuals are increasingly drawn to means/end thinking and action, *rationalization*. Rationalization is manifested in the escalating importance of technical proficiency, precision, and specialization. Talcott Parsons, in his introduction to Weber's *Sociology of Religion*, notes that increasing formal rationality "comprises the intellectual clarification, specification and systematization of ideas."[27] Formal rationality, in other words, becomes encoded in the ideas and practices of a culture.

Increasing rationalization, Weber argued, can be found in all spheres of human activity. As people and organizations realize that they can achieve valued ends through routinized procedures, these procedures become more and more attractive. Weber provided examples of increasing rationalization in a variety of arenas—law,[28] social norms,[29] sexuality,[30] and religion,[31] among others. Rationalization, for Weber, was a linear, macrohistorical trend, but proceeded at varying rates in different spheres of human endeavor: For example, some organizations quickly systematize their operating procedures, while others may take longer to do so. Even when rationalization is under way, it is usually an uneven, halting process, not a smooth, gradual one.[32]

In a discussion of Taylorism (or "scientific management"), Weber described rationalization in factory work using a tone that echoed Marx. Scientific management, he argued, demands that an individual factory worker adjust his "psycho-physical apparatus" to the machinery he works with: Workers must get "in line with the demands of the work procedure" and calibrate their thinking and behavior to correspond with the rhythm of the assembly line.[33] Weber concluded this section on discipline in economic organizations by noting that rationalization can stifle individuality—a substantively rational goal:

> This whole process of rationalization, in the factory as elsewhere, and especially in the bureaucratic state machine, par-

allels the centralization of the material implements of organization in the hands of the master. Thus, discipline inexorably takes over even larger areas as the satisfaction of political and economic needs is increasingly rationalized. This universal phenomenon more and more restricts the importance of charisma and of individually differentiated conduct.[34]

Consequences of Rationalization

Though Weber appreciated the positive aspects of rationalization, believing that means/end thinking often helps one accomplish immediate goals, his vision was ultimately a dismal one. He thought that rationalization in most spheres would, in the end, lead to alienation. Weber feared that increasing rationalization would deem spirituality, passion, and freedom superfluous or negligible.[35] In a 1909 debate he said:

> It is horrible to think that the world could one day be filled with nothing but those little cogs, little men clinging to little jobs and striving towards bigger ones. . . . This passion for bureaucracy . . . is enough to drive one to despair. It is as if in politics . . . we were deliberately to become men who need "order" and nothing but order, who become nervous and cowardly if for one moment this order wavers, and helpless if they are torn away from their total incorporation in it. That the world should know no men but these: it is in such an evolution that we are already caught up, and the great question is therefore not how we can promote and hasten it, but what can we oppose to this machinery in order to keep a portion of mankind free from this parcelling-out of the soul, from this supreme mastery of the bureaucratic way of life.[36]

As Barry Smart puts it, "the realm of values, of justice, freedom, beauty, and goodness lies beyond the perimeter of instrumental reason."[37]

Weber could not find a way out of this "iron cage" of rationalization, and the issue was a source of great intellectual torment for him. He considered the possibility that a leader with great charisma could disrupt the rationalization process by emphasizing values like freedom and spiritualism, and by challenging formally rational structures. Yet in the end, Weber believed that these types of interruptions could provide only temporary relief.[38]

Although Weber did not write about quantification outside of the context of business accounting and economic calculation, his thoughts on rationalization are directly related to the rise of statistical thinking in the West. As Herbert Marcuse notes, "progressive mathematization of experience and knowledge" is central to Weber's writings on instrumental rationality.[39] Increasing interest in demographic data, the quantification and categorization of behavioral acts, the diffusion of the census, and the tabulation of political opinions are all examples of rationalization. Assuming a Weberian perspective on these phenomena elicits a very useful series of questions about them. For example, if we view the history of quantification through the lens of rationalization, we are forced to focus on intentionality: Why do certain groups of individuals develop quantitative techniques, while others do not? What types of activities does calculation enable, and why is counting often seen as the most effective means for attaining particular goals?

Beyond intentionality, though, Weber's notion of the inevitable trade-off between formal and substantive rationality highlights the forms of social action *replaced* by quantification. Numerical descriptions of phenomena and statistical analysis enable the accomplishment of certain types of goals, but neglect the achievement of others. This is a theme we will return to in subsequent chapters, since quantitative forms of political communication supplant other types of action and discourse. For example, when newspaper journalists use the sample survey to describe public opinion on an issue, they are less likely to conduct in-depth interviews with knowledgeable citizens and political activists. One could argue that political activists, who are informed and passionate about particular issues, provide more valuable "data" than do the anonymous individuals included in the typical opinion poll sample. Weber's approach to social action illuminates, in a vivid fashion, the implications of increasing routinization. The benefits of quantification are obvious and immediate, since counting and statistical analysis provide data one can act upon. Yet we are much less likely to focus on the detrimental or "disenchanting" effects of formal rationality without the analytic tools Weber's work offers.

Weber's theorizing about rationalization and its effects influenced generations of philosophers and social critics. Several members of the Frankfurt School, a group of neo-Marxist German theorists, used Weberian notions of rationalization to inform their understanding of Western politics, economics, and culture.[40] Max Horkheimer, Theodor Adorno, Herbert Marcuse, and Jürgen Habermas have each explored the ways that instrumental rationality is woven into the fabric of corporate capitalism. Although these theorists generally disagreed with Weber's critique of socialism,[41] the conflict between formal and substantive rationality is a pivotal component of their writings. In this passage from an essay written in 1941, Marcuse argues that instrumental rationality and capitalism work together to shape our actions and thoughts:

> A man who travels by automobile to a distant place chooses his route from the highway maps. Towns, lakes and mountains appear as obstacles to be bypassed. The countryside is shaped and organized by the highway. Numerous signs and posters tell the traveler what to do and think; they even request his attention to the beauties of nature or the hallmarks of history. Others have done the thinking for him, and perhaps for the better. . . . Giant advertisements tell him when to stop and find the pause that refreshes. And all this is indeed for his benefit, safety and comfort; he receives what he wants. Business, technics, human needs and nature are welded together into one rational and expedient mechanism. He will fare best who follows its directions, subordinating his spontaneity to the anonymous wisdom which ordered everything for him.[42]

The Frankfurt School theorists were among the earliest to employ Weber's insights, yet other more contemporary scholars engaged the Weberian notion of rationalization as well. Michel Foucault (1926–1984), the French social theorist, was one writer who made rationalization central to his historical explorations of social practice. Even though Foucault did not acknowledge the impact of Weber's ideas on his own until late in his career, there are an extraordinary number of parallels between their theoretical perspectives. Foucault uses Weber as a starting point, recognizing the significance of rationalization, but builds on this foundation by introducing his own ideas about knowledge, discourse, and power. In order to explore the ties between Weber and Foucault, I begin with a brief review of Foucault's theory of power. After this initial analysis, I'll reintroduce Weberian theory and discuss the value of both theories for understanding quantification in politics.

Rationality, Discourse, and Power

Michel Foucault's innovative historical explorations of madness, criminality, sexuality, and other phenomena have made him one of the most influential and controversial social theorists in academe. He has borrowed concepts, insights, and methods from a variety of disciplines to create a unique and startling vision of culture and social life in the West. Throughout his career, Foucault intentionally avoided systematic theory construction, and chose instead to question the fundamental assumptions of other scholars. Those who wish to discover a grand theory embedded in Foucault's work will be frustrated, since his ideas evolved over time, and often contradict each other. [43]

One area of Foucault's theorizing which has been useful to students of politics and culture is his conceptualization of power. Even though Foucault never presented a formal theory of power, he spent considerable effort trying to redefine the term, questioning its traditional meaning in social theory. Unlike previous theorists and philosophers who viewed power as a *commodity*, held by the state or a social class, Foucault believed power to be a *set of practices*. Power is, more than anything, a strategy which is "exercised rather than possessed."[44] In one of his clearest explications of power, he wrote:

> By power, I do not mean "Power" as a group of institutions and mechanisms that ensure the subservience of the citizens of a given state. . . . It seems to me that power must be understood in the first instance as the multiplicity of force relations immanent in the sphere in which they operate and which constitute their own organization; as the process which, through ceaseless struggles and confrontations, transforms, strengthens, or reverses them. [45]

Foucault argues that power is located within the nexus of behavioral and discursive techniques found in any situation of domination. In his book *Discipline and Punish*, for example, Foucault traces the changing nature of punishment by focusing on the technologies of punishment—torture, incarceration, and observation, among others. It is through the study of these types of practices that one discerns who dominates, who becomes the subject of domination, and how these relationships evolve. A student of power, Foucault argues, needs to evaluate the texture and content of relationships between individuals or institutions acting together.[46]

If power is to be viewed as a strategy or process, one must understand the particular historical context in which it is found. This is why Foucault has concentrated his efforts on local manifestations of power, instead of developing a general theory of power which could be applied to a variety of periods or phenomena. Foucault argues that researchers should not look to the state and how it exercises power over citizens, but study the practices of power in local systems. He believes that one must evaluate power from "below":

> One must suppose [rather] that the manifold relationships of force that take shape and come into play in the machinery of production, in families, limited groups, and institutions, are the basis for wide-ranging effects of cleavage that run through the social body as a whole. These then form a general line of force that traverses the local oppositions and links them together; to be sure, they also bring about redistributions, realignments, homogenizations, serial arrangements, and convergences of the force relations.[47]

Foucault contends that the exercise of power is tied closely to two other processes—the production of knowledge and the creation of observational techniques. Both of these linkages are critical to Foucault's empirical work, and each is useful to students of political action and discourse.

In contrast to theorists who believe that powerful individuals and institutions determine the bounds of legitimated knowledge, Foucault argues that knowledge and power are produced simultaneously: They "reinforce one another in a circular process."[48] What is accepted as "truth" in any given society emerges with transformations in the social structure. For Foucault, power and knowledge are closely correlated, but there is no discernible causal relation between the two, since they appear at the same historical moment:

> We should abandon a whole tradition that allows us to imagine that knowledge can develop only outside its injunctions,

its demands and its interests. Perhaps we should abandon the belief that power makes mad and that, by the same token, the renunciation of power is one of the conditions of knowledge. We should admit rather that power produces knowledge . . . that there is no power relation without the correlative constitution of a field of knowledge, nor any knowledge that does not presuppose and constitute at the same time power relations.[49]

Along these lines, Foucault has written extensively about the ways that the human and medical sciences (e.g., psychiatry or criminology) exemplify the mutual dependence of knowledge and power. As these disciplines developed, they were able to refine their tools of observation, measurement, and categorization, although they did not seek "truth" as we generally understand it. These disciplinary techniques and bodies of knowledge were created for purposes of social control, and control was enhanced through their development.[50] In *Madness and Civilization,* Foucault argues that doctors did not try to *understand* madness—they simply learned to *master* and control it.[51] To use Weberian terminology, the development of the human sciences is an example of the irrationality of rationalization: Methodologies were routinized, but the goals of scientists were not inspired by substantive rationality.

Power and knowledge come together most clearly in the content of *discourse*. In a passage reminiscent of Mikhail Bakhtin's writings on heteroglossia,[52] Foucault argues that multiple discourses are found in situations where power is exercised. Discourses are used by individuals and institutions to shape reality, obscure motivations or interests, and resist domination. In *The History of Sexuality,* Foucault writes:

We must not imagine a world of discourse divided between accepted discourse and excluded discourse, or between the dominant discourse and the dominated one; but as a multiplicity of discursive elements that can come into play in various strategies. It is this distribution that we must reconstruct, with the things said and those concealed, the enunciations required and those forbidden, that it comprises. . . . Discourses are not once and for all subservient to power or raised up against it, any more than silences are.[53]

In describing talk about homosexuality in the nineteenth century, for example, Foucault argues that the same discourses used to "disqualify" homosexuality were also used to legitimate it: Categories of sexual behavior created by medical science were employed by a variety of parties to justify and to condemn the same practices.[54]

Although we will return to Foucault's ideas about discourse in subsequent chapters, their usefulness to students of politics cannot be overemphasized. Rhetorics do not by themselves dominate or become subverted: They are adopted by actors who perceive these discourses to be useful weapons in battle. Foucault's ideas about the "polyvalence of discourses" help us understand how language is "stolen" or manipulated by those who find themselves in situations where power is exercised. It is in his work on discourse that Foucault underlines the importance of bridging levels of analysis—the real exercise of power and the discourses surrounding it.

Knowledge and power are inextricably intertwined, but for Foucault, there is a third element of contemporary dominance—surveillance. Over the past few centuries, a new form of power has emerged. This *disciplinary* power, Foucault posits, is exercised on individuals' bodies, not on their property. An example of this type of dominance is the Panopticon, an architectural design introduced by Jeremy Bentham in the mid-nineteenth century.

A Panopticon is a plan for prisons, with an observation tower at the center of a large circular room of cells. The placement of the tower and the use of backlighting enable a supervisor to see all inmates, but remain unseen himself. Furthermore, the inmates cannot view each other. The beauty of the design, as a means of social control, is that prisoners are unsure of whether or when they are being observed. As a result, subjects tend to internalize rules and norms for behavior.[55] The Panopticon—a place where one is observed but cannot see—is an ideal type of dominance in Foucault's view. The technique captures the essence of modern power, and the theory underlying it can be applied to other innovations: Technologies of surveillance, from wiretaps to satellite photography, prevent us from knowing whether our behavior is being monitored. Foucault sees the Panopticon as a metaphor for discipline in contemporary life: "Our society is one not of spectacle, but of surveillance."[56] Panopticism is ritualized dominance, a form of power which can be "depersonalized, diffused, relational and anonymous, while at the same time totalizing more and more dimensions of social life."[57]

For our purposes, the idea of disciplinary power is particularly useful because the basis of this force is in observation, measurement, and calculation. Although Foucault spends most of his effort describing the treatment of prisoners, the insane, children, and other more or less helpless beings, his insights can be applied to a variety of situations. The methodologies of investigation and observation in the human sciences are subtle mechanisms of social control: If one can observe and measure a phenomenon, one can regulate it as well. Foucault's ideas about the power/surveillance relationship enhance the history of quantification because they introduce a new level of complexity into that history. Early statisticians sought social control through the observation of the body. Yet this was not an obvious application of power. It was power gained through knowledge, and the ability to watch and to count.

A New Framework for the Study of Public Opinion

Taken together, Weber's notion of rationalization and Foucault's writings on power yield valuable tools for analyzing the role of numbers in political discourse. Although the two theorists saw the process of rationalization in social life differently,[58] their views of history prompt an interesting set of questions about the rise of quantification in politics. These are queries which animate the empirical studies of subsequent chapters, and I will return to them throughout the book: How is it that numbers are used to dominate or resist domination in the political sphere? Why are quantitative discourses viewed as authoritative during particular periods in American political history? And finally, what are the implications of accelerated measurement, calculation, and quantification for political life?

There are three areas of overlap between Weberian and Foucauldian theory which are most relevant to students of public opinion history: the advent of instrumental rationality, the notion of power as strategy, and the relationship between measurement and legitimate social control. Each set of ideas informs our understanding of how politics and opinion communication have changed over time.

Max Weber was not the first to write about rationality, since the concept was already firmly rooted in the tradition of German social theory. Yet Weber's central insights—the inevitable trade-offs between instrumental and substantive rationality, and increasing rationalization—illuminate a tremendous number of recent developments in American politics. The decline of the parties and the rise of political consulting, the pervasiveness of the public opinion poll, and the dominance of the electronic media each exemplify the trend toward routinization and systematization. Once these developments are viewed through the lens of Weber's theory, new questions are raised: Will these trends end in disenchantment? What is lost with the advent of rationalized political communication? Weber prods us to ask these rather broad historical questions, but Foucault directs us to make detailed studies of *particular instances* of rationalization: Since systematization and routinization are often complex, multifaceted phenomena, the student of political history must focus on narrow instances within that history. The annals of public opinion expression and measurement are a rich arena for inquiries about rationalization, since quantification has been so thorough and so dramatic in that particular sphere.

One need not give up the notion that power may, in certain circumstances, be viewed as a commodity or property. Yet considering power as a set of practices enables students of politics to focus their inquiries much more sharply. Until Foucault wrote about a wide-ranging set of disciplinary techniques, theorists did not concentrate on the techniques associated with the exercise of power. The value of studying these technologies is enormous: The exercise of power is an uneven process which often succeeds, but also often fails. If we fix our attention on the strategies of power, we can observe the ways that individuals or institutions attempt to dominate, but also the ways these actions are resisted. In fact, the perpetual nature of resistance to power is a critical element of Foucault's writings. He argues that

> where there is power, there is resistance. . . . [The existence of power relations] depends on a multiplicity of points of resistance: these play the role of adversary, target, support, or handle in power relations. These points of resistance are present everywhere in the power network. Hence there is no single locus of great Refusal, no soul of revolt, source of all rebellions, or pure law of the revolutionary. Instead there is a plurality of resistances, each of them a special case: re-

sistances that are possible, necessary, improbable; others that are spontaneous, savage, solitary, concerted, rampant, or violent; still others that are quick to compromise, interested, or sacrificial; by definition, they can only exist in the strategic field of power relations.[59]

The application of power strategies and resistance to them is a constant throughout the history of public opinion. We will observe this process in the empirical case studies that follow, but recent, vivid illustrations come to mind easily. Near the end of the 1988 presidential election campaign, for example, Michael Dukakis (like Harry Truman before him) urged voters not to listen to the political campaign managers and pollsters who predicted the Democrat's demise. He asked that they evaluate the two candidates and their issue positions instead of allowing political professionals to shape the election process.[60] It is possible that these sorts of rhetorical pleas will become increasingly popular, as national campaigns grow even more rationalized.[61]

Finally, the relationship between measurement or calculation and the production of legitimate knowledge is one which permeates the lengthy history of public opinion communication. As we shall see in chapter 3, numerical descriptions of public opinion gained authority beginning in the early nineteenth century with the diffusion of the general election and the use of straw polls in election campaigns. A brief example of the authority associated with quantification is appropriate here, though. In his book *The Captive Public*, Benjamin Ginsberg argues that opinion polls are often used by American presidents and interest groups to delegitimate claims they want to discredit. Most often those who are discredited are minority groups or marginalized populations who lack the ability and resources to conduct opinion polls. Ginsberg believes that the scientific aura of polls—and the pollsters' insistence on rigorous, precise measurement—explains their attraction: Polls produce authoritative knowledge because they seem to be conducted in an "objective," value-neutral manner.[62] Although survey researchers themselves are well aware of the inadequacies of these measures, qualifications about the results of polls seem to get lost in public discourse.[63]

In this chapter, we reviewed the history of quantification and the different conceptual approaches one can bring to this history.

Yet the instrumental use of numbers is only part of their appeal in the political sphere. Statistics and quantitative descriptions of the public have great symbolic worth, as well. Although their symbolic allure is tied to their instrumental value, the use of quantitative data is a powerful ritual process. It is to the symbolic force of numbers that we now turn.

CHAPTER TWO

Numbers and Symbolic Politics

Like the symbols of language and of art, mathematical symbols
are from the beginning surrounded by a sort of magical atmo-
sphere. They are looked upon with religious awe and
veneration.

Ernst Cassirer
An Essay on Man, 1944

THE PHILOSOPHER Ernst Cassirer believed mathematical
symbols to be the most interesting symbols of all. Unlike
words or most visual symbols, numbers enable the complete
objectification of experience. Many symbols help us achieve
the distance necessary for understanding social action, but numbers permit us to discover order and system in the world. Today, as
in the days of the Pythagorean thinkers Cassirer studied, numbers
have a mystical quality. Quantitative data are precise and elegant in
ways that the most exacting language can never be.

In the previous chapter, we explored the instrumental functions of quantification—the straightforward, manifest uses of numerical data. Yet quantitative data also serve symbolic purposes,
which cannot always be determined in advance. The instrumental
functions of opinion polls, for example, are usually discussed and
outlined *before* surveys are conducted: Pollsters collect a particular
type of data and usually have concrete reasons for doing so. Pollsters' clients, such as news organizations, commission or purchase
these survey data because the results may attract the attention of
readers and viewers. Symbolic uses of the data these organizations
collect—by legislators, interest group leaders, or citizen activists—
are much more difficult to predict. In fact, the symbolic value of
public opinion data emerges *during* public debate. It is only in the

context of political discourse and ritual that the true rhetorical value of numbers becomes apparent.

Most often, quantification is considered in the context of its instrumental value. In this chapter, though, we explore the more ambiguous, symbolic functions of public opinion data. These two functions, instrumental and symbolic, are so closely intertwined that they are often difficult to isolate empirically.[1] In many cases different parties seize the same data, embed these data in distinctive ideological rhetorics, and then use the numbers for very different purposes. Those who conduct polls for specific reasons do not always control the numbers they produce, so professional survey researchers are often frustrated by the ways their findings are cited in public discourse.

In subsequent chapters I will analyze different episodes in the history of public opinion where numbers served both instrumental and symbolic functions. First, however, we must explore the nature of symbolic communication itself. A brief review of the extensive scholarly literature on symbols will allow us to determine how numbers have come to play such a vital role in political dialogue. In the first section, I examine the character of symbols themselves: What are symbols, and why have they been a central focus of inquiry across academic disciplines? Next I analyze how and why symbols are used in politics to construct the bounds of public debate. Last, we turn to symbols of public opinion. What are symbols of public opinion? And why have numerical symbols of popular sentiment been so compelling throughout American political history? Numerical descriptions of the nebulous public mood seem precise and objective, but exactly how have they become so definitive?

The Nature of Symbols

Scholars have defined symbols in a variety of ways since the turn of the century. Theorists from Sigmund Freud to Kenneth Burke have studied how symbols are used, consciously or unconsciously, by individuals and institutions wishing to express themselves. The words "symbol" and "symbolic" are also widely used in everyday conversation, as people try to find meaning in the actions of others.

Although a variety of theorists have written about symbolic expression, Freud was one of the earliest. He described, for example, the roles of symbols in dream work, and how these symbols could be used by the psychoanalyst in therapy. In a lecture titled "Symbolism in Dreams," Freud explained that

> symbolism is perhaps the most remarkable part of our theory of dreams. . . . Symbols make it possible for us in certain circumstances to interpret a dream without questioning the dreamer, who indeed in any case can tell us nothing about the symbols. If the symbols commonly appearing in dreams are known, and also the personality of the dreamer, the conditions under which he lives, and the impressions in his mind after which his dream occurred, we are often in a position to interpret it straightaway; to translate it at sight, as it were.[2]

Freud viewed symbols as indicative of discord and unhappiness on the part of the dreamer. In dreams, Freud argued, there are a limited number of things which are represented symbolically: Most often, symbols represent the body, family members, birth, death, and other such significant people and events. In Freud's theory there was a regular correspondence, across individuals, between particular symbols and the phenomena they signified. For example, journeys or traveling represent death, while small animals and vermin tend to represent children or siblings. Although Freud's specific correspondences are now viewed by many as dubious and somewhat culture-bound, the notion that symbol use is critical to individual cognition is widely accepted.[3]

Freud influenced theorizing about symbolism in psychology, but Émile Durkheim set the research agenda for work on symbols in sociology and anthropology. Durkheim studied symbolism primarily among groups or societies, and not within the context of the individual psyche. Unlike Freud, Durkheim argued that symbols "were expressive of consonance, of solidarity of the individual with his society," and not of disharmony.[4] For Durkheim, symbolic communication was a component of social process: Symbols could elicit strong feeling and also serve as bases for individual and institutional action. Symbols are powerful, Durkheim posited, because they enable the "transference of sentiments." His famous discussion of emotion and symbols is worth quoting at length:

> The idea of a thing and the idea of its symbol are closely united in our minds; the result is that the emotions provoked

by the one extend contagiously to the other. But this contagion, which takes place in every case to a certain degree, is much more complete and more marked when the symbol is something simple, definite and easily representable, while the thing itself, owing to its dimensions, the number of its parts and the complexity of their arrangement, is difficult to hold in the mind. . . . The soldier who dies for his flag, dies for his country; but as a matter of fact, in his own consciousness, it is the flag that has the first place. . . . He loses sight of the fact that the flag is only a sign, and that it has no value in itself, but only brings to mind the reality that it represents; it is treated as if it were this reality itself.[5]

Since Durkheim wrote, a variety of anthropologists, many of whom conducted fieldwork in non-Western societies, have engaged in the rigorous study of symbolism. Edward Sapir, who wrote a remarkably influential essay on symbolism in 1934, drew upon psychoanalytic and linguistic theory in order to define and operationalize symbols.[6] Sapir distinguished between signs—which simply indicate something—and symbols, which represent more complex ideas. For Sapir, there were two types of symbols: referential and condensation. Some symbols, like the ticking of the telegraph, simply refer to meanings. They are substitutes for ideas, and are therefore very economical forms of communication. Condensation symbols are those which allow us to refer to abstract, intricate ideas, and also to the profound emotions associated with those ideas. In discussing these symbols, which often seem trivial on their surfaces, Sapir's debt to Freud becomes clear: Condensation symbols reflect strong feelings that are often unacknowledged by the conscious mind.[7]

Symbols frequently operate on both the referential and condensation levels. The flag, an example used by many theorists, signifies or directly represents a nation, but can also stir emotions or communicate a particular type of patriotism. Since flags work as symbols on these two levels, they are extremely popular icons: American flags can be found on clothing, in newspaper mastheads, imprinted on consumer goods, and in a multitude of other places. Symbols of public opinion, in the form of poll results, also function on both referential and condensational symbolic levels. Take, for example, a very common type of poll—the presidential popularity poll. Good standing in a popularity poll indicates that a president is well liked by many, but also may indicate great faith or pride in government. During times of national crisis, presidential popularity ratings often soar, because patriotic sentiment runs high at these moments.[8]

Since symbols are multitiered forms of expression, theorists in the communications field have always been drawn to them. One of the earliest of these researchers was the sociologist George Herbert Mead. Mead believed that the "self" and society both evolve through the communication of what he called "significant symbols." Thinking, for Mead, was impossible without symbols, and symbols themselves are socially constructed. Mead argued that communication with others was based on shared symbolic repertoires:

> Thinking always implies a symbol which will call out the same response in another that it calls out in the thinker. Such a symbol is a universal of discourse; it is universal in its character. We always assume that the symbol we use is one which will call out in the other person the same response, provided it is a part of his mechanism of conduct. A person who is saying something is saying to himself what he says to others; otherwise he does not know what he is talking about.[9]

Our internal use of symbols, in other words, is inextricably tied to our public use of symbols. Mead's insights emphasize the relationship between the structure of symbol use on the individual, psychological level and the use of symbols in public discourse. Symbols are meaningful because of their *social* resonance, because they provide a focal point for the experiences, feelings, and ideas of many. In the aesthetic realm, a work of art is powerful when it employs profound, widely shared symbols. Writing about symbols and literature, Kenneth Burke defines symbols as "the verbal parallel to a pattern of experience."[10] He argues that patterns of experience are often turned into symbols by artists and writers, and that the "symbol is perhaps most overwhelming in its effect when the artist's and the reader's patterns of experience closely coincide."[11]

For our purposes, anthropologist Raymond Firth's definition of *symbol* is most useful, since it is broad enough to encompass many of the theoretical insights discussed above. Firth argues that a symbol is a sign which has a complex series of associations, often of the emotional kind, and difficult (some would say, impossible) to describe in terms other than partial representation. The aspect of personal or social construction in meaning may be marked, so no sensory likeness of symbol to object may be apparent to an observer, and imputation of relationship may seem arbitrary.[12]

Symbols, Politics, and Social Action

The study of political symbols has long been central to fieldwork and theory building in cultural anthropology, but beginning in the late 1950s, political scientists started to study these types of symbols as well. Growing attention to political socialization was partially responsible for increased concern with the symbols of politics. Those who studied the evolving belief systems of children found that symbols of authority—the president or the mayor of a child's city—were recurring and salient.[13] Early in their lives children learn to venerate the office of the presidency and the man who occupies it, but they also develop a more generalized respect for the political system itself. Symbols of authority, and other American icons such as the flag, contribute to what political scientists have called "diffuse system support."[14]

Studies of political socialization in the 1950s and 1960s led researchers to the analysis of significant symbols, but so did the development of major social movements. The civil rights movement, the antiwar movement, and, later, the women's liberation movement each underscored the importance of symbolic communication in political life. Rituals of dissent which incorporated symbols—flag burning, the destruction of draft cards, bra burning—were vivid and powerful. Television was particularly adept at transmitting these ritual displays, and the medium accelerated the dramatic use of political symbols beginning in the 1960s.[15]

There are a variety of connections between the use of symbols and the structure of power in any given community or state. Symbols are used by those in power to legitimate their rule, but symbols also serve as bases for movements which question the status quo. C. Wright Mills has argued that certain "master symbols"—such as "the will of the people" or "the vote of the majority"—are often independent variables in the analysis of political action: Appeals to these symbolic manifestations of values can direct the behaviors of individuals and institutions.[16] Of particular interest to students of politics are three functions of symbols. Symbols are useful to regimes who wish to legitimate themselves or to delegitimate the claims of others. They are also meaningful to groups who challenge the political status quo, hoping to mobilize a constituency for political action.

Much of the literature on ritual in anthropology, sociology, and political science focuses on the ways that regimes legitimate themselves. Sociologists, such as Mills and Hans Gerth, argue that institutions generate "symbol spheres" which justify their existence. Symbol spheres are "universes of discourse—the vocabularies, pronunciations, emblems, formulas and types of conversation which are typical of an institutionalized order."[17] Very often, master symbols associated with a particular institution are so "deeply internalized" by individuals that their significance and meaning remain unquestioned and unchallenged. Examples of political institutions and their concomitant symbol spheres abound. The U.S. flag, a favorite example of political theorists, is certainly a master symbol closely associated with the American polity and military. Furthermore, the flag is most often used for ceremonial purposes by those who *already support* the polity. As Peter Berger and Thomas Luckmann note, institutions which are already powerful use symbols to reach an even higher plane of authority. Legitimation through symbol use "produces new meanings that serve to integrate the meanings already attached to disparate institutional processes. The function of legitimation is to make objectively available and subjectively plausible the 'first-order' objectivations that have been institutionalized."[18] In the cases of the flag, the bald eagle, the White House, and other such icons, the legitimacy of the polity has been transferred to the symbol.[19] Each of these items—a colored cloth, a bird, and a building—has very little meaning in itself. It is the constant association of these symbols with the polity that gives them their significance. People recognize these symbols as referring to the government, and they can be used as advertisements for the natural place of that institution in our lives. Perhaps Carlton Hayes best describes how the flag operates as a legitimating symbol:

There are universal liturgical forms for "saluting" the flag, for "dipping" the flag, for "lowering" the flag, and for "hoisting" the flag. Men bare their heads when the flag passes by; and in praise of the flag poets write odes, and to it children sing hymns and pledge allegiance. In all solemn feasts and fasts of nationalism, the flag is in evidence, and with it that other sacred thing, the national anthem. . . . Worshippers stand when it is intoned, the military at "attention," and the male civilians with uncovered heads, all with external show of respect and veneration.[20]

Those in government may also use significant symbols to marginalize and disparage particular groups or policies. Gerth and Mills note that although many Americans support certain socialist-inspired policies, the application of labels such as "socialist" or "communist" can completely discredit these same policies.[21] This sort of symbolic assault is exemplified by former president Reagan's rhetoric describing the Sandinista government in Nicaragua, headed in the 1980s by President Daniel Ortega. Although Nicaragua did have ties with Cuba, the Soviet Union, and other communist-bloc nations, Reagan repeatedly emphasized the socialistic, noncapitalist nature of the Sandinista regime. By continually emphasizing the lack of free elections and a free press in Nicaragua, and by labeling the country "communist," Reagan believed he could discredit the Sandinistas in the eyes of Congress and the general public.[22]

Beginning in the 1960s, the flag and other symbols normally associated with the legitimacy of government were transformed into symbols of protest. These master symbols were often used as expressions of dissent, and along with other strategies, helped to mobilize individuals who opposed U.S. involvement in Vietnam. Todd Gitlin has argued that the media were attracted to the most "colorful" forms of symbolic communication in the late 1960s, since expectations for antiwar drama ran high. As a result, Gitlin believes, media attention drove certain antiwar activists to great feats of flamboyant, ritual protest—flag burning among them.[23]

As Murray Edelman and others have pointed out, symbolic communication and rhetoric actually *construct* the political sphere. Labels and icons are regularly employed by those inside and outside institutional structures to frame actions and advocate positions.[24] With the diffusion of visual media, and television in particular, symbolic communication has become more complex and more universal. Advertisers are especially sensitive to the compelling nature of patriotic symbols (e.g., flags, the likenesses of George Washington and Abraham Lincoln, and images of national monuments) to sell ideas and commodities to a sympathetic public.[25]

Symbols of Public Opinion

Since public opinion expression is viewed as central to the democratic process in America, symbols of public opinion are pervasive. One could argue that many of the patriotic symbols discussed above are also symbols of public opinion. The flag, for example, is powerful in certain contexts because it represents the *entire* nation—the unity that is America: A flag implies universality of belief in country, and all are expected to stand during the moments we pledge our allegiance to it. Another popular symbol which represents democracy, but also the public will, is the U.S. Constitution. This document, which Wilbur Zelinsky calls "a divine national scripture," is widely venerated, and operates, in a way, as America's social contract.[26] For Rousseau, the general will was manifested in the social contract, and in a similar sense, the public sentiment is the basis for the constitution.

One problematic aspect of studying symbols of public opinion is that they are often conflated with symbols of patriotism and nationalism. An example is the yellow ribbon, used extensively during the Persian Gulf War to signify support for American troops stationed in Saudi Arabia. The ribbon was displayed by parties who supported American policy, and also by those who objected to U.S. military involvement in the conflict. The yellow ribbon worked particularly well for those protesting U.S. policy in the Persian Gulf because it signified allegiance, but not agreement with Bush administration actions. One could argue that yellow ribbons connoted support for the troops, and were also rather general indicators of patriotic public opinion.

There is one set of symbols which is more directly associated with public opinion itself—those numbers derived from survey research. Quantitative data from polls and surveys are numerical symbols which have proven to be powerful, multilayered ones when used in political discourse. On one level, numbers have the "magical" quality Cassirer alluded to: They are precise, elegant, and above all, scientific. Numbers enable objectivity, and objectivity is one road to enlightenment.[27] Data about public opinion benefit from the general respect accorded numerical symbols. Polling data, as many have noted, are considered so important and so newsworthy that journalists write stories *around* the release of these statistics.[28] With the diffusion of the sample survey, politicians, journalists, and a variety of others have come to believe that discerning public opinion is not a particularly difficult task: One need only draw a representative sample, design standardized questionnaires, and properly train interviewers. This procedure yields valuable data, rigorously gathered and seemingly "scientific."

On another level, numbers which describe the public mood are democratic symbols. The theory and practice of sampling dictate that all members of the population have an equal opportunity to be chosen for participation in a survey. Although most Americans may not understand the actual logistics and procedures necessary for drawing a national random sample, most probably understand the notion that surveys are meant to be representative.[29] The reason that polls are so pervasive is that they work symbolically on two levels at once: They are scientifically derived data, *and* they are representative of general public sentiment. Sampling itself is a democratic notion. So while there are (and, no doubt, will always be) complaints about and assaults on polls in public discourse, these data are omnipresent symbols nonetheless.

Why quantitative representations of opinion have become so pervasive is a complex question, but the answer seems to have much to do with the simplicity of symbolic communication. Numerical techniques for the description of popular sentiment are unambiguous, and they purport to measure an extremely nebulous and transient phenomenon. In the days before sampling, as Benjamin Ginsberg has pointed out, people were forced to express themselves through action, and leaders tried to comprehend the public mood by monitoring a large variety of occurrences.[30] Yet with the development of aggregation techniques for measuring opinion, communication of the popular will became much less complicated: Quantification is an extraordinarily economical method for condensing complex political beliefs.

Numerical symbols of mass belief are valuable because they are labels for the amorphous entity we call "public opinion." Quantitative data enable us to speak, in a very succinct manner, about public moods. In comparison, the behavior of a crowd at a protest rally—one forum for the expression of public opinion—is much more difficult to describe. It takes more effort and subtlety to characterize the actions of a large number of people engaging in a range of behaviors than to aggregate verbal opinions expressed in response to a standard form. Numbers allow us to communicate directly about the abstract notion of public opinion, just as IQ test scores have enabled educators to discuss something called "intelligence."[31] Much of the texture and complexity of political attitudes is lost in the polling process, yet much is gained in the way of public discourse, since poll data are so easily communicated.

Opinion Data: Instrumental versus Symbolic Uses

Symbols of public opinion, quantitative and qualitative, are part of a larger ritual process in American politics. When an issue becomes the focus of public debate, politicians and journalists inevitably ask themselves how the public feels about that issue. For elected officials, understanding the popular sentiment is part of their job, and for reporters this is also the case. But even beyond these responsibilities, communication about public opinion has become habitual in America.

To understand the varied uses of opinion data, these numbers need to be evaluated from both symbolic and instrumental perspectives. Each of these frameworks forces us to examine different aspects of the public opinion expression process, and each is extremely valuable. As I noted in the previous chapter, an understanding of the means/end rationality of public opinion measurement highlights issues of social control, power, and surveillance. An emphasis on instrumental uses of public opinion data underscores the obvious and sometimes critical functions these numbers serve for statesmen, journalists, political activists, and, occasionally, average citizens.

The symbolic uses of numbers are much less obvious than the instrumental ones, yet they are just as important. Opinion data are not always used in a calculated, rational manner, and they are not necessarily used in the way one may have originally planned. A focus on instrumental rationality accents the mechanics of the public opinion expression and measurement process—the plans one makes to collect and utilize data to achieve ends. A focus on the symbolic use of numbers demands that we shift the emphasis of our analysis. Symbolic communication revolves around *emotional* appeal, a type of rhetoric which lies outside of the Weberian notion of instrumental reason. Symbols stir feelings, and capitalize on passions which are difficult to incorporate into a rational calculus about policy or anything else.

In his study of political ritual, David Kertzer argues that research on symbols is difficult because symbols themselves are ambiguous and multivocal: The same symbols are used by different people, in different contexts, for different purposes. He also points out that symbolic communication and the ritual use of symbols are central to political life. Kertzer notes:

> The image of "political man" as a rational actor who carefully weighs his or her objective circumstances and decides on a course of action based on an instrumental calculation of self-interest leaves out culture and all that makes us human. Though we are rooted in the physical world and much affected by material forces, we perceive and evaluate them through our symbolic apparatus.[32]

From this perspective, people are symbol-using beings who often opt for the dramatic or compelling argument over the one arrived at through reason. Kertzer, in the tradition of symbol theorists who came before him, recognizes that a full understanding of politics demands that one examine at least two sides of behavior—the instrumentally rational side, and the more affect-driven side.

In exploring the instrumental uses of quantitative opinion data, we turned to two theorists of rationality—Max Weber and Michel Foucault. Not surprisingly, both of these theorists understood that there was another, less rational dimension of social action as well. Weber wrote about the power of substantive rationality—appeals to values, to tradition, and to charisma. In his work, Foucault emphasized how knowledge and our categories for understanding human action are, at their roots, irrationally and idiosyncratically constructed.

One might argue that symbols of public opinion are often used instrumentally in political discourse, since they are means to ends. But as so many scholars have pointed out, the meaning of a symbol is never concrete enough to be used in this fashion: A variety of meanings may be ascribed to the same symbol. One cannot predict just how symbols will be exploited, manipulated, or imitated, after they are created. If one is to study symbolic communication in the area of public opinion, it is important to look beyond the means/ ends equation. How are opinion data used in the context of ideological or partisan debate? How is it that quantitative data, which seem so objective and precise in their meanings, can be used to stir the emotions? These are questions to which we return throughout this study, as we analyze the multidimensional nature of opinion expression in American political history.

Symbols and the Study of Public Opinion

The large majority of students of public opinion have been more interested in attitude measurement than in the symbolic role of measurement itself.[33] Although survey researchers are beginning to analyze the ways poll data are used in the judicial system,[34] in government agencies,[35] and in business,[36] the uses of opinion data in political debate are still understudied. As a result, *theory* about the ways that quantitative data are employed in public life is sorely lacking: Researchers have refined methods for measuring opinion, but still do not know how the products of their efforts are managed in the political arena. If students of politics are to understand this aspect of the opinion communication process, they must begin by examining the specific, historical contexts in which public preference data have been used.

There is a dearth of research on the symbolic uses of opinion data in contemporary discourse, but historical perspectives on the phenomenon are lacking as well. As the previous chapter details, quantitative techniques for assessing public opinion have a long history. Yet the ways in which numerical opinion data have been used over the course of time have not been a focus of scholarly research. In subsequent chapters of this book, I document the ways in which quantitative opinion data have been used by partisan journalists of the nineteenth century, U.S. congressmen and reporters in the 1930s and 1940s, and political journalists writing today. Studying the uses of opinion data over time highlights the ways methodologies have evolved, but also the ways American politics has changed.

Quantitative data may, on occasion, provide vivid, reliable portraits of public opinion. Yet the collection and communication of numerical data does not always answer questions about the public mood on important political matters. Often these data initiate conflict, instead of preventing or suppressing it. As we shall see in the case studies which follow, the objective, precise character of numbers has not created a more rational political sphere ruled by instrumental reason. On the contrary, instead of becoming tools for the *resolution* of ideological or policy conflicts, quantitative data have often been the *source* of such struggles throughout American political history.

CHAPTER THREE

Techniques of Opinion
Expression and Measurement

D URING ANY PERIOD the methods used to measure popular sentiment, the ways attitudes are expressed, and the meaning of public opinion itself are all tightly interwoven. In fact, behind every technique for articulating or measuring public opinion is a statement about the nature of the opinion communication process. Modern public opinion polling, for example, assumes that public opinion is an aggregation of many individual opinions. The use of the sample survey also presumes that the confidential exchange between pollster and informant is ultimately a "public" expression process, even though poll respondents and their corresponding opinions are never identified.

This chapter traces the history of public opinion by focusing on the changing techniques for expression and measurement. If we are to understand the quantification of public opinion, which accelerated in early nineteenth century America, we must first understand the larger historical progression of opinion techniques. This macrohistorical perspective reveals trends in opinion expression over time, as well as radical changes in the meaning of public opinion.

I begin this inquiry by defining two key terms: *public opinion* and *technique*. *Public opinion* has been a particularly difficult phrase to define, and a multiplicity of distinct conceptualizations can be found in the social science literature. After this discussion of terminology, we turn to the history of public opinion technologies. Questions are posed about this history: Have opinion techniques become increasingly rationalized over time, as Weber predicted? And does the history of public opinion technology echo Michel Foucault's work on surveillance and social control? Throughout this trend analysis, I evaluate the public opinion poll: In light of previous techniques for expression and measurement, how is the poll different from its ancestors, and what does it have in common with these older technologies?

Defining Public Opinion

In 1965, a researcher named Harwood Childs reviewed the definitions of public opinion in the academic literature. Instead of consensus, however, Childs discovered scores of different definitions. Some of the definitions stated that public opinion was the collective attitude of political elites, involved and interested in policy. Other definitions assumed public opinion to be the aggregation of all opinions, regardless of their origin. Still others, like the political scientist V. O. Key, believed public opinion to be the set of important popular attitudes to which governments attend.[1]

The reason why Childs found so many definitions is obvious: Social theorists and researchers who provided the definitions were interested in different aspects of the opinion communication process. Some studied the way opinions are formed, or how our attitudes are influenced by those around us. Others were concerned with the relationship between public opinion and public policy— how and whether mass opinion is reflected in legislative action or the nature of political systems. Finally, many of the researchers were interested in the ways in which opinions toward particular issues changed over time. Each of these projects demanded a unique definition of public opinion. For example, if one is interested in political socialization, one must conceptualize public opinion as a dynamic, potentially malleable phenomenon. On the other hand, if a researcher wants to understand the correlation between the nature of mass opinion in a particular nation and the type of regime it supports, he or she will be drawn to the stable elements of public opinion as well as the dynamic ones.

In general, the various meanings of public opinion can be sorted into four definitional categories: Aggregation, Majoritarian, Discursive/Consensual, and Reification.[2]

Today we tend to think of public opinion as the aggregation of anonymously expressed opinions. The opinion poll is the primary tool that journalists, politicians, and others employ in order to understand the character of public sentiment. When "the public" or "public opinion" is invoked in popular discourse, the speaker or writer is often referring to the results of a survey.[3] Voting was the earliest form of opinion aggregation, but the practice of counting individual attitudes accelerated with the introduction of the straw poll in the 1820s. An exemplar of aggregation-oriented theorizing about public opinion is George Gallup and Saul Rae's polemical argument for the use of opinion polls, titled *The Pulse of Democracy*. Here Gallup and Rae argue that public opinion is best ascertained by posing questions to a variety of individuals, regardless of their involvement in politics or knowledge about issues. With the help of sampling, the authors argue, public opinion could be discerned simply by "sounding the opinions of a relatively small number of persons, proportionate to each major population group in every section of the country."[4]

A second category of definitions might best be described as majoritarian. These conceptualizations assume that the opinions of most consequence are those expressed by the largest number of citizens. This approach is also aggregation-oriented, but does not treat all opinions equally: It assumes that minority opinion is less significant than majority opinion. An example is the definition of public opinion that A. Lawrence Lowell gave in his 1913 book, *Public Opinion and Popular Government:* "A majority is not enough, and unanimity is not required, but the opinion must be such that while the minority may not share it, they feel bound, by conviction, not by fear, to accept it."[5]

A third category of definitions includes those which revolve around consensus and communication. The most famous of these is Jean-Jacques Rousseau's conception of the "general will," which served as the basis for the social contract.[6] John Locke also wrote of norms and consensus in *An Essay Concerning Human Understanding*. He argued that there are three types of law which govern people—divine law or the law of God, civil law, and the law of "opinion or reputation."[7] Locke believed that the law of opinion, what we now call social norms, is by far the most powerful: Those who flout accepted manners or opinion risk becoming outcasts within their own communities. More recently, Elisabeth Noelle-Neumann has drawn upon these definitions to put forth a theory of opinion formation and change. In her book *The Spiral of Silence*, Noelle-Neumann posits that public opinion is a societal consensus which binds individuals together, but also oppresses them.[8]

The definitions in this third category all emphasize the role of communication in the public opinion process. In order for people to know when they have stepped outside the bounds of acceptable behavior, they must understand the extent of these bounds. As a result, the sending of cues is constant for consensus theorists: People are almost always engaged in the verbal or nonverbal communication of opinion.

A fourth category of definitions assumes public opinion to be a fiction or a reification. Writers such as Walter Lippmann believed that public opinion is a *projection* of media or elite opinion.[9] In fact, public opinion is a "phantom" manipulated by a variety of parties who wish to legitimate their positions or actions. The French sociologist Pierre Bourdieu has updated Lippmann's critique, arguing that public opinion simply does not exist. Citizens are rarely interested or educated enough to articulate informed opinions, Bourdieu argues, and to believe otherwise is to be naive about the democratic process.[10] The theorists who compose this fourth category are an eclectic group, and many of them are severe critics of modern survey research.

In this book, I avoid choosing among these categories and instead recognize that "public opinion" has different meanings during different periods. As Habermas has noted, the terms "public sphere" and "public opinion" are extremely time-bound: Both concepts "acquire their specific meaning from a concrete historical situation."[11] Indeed, the conception of public opinion in a particular era is a function of social, political, and technological context. Locke's "law of opinion" may not be useful in understanding contemporary *mass* opinion formation processes, but it might describe very well the nature of opinion communication in smaller communities. Similarly, the phrase *public opinion* may be used in a polemical fashion by a politician even if he has neither qualitative nor quantitative evidence to support his arguments. In a case like this, public opinion does appear to be a fiction of sorts, invoked for rhetorical purposes.

Techniques and Technologies

Public opinion "techniques" or "technologies" are simply the tools that people use to express or measure attitudes. These techniques, which historian Charles Tilly has named "repertoires," are utilized by political actors, at different times, for a variety of purposes. Below I discuss the many techniques people have employed to communicate their opinions, either to each other or to their leaders. Theorists disagree over the proper definition of *technology*.[12] As in the debate over the meaning of public opinion, much of the problem stems from the different theoretical and empirical approaches employed by those studying technology. Here I will use Jacques Ellul's definition of *la technique*: *"the totality of methods rationally arrived at and having absolute efficiency* (for a given stage of development) *in every* field of human activity."[13] Ellul's definition is particularly valuable for our purposes, since he underlines the intentionality of technology use. People and institutions develop tools to express or assess public opinion because they *need* to do so promptly and effectively. Ellul also believed that techniques for completing tasks are used in all areas of human endeavor. Technology is not found solely in the realms of engineering or medicine. Thinking about peoples' actions and channels of communication as techniques of expression forces one to look more carefully at the motivations and goals of those individuals.

Techniques of public opinion are two-dimensional. The tools that are used to measure popular attitudes are techniques of expression as well. Although a survey research supplier measures opinion about an issue so that it can sell these data to newspapers and other organizations, the poll also enables the articulation of opinion. Similarly, newspapers themselves are technologies which assess public opinion, but they also give voice to public opinion.

A Brief History of Opinion Techniques

Several scholars have written about the different ways people have expressed their opinions over the course of time. Wilhelm Bauer, a German historian who wrote a lengthy history of public opinion in 1914, traced the communication of popular sentiment from ancient Greece to the early twentieth century. Charles Tilly has challenged public opinion researchers to think about their work from a historical perspective, and has explored attitude expression before the age of survey research. The most recent scholar to work in this historical tradition is Benjamin Ginsberg, who has argued that general elections and polls were introduced by regimes who sought to "domesticate" a volatile public, beginning in the late eighteenth and early nineteenth centuries.

A complete history of public opinion has never been written, partly because the subject is so broad, and partly because the history is an exceedingly long one. Here I will review a few of the major periods and developments in the history of opinion expression—moments which historians of public opinion believe to be the most significant. Although a variety of philosophers, from Plato to Habermas, have written about the nature of public opinion, I will refer to their works only occasionally in the body of the text as I evaluate development of public opinion technology. Table 3.1 is a compilation of many of the major technologies for the assessment and expression of public opinion. The list is drawn from the vast scholarly literature in public opinion history, and indicates the approximate period of appearance for each of the techniques.

TABLE 3.1 Historical Techniques for the Expression
and Assessment of Public Opinion

Techniques[a]	Time of Appearance[b]
Oratory/Rhetoric	5th century B.C.
Printing	16th century
Crowds	17th century
Petitions	Late 17th century
Salons	Late 17th century
Coffeehouses	18th century
Revolutionary Movements	Late 18th century
Strikes	19th century
General Elections	19th century
Straw Polls	1820s
Modern Newspapers	Mid-19th century
Letters to Public Officials & Editors	Mid-19th century
Mass Media Programming (Political)	1920s–1930s
Sample Survey	1930s

[a]The list of techniques in this table is far from complete, however, I have attempted to include those techniques cited most often by scholars in a range of disciplines. In order to compile the list, I drew from all significant histories of public opinion in the political science, sociology, communication, and history literatures. Some of these are: Bauer 1930, Coser 1970, Ginsberg 1986, Habermas 1989, Martin 1984, Palmer 1967, Sussmann 1963, and Tilly 1984.

[b]These dates represent crude approximations of when each technology was first employed.

Ancient Roots of Public Opinion Expression

The philosophers of ancient Greece were the first to write about public opinion. Plato, who harbored a general distrust of the public, was much less sympathetic to public opinion than Aristotle, who wrote:

> It is possible that the many, no one of whom taken singly is a good man, may yet taken all together be better than the few, not individually but collectively, in the same way that a feast to which all contribute is better than one given at one man's expense. For where there are many people, each has some share of goodness and intelligence, and when these are brought together, they become as it were one multiple man with many pairs of feet and hands and many minds. So too in regard to character and the powers of perception. That is why the general public is a better judge of works of music and poetry; some judge some parts, some others, but their joint pronouncement is a verdict upon the whole. And it is this assembling in one what was before separate that gives the good man his superiority over any individual man from the masses.[14]

Aristotle viewed public opinion as a "collective will" which evolved naturally over time.[15] Public opinion could be wise, and was certainly superior to the opinions of individual men: It is through aggregation, he argued, that wisdom appears. Plato saw public opinion quite differently, arguing that the collectivity was not capable of debating or deciding matters of policy.[16]

As Bauer points out, there were numerous techniques for the communication of public opinion in ancient Greece. Besides limited elections, there were Panhellenic festivals, pamphlets, and dramatic performances. The most important technique developed in Greece, though, was oratory. Oratory and rhetoric were believed to be extremely powerful tools for mobilizing the population or placating the public. In the marketplaces of ancient Greece, where citizens assembled "oratory rapidly developed as the technique best suited to the manipulation of public opinion and continued throughout later Greek and Roman times as the most powerful instrument of political propaganda and agitation."[17] In Roman history, techniques of opinion expression and assessment developed by the Greeks were widely employed, and a sophisticated transportation system accelerated the discussion of political issues and the exchange of ideas.[18] Paul Palmer notes that classical Roman writers "had little respect for the *vulgus*," but it seems that public opinion had become an important and identifiable quantity during that time.[19]

Most histories of public opinion contain wide gaps between the fall of the Roman Empire and the invention of the printing press. Bauer believes that the spread of news about politics, and the communication of ideas more generally, suffered during this period because the population was largely scattered across the European countryside. Decentralization of the populace combined with widespread illiteracy resulted in a dramatic remission of political discourse.[20]

There were two major events in the history of public opinion during the sixteenth century, both with enormous political impacts: Niccolò Machiavelli wrote *The Prince* and *The Discourses*, and the technology of printing diffused.

Much of *The Prince* either directly or indirectly addressed the subject of public opinion. Machiavelli believed that if a ruler was to gain control over the populace, he must seem humane to the masses regardless of his true feelings about them. He viewed people as "thankless, fickle, false, studious to avoid danger, and greedy," among other things.[21] The successful prince, Machiavelli wrote, is feared but not hated by the public, and is careful to appear merciful and benevolent. In the realm of public opinion persuasion and manipulation, superficial appearances matter most of all: These appearances can be the source of great triumph for the prince or the source of miserable failure. Machiavelli reminded the prince, "Every one sees what you seem, but few know what you are, and these few dare not oppose themselves to the opinion of many who have the majesty of the State to back them up."[22] It seems that Machiavelli was not only an early practitioner of what we now call "image management." He was also attuned to the power a public exerts on its own members well before Locke wrote about the laws of opinion and fashion.

Publics and Crowds

During the century in which *The Prince* was published a revolutionary communication technology emerged—the printing press.

As the historian Elizabeth Eisenstein has argued, the invention of the printing press enabled the birth of the modern public, as distinct from the crowd: In a public, compared to a crowd, individuals are connected through the communication of ideas and not by physical proximity. Until the press appeared, opinions were communicated orally, but printing made sustained, complex political discussion possible. She also argues that reading drew individuals away from their communities, yet at the same time facilitated the establishment of new ones:

> By its very nature, a reading public was not only more dispersed; it was also more atomistic and individualistic than a hearing one. Insofar as a traditional sense of community entailed frequent gathering together to receive a given message, this sense was probably weakened by the duplication of identical messages which brought the solitary reader to the fore. . . . But even while communal solidarity was diminished, vicarious participation in more distant events was also enhanced; and even while local ties were loosened, links to larger collective units were being forged. Printed materials encouraged silent adherence to causes whose advocates could not be found in any one parish and who addressed an invisible public from afar.[23]

Although printing brought about revolutionary changes in the way political opinions were advanced and absorbed, illiteracy was still widespread. Since many could not take advantage of print as a technique for expressing their opinions, oral techniques remained popular. As Tilly, E. P. Thompson, and Robert Darnton have pointed out, the riot, the parade, the comical public ritual, and other such techniques of expression were very popular beginning in the seventeenth century. Tilly notes that techniques or "repertoires" for expressing public opinion were largely of one type:

> Broadly speaking, the repertoire of the seventeenth to nineteenth centuries held to a *parochial* scope: It addressed local actors or the local representatives of national actors. It also relied heavily on *patronage*—appealing to immediately available power holders to convey grievances or settle disputes, temporarily acting in the place of unworthy or inactive

power holders only to abandon power once the action was done.[24]

Darnton found many examples of creative public polemics in late seventeenth and early eighteenth century France. He writes of one instance where workers who were poorly treated by shop masters used cats to symbolize the bourgeoisie in elaborate rituals of dissent. At one point, two young men initiated a cat massacre of sorts. After many of their masters' cats were murdered, "they dumped sackloads of half-dead cats in the courtyard. Then the entire workshop gathered round and staged a mock trial, complete with guards, a confessor, and a public executioner. After pronouncing the animals guilty and administering last rites, they strung them up on an improvised gallows."[25] Parades and demonstrations of this period were often conducted during "carnival," a time before Lent when extraordinary behavior was the norm and rules of social behavior were temporarily abandoned.

In the mid-seventeenth century another, more orderly, form of public opinion expression emerged: the petition. As early as 1640, English citizens petitioned Parliament on a variety of topics from the abuses of monopolies to the importance of peace. The petitions did not go unnoticed by members of Parliament. In fact, those citizens who signed a petition would often form an unruly mob, marching toward Parliament with their grievances in hand. Eventually, as Cecil Emden points out,

> both Houses made declarations in 1648 against petitions being presented in a tumultuous manner. Shortly after the Restoration a statute was passed regulating tumultuous petitions and providing that no petition should be presented by more than twenty persons unless with the consent of three or more justices of the peace.[26]

Although petitioning of the government continued after the 1648 statutes, the Parliament was still wary of the public spectacles which often accompanied the presentation of grievances. In 1698 and 1699 legislation was passed which required that petitions be presented by a member of Parliament, and not by the petitioners themselves.[27] These legislative acts foreshadowed the larger role the state would eventually assume in the public opinion communication process.

Civilized Expression: French Salons and English Coffeehouses

The salons of prerevolutionary France and the coffeehouses of eighteenth and nineteenth century London were both critical to elite intellectual life during these periods. Yet both were also important venues for public opinion expression and measurement. Ideas about religion, politics, and art were generated in both arenas, and the content of conversations in these forums eventually became part of public discourse.

Many scholars have written about the character of Parisian salons during the eighteenth century.[28] At these small gatherings, writers, statesmen, artists, and other assorted intellectuals congregated to discuss books and ideas. Rousseau, Diderot, and other philosophes used the forum of the salon to develop their theories, although many found the pretension and formality of these meetings stifling. Wit and provocative banter were valued most in the salons where literary men in poor financial circumstances mingled with the nobility and political elites. Philosophers and writers benefited from participation in the salons, since the powerful women who organized them could help these men attain academic positions and literary prizes.[29]

A typical salon of the period was that of Madame D'Épinay, friend to such luminaries as Voltaire, Rousseau, and Duclos. D'Épinay was not particularly well educated or wealthy, but like many salon keepers, understood the value of ideas. Helen Clergue notes that the conversation in Madame D'Épinay's salon focused on politics, philosophy, and ethics. In her drawing room, during the 1760s, foreign visitors, men of letters, and politicians engaged in wide-ranging, lively political discourse.[30]

The development of salons represents a critical chapter in the history of public opinion. The dialogue in these drawing rooms influenced the nature of public opinion in France, but the salon was also a forum for opinion assessment: Talk in the salons was often monitored by the regime. Jacques Necker, finance minister under Louis XVI, was the first to note the power of salons to influence public opinion: "He [Necker] remarked that during the reigns of Louis XV and Louis XVI the courtiers and even the ministers would have risked displeasing the royal family in preference to exposing themselves to an unwelcome reception in the leading *salons* of Paris."[31]

FIGURE 3.1 Madame d'Épinay, from the painting by Jean-Etienne Liotard (1759). D'Épinay, who organized one of the most famous philosophical salons of the eighteenth century, was friend to Rousseau, Grimm, and other luminaries. Courtesy of the Museé d'art et d'histoire, Geneva.

Necker believed that "public opinion" described the elite group sentiment of the salons, rather than the opinions of the entire population of French citizens, whom he called the "toute sauvage."[32] Lewis Coser notes that the salon was not simply a forum for witty conversation and flirtation: "[The *salon*] attempted . . . to mold the world of letters as well as public opinion and to assist at the birth of new ideas."[33] More recently, Jürgen Habermas has argued that the salon was one catalyst for the development of the "public sphere" during this period. These middle-and upper-class gatherings were forums where people, many of whom played no role in government, criticized the state in a sustained manner for the first time.[34]

The salons of eighteenth century France were overshadowed by more varied expressions of public opinion which emerged in the days before the Revolution. During these years and during the Revolution itself, political activists circulated newspapers, organized antigovernment parades, and distributed political cartoons, among other things, in order to mobilize public opinion against the monarchy.[35] Indeed, the French Revolution is one of the most interesting events in the history of public opinion because it was the first truly popular revolution, the first time when a massive uprising of public sentiment changed the course of government. Several French intellectuals, including Rousseau, emphasized how important public opinion could be as a revolutionary force. The historian Keith Baker notes that

> the idea of the emergence of enlightened public opinion as a political force was perhaps put most succinctly [in 1782] by that remarkably informative observer of French political culture at the end of the Old Regime, Louis-Sébastien Mercier. . . . "Today, public opinion has a preponderant force in Europe that cannot be resisted. Thus in assessing the progress of enlightenment and the change it must bring about, we may hope that it will bring the greatest good to the world and that tyrants of all stripes will tremble before this universal cry that continuously rings out to fill and awaken Europe."[36]

During these years of violent change in France, a technique of public opinion expression similar to the salon gained popularity in London. The coffeehouse became a gathering place for writers, intellectuals, and common citizens. Access to coffeehouses was not

FIGURE 3.2 The Conversazione From Samuel Hoole's *Modern Manners* (1782). The salons of eighteenth century France were critical to the communication of public opinion during the Old Regime.

limited as it was in the salons, since one paid a very small price to join the coffeehouse conversation. Opinions were debated in coffeehouses, and these dialogues often found their way into the pages of popular magazines. In fact, as Lewis Coser has noted, Steele, Addison, and others published excerpts from coffeehouse conversation in *The Spectator, The Tatler, The Guardian,* and other such magazines. Coser writes about the influence of London coffeehouses:

> A common opinion cannot be developed before people have an occasion to discuss with one another, before they have been drawn from the isolation of lonely thought into a public world in which individual opinion can be sharpened and tested in discussion with others. The coffeehouse helped to crystallize a common opinion from a multitude of individual opinions and to give it form and stability.[37]

Techniques of Aggregation and the Emergence of Modern Notions of Public Opinion

Beginning in the late eighteenth and early nineteenth centuries, modern techniques of public opinion measurement and expression began to appear. One of the most important of these techniques was the general election.[38] Elections represent a turning point in the history of opinion expression because they require private communication of opinion. Although the earliest secret ballot was employed before 300 B.C. in India, America's system of secret balloting in colonial elections was the first large-scale program for recording opinion, and served as a model for other national election systems.[39] After elections were in place, the straw poll emerged as a way to predict election outcomes. The conduct of straw polls and the ways they were used by journalists and political activists are the subjects of the next chapter.

The general election, and the theory behind it, paved the way for other aggregation approaches to public opinion. Newspaper circulation figures and, later, ratings for radio and television programs eventually became critical indicators of public opinion. That public opinion might be construed as the sum of many *atomized* individual opinions or actions was not a new idea, but it seemed to catch on as never before in the early nineteenth century. Previously, notions of

FIGURE 3.3 Lloyd's Coffeehouse in London, 1798. The coffeehouse of the eighteenth century, which was far more accessible to common citizens than the Parisian salons, was the site of political and literary debate. Used by permission of Viking Penguin.

public opinion were associated with the activities of crowds or communities. Public opinion was thought to be a consensus of individuals, engaged in an *interactive* communication process. Yet new techniques of aggregation seemed more appropriate for a large, rapidly growing American democracy. Widespread political participation, and equality (for some), were viewed as critical, so aggregation provided an efficient, reasonable method for the expression of sentiment.

As techniques of aggregation diffused, modern views of public opinion began to emerge. It was during the mid-nineteenth century that Tocqueville wrote about the "tyranny of the majority," which echoed and extended themes in *The Federalist Papers*. Much scholarly effort has been devoted to explicating Tocqueville's work, but less attention has been accorded to James Bryce, a British visitor to the United States who published the encyclopedic *American Commonwealth* in 1891. Bryce's work is particularly interesting to students of public opinion because he focused on the dynamic relationship between the press and public opinion. While he seemed to consider public opinion a sum of individual opinions, Bryce could not predict the development of the sample survey:

> How is the will of the majority to be ascertained except by counting votes? . . . No country has yet surmounted these inconveniences, though little Switzerland with its *Referendum* has faced and dealt with some of them. But what I desire to point out is that even where the machinery for weighing or measuring the popular will from week to week or month to month has not been, and is not likely to be, invented, there may nevertheless be a disposition on the part of rulers . . . to look incessantly for manifestations of current popular opinion, and to shape their course in accordance with their reading of those manifestations.[40]

Although he thought often about different ways one might assess public opinion (e.g., elections, political party platforms, etc.), Bryce believed that newspapers were powerful channels of opinion communication. Dailies were "narrators" that reported on events, "advocates" that argued ideological positions, and "weathercocks" that sensed shifts in the direction of public opinion.[41]

Bryce, like many contemporary theorists, treated public opinion as a concrete phenomenon—public opinion *acted*. Opinion for Bryce was an independent variable in a multitude of ways: Public sentiment caused politicians to perform, served as the basis for legislative change, and mobilized individual citizens. For Bryce, public opinion was not a phantom, as it was for Lippmann three decades later. It was a force to be reckoned with—an institution as critical as the parties and the presidency.

Trends in the History of Opinion Techniques

Table 3.2 replicates the list of the major techniques for opinion expression and assessment, and then categorizes these techniques according to the type of expression each enables. This sort of analysis is crude, since countless variations of each technique can be found in the historical literature, but it does help us detect trends in expression of opinion over time. Weber's theory of rationalization and Foucault's writings on disciplinary technology prove to be particularly useful as analytic tools in this regard. Both theorists emphasized the relationship between technology and social control: Weber wrote about factories and bureaucratic regulation, while Foucault concentrated on techniques of punishment and incarceration. We can apply these same ideas to this history of public opinion techniques.

The Weberian notion of increasing rationalization predicts that the more recent public opinion technologies should encourage more structured opinion expression than older techniques. In order to get at the degree of rationalization embodied in each technology on this list, I ask whether the opinion expression *enabled* by the technology is more structured than unstructured. Does the technique allow an individual to create his or her own questions and answers, or does it tend to constrain one to established choices?

It seems that techniques for expression and assessment of public opinion have become more structured over time. Salons, coffeehouses, frequent rioting, street demonstrations, and other early means of expression allowed for very free-flowing discussion of political and social issues. Yet, the introduction of the general election in the late eighteenth and early nineteenth centuries represents a turning point—a point where public opinion rationalization accelerated.

TABLE 3.2 Techniques of Public Opinion and Type
of Expression Enabled

Techniques	Structured or Unstructured	Public or Private
Oratory/Rhetoric	Unstructured	Public
Printing	Unstructured	Public & private[a]
Crowds	Unstructured	Public
Petitions	Unstructured & structured[b]	Public
Salons	Unstructured	Public
Coffeehouses	Unstructured	Public
Revolutionary Movements	Unstructured	Public
Strikes	Unstructured	Public
General elections	Structured	Private
Straw polls	Structured	Private
Modern newspapers	Structured	Public & private
Letters to public officials & editors	Unstructured	Public & private (unsigned letters)
Mass media programming (political)	Structured	Public & private
Sample survey	Structured	Private

[a]Printing enabled one to read privately, although printed material often became part of public discourse.

[b]Although petitions were drawn up at mass meetings where there was much discussion and argument (see Emden 1956), the expression they ultimately enabled was structured—either one signed a petition or one chose not to.

Let us compare two of the techniques for expressing opinion: rioting, a largely unstructured activity, and the sample survey, a structured one. Although it is the case that one's ability to send subtle or complex messages is limited during a demonstration (especially a violent one), the amount of expressive freedom enabled by the technology is great compared to that of the poll. Historians like Tilly, who have studied public expression before the nineteenth century, have provided colorful, detailed evidence indicating that collective action could be extremely powerful *because* it was diverse and creative. Collective action during the seventeenth and eighteenth centuries generally allowed individuals to demonstrate whenever and however they needed to, while directing their actions at particular parties (certain elites, authorities, etc.). Furthermore, multiple potential leaders existed for these demonstrations—charisma and not position qualified one to lead a revolt.

When one compares these actions to the sample survey, it is clear that polls constrain people in a way riots did not. Rioting as a technology was flexible enough so that an individual or group with a grievance could (potentially) stimulate action at any time, for any reason, with a variety of targets. The sample survey, on the other hand, is a technology which demands statistical expertise, substantial planning, the investment of large monetary resources, and access to the national media if one is to broadcast one's results. As Ginsberg has pointed out, few common citizens, labor groups, or grass-roots political activists are able to afford such means of public opinion measurement and expression.[42]

Elections, straw polls, and the sample survey all define the issues we express opinions on and the responses we can choose. Mass media (newspapers, radio, and television talk programs concerning politics) are more complex in their structuring of public opinion, but they nonetheless enable expression which is limited in nature. Although communications scholars have found that the meaning of a text is negotiated by the reader/audience, there are often limitations or boundaries for interpretation inherent in the text itself.[43]

From the perspective of media industry executives and producers, circulation figures for newspapers and ratings of radio and television political programs represent the opinion expression enabled by mass media technologies: These statistics were designed to represent audience approval or disapproval of media political content. Although many people are no doubt dissatisfied with the media products available to them, their voices are rarely heard. Letters to public officials and editors seem to be one of the few modern exceptions to the pattern of increasing rationalization of expression. Yet these too are subject to the selectivity of editors and to the limitations on space devoted to letters in most newspapers and magazines.

I should emphasize that the more recent public opinion techniques, such as the sample survey, have *not* by any means *replaced* previous strategies. They have, however, become more closely associated with public opinion expression than the previous techniques. Living room discussions of politics and art, similar to those of the salons, still occur. The issue is whether or not they are viewed, *in political discourse*, as dominant forms of public opinion expression. As noted above, scholars writing from the 1940s to the present have been forced to contend with the notion that polls are becoming synonymous with public opinion.

One reason why Weber's theory of rationalization is particularly useful to students of public opinion is that it highlights issues of social control. Rationalization is not an abstract phenomenon: It is the process by which institutions and individuals, in the case of public opinion measurement, systematize their practices in order to conduct a more effective surveillance of the population. Although my evidence is not conclusive, there are strong indications of a movement away from "bottom-up" expression techniques and toward "top-down" strategies controlled by the state or by private industry forces. Writing about new "mass feedback technologies," such as opinion surveys and television ratings, James Beniger has noted that

> the impetus for new technologies of mass feedback, between the turn of the century and World War II, came from business and government, not from citizens and consumers looking for new ways to "speak their minds." . . . It was not only that people shifted the focus of their communication from local audiences to national ones, it was also that the audiences themselves, especially big business and big government, were increasingly listening to what people had on their minds— and increasingly listening (thanks to the new mass feedback technologies) whether people intended to tell or not.[44]

Here Beniger echoes Foucault's work on disciplinary techniques. Although modern opinion techniques are not quite as unobtrusive as the Panopticon, they are not particularly invasive either. Table 3.2 indicates that opinion techniques which allow for a great deal of observation without substantial intervention have become more prevalent over time. For example, television ratings, which are usually gathered through minor alteration of broadcast technology, allow companies to accumulate public opinion data easily and unobtrusively. How much people watch particular types of programming is valuable information for television networks, political leaders, and students of contemporary social life. Another method, the sample survey, is also a fairly unobtrusive observational technique. In a typical national poll, hundreds (or thousands) are interviewed, but the opinions of the entire populace are thought to be represented by these data. From the perspective of Foucauldian theory, surveillance of the whole population is achieved painlessly and quietly.

Public Opinion and Private Opinion

Beyond the rationalization of public opinion techniques, I have also attempted to explore changes in the openness or *public* nature of expression. For each technique listed in table 3.2, I have classified the technique as "public" or "private" according to whether it *enables* an individual to speak publicly or privately when expressing himself or herself. When individuals speak publicly, their intention is to reach others in an open forum, and when they speak privately, they do not expect *their* opinions to be widely communicated.

I take up the issue of public versus private opinion expression because it is central to classical theories of democracy. If the common good is to be discussed and understood, there must be multiple channels for public expression and debate. In her compelling explication of unitary versus adversary democracy, Jane Mansbridge notes that face-to-face meetings and discussions were a crucial part of deliberation about the common good in Athens.[45]

Table 3.2 indicates that public opinion expression became more private over the course of history. This pattern is consistent with notions of mass society—i.e., that industrialization in the mid-nineteenth century led to weakening of social ties in local communities and the decay of public life. Many mass society theorists have argued that the public sphere began to shrink as individuals turned inward to the nuclear family, and gradually minimized ties with others in their communities.[46]

Although a public/private distinction is important for understanding technological trends, it should be noted that these concepts are closely related to those of anonymity and attribution. These two sets of concepts are so closely correlated, in fact, that separation is problematic and often practically impossible.

Let us take the public opinion poll, which is both private and anonymous, as an example. When one converses with a survey interviewer on the telephone (much contemporary polling is conducted by phone since the diffusion of that instrument and the advent of random digit dialing), the conversation is a private one. Although one might know that his or her opinion will be aggregated, and perhaps widely publicized by a newspaper or television network, the actual expression of opinions is done in a private setting. One might argue that since the *expression* is made public, the sample survey is not a private means of expression. Yet the anonymity and confidentiality of the sample survey enables the individual to deny ever expressing a particular opinion: He or she need never claim credit for one of the many opinions aggregated by the pollster.

Riots are another case where anonymity and privacy become conceptually intertwined. If one participates in a riot, one is most definitely engaged in a public act, yet may somehow be able to maintain anonymity in a large crowd. Here, as compared to the case of the poll above, the initial expression is public and the resulting expression may be either anonymous or attributed. I would argue, however, that attribution of an opinion to a person under these circumstances is more likely than not.

Polls and Political Expression

The development of public opinion expression and measurement techniques over time indicates that public opinion has become a more structured, private type of participation in politics. Yet how does the public opinion poll, which employs routinized data collection procedures and assures respondents of the confidentiality of their opinions, affect the nature of political expression?

It seems clear that the sample survey is designed to maximize political participation in mass societies. Techniques of representative sampling were conceived to make public opinion articulation and assessment manageable and fair in a society where holding constant referenda presents countless logistical difficulties. Yet while polling is an attempt to maximize a "top-down" form of mass political participation, it may fail to improve debate and discussion in democratic societies as compared to public opinion techniques of the past. In fact, by structuring individual expression and by turning public opinion expression into a private process, the sample survey may distance us from classical democratic notions of participation.

Although the effects of opinion polls on democratic communication are the subject of chapter 8, a brief illustration of my argument is germane here. Let us take two opinion techniques as ideal types—the salon and the opinion poll. The salons of the eighteenth century and the coffeehouses of the same period were oriented around free, unstructured expression of opinion. From most accounts describing the salons and coffeehouses, it seems that nearly all participants were involved in a reciprocal communication process where they spoke, listened, and spoke again. There was no final word, no final opinion expressed—a dynamic opinion formation process was the element fundamental to the operation of the salon and the café.

In contrast, even if an individual feels confident that he or she has answered a pollster's questions to the best of his or her ability, that individual has not, in most cases, used his or her own words or concepts.[47] The picture of public expression drawn by Bourdieu—where pollsters direct public discourse by selecting the questions and dictating respondents' choices—is uniquely tied to modern, rationalized conceptions and techniques of public opinion. If we think about polling in contrast with earlier techniques, its ability to structure both the expression and the discernment of attitudes becomes even more vivid.

Although many options for public expression exist in democratic societies, polling is a dominant form of opinion articulation. Like voting, it is characterized by confidentiality and privacy of expression. With the sample survey interview, one expresses his or her opinion exclusively to the pollster: Opinions are not articulated in a forum for others to consider and debate. The private nature of opinion expression encouraged by polls and the rigidity of the expression both contradict tenets of political participation as embodied in classical democratic theory. Interestingly, though, polls do attempt to maximize a certain (narrow) type of political participation indirectly, by estimating the views of the entire population through statistical analysis.

The diffusion of the sample survey has helped political leaders monitor the feelings of the entire populace more effectively, and at the same time gives citizens a mechanism for social comparison. We can get a sense from poll data of how our fellow citizens feel about issues. Yet the question for social theorists is whether or not the ability to increase the sheer number of opinions represented outweighs a potential decay in the "public" nature of public opinion.

The sample survey is the most recent addition to a lengthy list of opinion technologies, employed by a variety of individuals and institutions over time. These different techniques served different purposes: Some were channels for dissent (e.g., the riot), while others could be used to manipulate or control the citizenry (e.g., rhetoric). None of the techniques was used in a consistent manner, but the character of these techniques tended to facilitate different types of expression.

One question raised early in this chapter concerned the meaning of public opinion. The historical sketch here confirms Habermas's argument that our ideas about public opinion are perpetually in flux: What we call public expression has much to do with *how* we express and measure the phenomenon.

As in the cases of technology Foucault studied, it is impossible to argue that any of these opinion techniques *caused* us to think about public opinion in a certain manner, or that an intellectual shift brought about a technological one. In every case, assumptions about the nature of public opinion evolved with the technology itself. For example, the idea that public opinion is an aggregation of many equal opinions existed before the diffusion of the straw poll, since the practice of summing opinions has its roots in ancient Greece. Yet widespread political involvement was thought to be extremely valuable and important in the nineteenth century, so the development of the straw poll made perfect sense.[48]

This chapter has only outlined the parameters of the history of public opinion. But this synopsis, and the detection of general trends in the development of opinion techniques, provides a context for understanding the way opinion has been expressed in America from the mid-nineteenth century to the present. The primary subject of this book is not the long history of public opinion, but the ways that quantitative expression techniques have evolved over the last two centuries. To study these techniques, we must narrow our focus considerably, and concentrate on particular cases of opinion expression. Our first case is that of the straw poll, an early and important technique of public opinion expression and assessment.

CHAPTER FOUR

Partisan Politics and the Symbolic Use of Straw Polls, 1856–1936

Ａ
LTHOUGH POLITICIANS have always tested the waters of public opinion before elections, early nineteenth century party workers, politicians, and journalists became enamored with a crude, quantitative opinion measurement technique—the straw poll. As elections became more competitive, and as mass participation in politics accelerated, straw polls became a ubiquitous tool for predicting the outcomes of local and national political contests.[1] These "straws," as they were called by the press, enabled partisans and reporters to get a sense of a candidate's chances for success in an upcoming election, but were also used to denigrate opposing candidates or boost the morale of the rank and file in one's own party. The quantitative data derived from straw polling were most often used in political debate as authoritative evidence about the nature of public opinion: By the mid-nineteenth century, survey results were viewed as symbolic assets by journalists and party officials seeking legitimation of their ideological positions.

Straw polls are opinion surveys, conducted orally or with pen and paper, which are used to determine the popularity of a particular candidate or policy. Although these sorts of polls are still commonly found today (e.g., "call-in" polls conducted by radio and television stations), professional pollsters, political consultants, and journalists now use statistical sampling to gain a more accurate understanding of the popular sentiment.[2] Despite the differences between the two methodologies—the straw poll and the sample survey—the straw was a precursor to the modern public opinion survey. George Gallup, who popularized sample surveying and wrote extensively on the role of the survey in contemporary democracies, claimed that the earliest straw poll was published in 1824 by the *Harrisburg Pennsylvanian*.[3] However, closer scrutiny of early polls by opinion researcher Tom Smith revealed that these polls were actually conducted by party workers and ordinary citizens. Smith also noted that the polls conducted during the 1824 presidential election campaign were of great interest to journalists and the general public: These polls "stirred up at least as much controversy as do preelection polls in the mid-twentieth century."[4]

The most famous straw polls in American history, though, were the ones conducted by the *Literary Digest* in the 1920s and 1930s. The *Digest* mailed and tabulated millions of ballots during presidential election campaigns, and its predictions were monitored with great interest by politicians and the general public. *Digest* editors often celebrated the success and wide recognition of their poll by publishing cartoons about the survey that appeared in other magazines and newspapers (see figure 4.1). For many years the poll was a success. The *Digest* accurately predicted both the winners and vote differentials for the presidential elections of 1920, 1924, 1928, and 1932, but failed to anticipate Roosevelt's defeat of Landon in 1936. Due to an oversampling of Republican voters, *Digest* editors projected a great victory for Landon, and were later forced to explain the faulty prediction to readers (see figure 4.2). Although the magazine claimed it would continue to conduct polls, the 1936 survey was the *Digest's* last. The magazine ceased publication the following year.[5]

Many scholars have described the development of polling after the *Literary Digest's* costly error, but the numerous straw polls conducted before the 1930s have received far less attention.[6] From the 1820s on, newspapers commonly published the results of straw polls, and readers came to think of these data as news. This chapter describes how journalists used straw polls in presidential campaign reports from the Civil War era through the 1936 contest between Roosevelt and Landon. Of particular interest are the ways that reporters and editors wove the results of straw polls into stories about upcoming elections, and into their own ideological discourses about politics. Before turning to the issue of quantification in nineteenth and early twentieth century political journalism, however, it is necessary to set the scene: We begin with a brief discussion of the roles newspapers played in the public opinion expression process during the mid-nineteenth century.

ARRIVAL OF THE EDITOR WHO IS
ALWAYS TAKING STRAW-VOTES

FIGURE 4.1   A cartoon published in the *Literary Digest* November 1,
1924.

Public Opinion, Politics, and Newspapers in Nineteenth-Century America

Beginning in the mid-nineteenth century, citizens, journalists, and
political parties began to experiment with quantitative techniques
for assessing public opinion, but this period also marks the com-
mencement of modern theorizing about the popular sentiment.
Some of the most comprehensive descriptions of the political process and public opinion were those provided by a pair of visitors to
the United States—Alexis de Tocqueville and James Bryce. Both

The Literary Digest

NOVEMBER 14, 1936   Thirty ~~TEN~~ CENTS

IS OUR FACE RED!

The following telegram was received by The Literary Digest: "With full and sympathetic appreciation of the rather tough spot you now find yourselves in, we offer the following suggestion as a piece of strategy to turn seeming defeat into victory and put name of Literary Digest on every tongue in America in a most favorable manner in your next issue— print the front cover in red except for a small circular space in the center; in this space print the words 'And is our face red!' The people of America like a good sport and will like you accordingly." Signed: George Bennitt, A. C. Johnston and Al Devore; 625 State Street, El Centro, California.

[Editor's Note: We appreciate the suggestion, which arrived when this issue's cover was on the presses, so the above is offered.]

FIGURE 4.2   From the article, "What Went Wrong With the Polls?" In the *Literary Digest*, November 14, 1936.

were fascinated with the central role of popular opinion in American political life, and both wrote extensively about its contributions and problems.

Tocqueville recognized the power of the public and expressed fears about the "tyranny of the majority." He argued that "while the majority is in doubt, one talks; but when it has irrevocably pronounced everyone is silent and friends and enemies alike seem to make for its bandwagon."[7] Although Bryce, writing years later, displayed some concern about the problems associated with public opinion, he was much more optimistic about the place of this type of expression in democratic states. Most important, Bryce believed that newspapers were the central organs of public opinion expression at the end of the century. He noted that newspapers report, persuade, and often reflect the will of the people. He wrote:

> It is chiefly in its [third] capacity as an index and mirror of the public opinion that the press is looked to. This is the function it chiefly aims at discharging; and the public men feel that in showing deference to it they are propitiating, and inviting the commands of, public opinion itself. In worshipping the deity you learn to conciliate the priest.[8]

Although contemporary newspapers have experienced a steady decline in readership, newspapers were a critical part of American political discourse during the nineteenth and early twentieth centuries. Perhaps the upheavals in American life during this period— changes in transportation, the mechanization of production processes, and transformations in family life—helped to establish the press as a constant, reliable source of information.[9] As many scholars have noted, the rise of the penny press and the growth of mass circulation magazines were responsible, in part, for an expansion of discourse in the public sphere.[10] Morton Keller points out that people became "less parochial" during the last years of the century, reaching out for printed information which could take them beyond the bounds of their local communities. New popular magazines, applauding an educated and articulate public, with "revealing" titles like *Public Opinion*, *Everybody's*, and *Cosmopolitan*, were first published during this era.[11]

There is much scholarly debate about when and how objectivity became an important journalistic norm, but it is clear that most newspapers had distinct ideological perspectives in the mid-nineteenth century. As Mott notes, only five percent of newspapers listed in the 1850 census could be labeled "neutral" or "independent."[12] In fact, Michael Schudson has argued that journalistic opinion leaders did not seriously grapple with the problems of political bias and objectivity until after the First World War. He explained:

> Not until after World War I, when the worth of the democratic market society was itself radically questioned and its internal logic laid bare, did leaders in journalism and other fields, like the social sciences, fully experience the doubting and skepticism democracy and the market encouraged. Only then did the ideal of objectivity as consensually validated statements about the world, predicated on a radical separation of facts and values, arise.[13]

Journalistic discourse in the mid-nineteenth century was infused with partisan ideology, but these biases became most obvious during presidential election contests.

Reporting Public Opinion During Elections

There was no scarcity of public gatherings during a typical mid-nineteenth century presidential race, so journalists were always able to locate newsworthy events as election day drew near. Rallies, parades, pole raisings, and other forms of partisan expression were commonplace, and a great many of these occurrences were described either briefly or in great detail by the daily paper.[14] Public gatherings provided opportunities for journalists to gauge popular sentiment, and reporters often conducted straw polls as people arrived at or departed from political meetings.

In general, high voter turnout rates and an animated interest in election results characterized this era in party politics. Robert Dinkin noted that

> unlike the present situation, where many voters are independent or only nominally linked to a political organization, those of the last half of the nineteenth century felt deeply committed to their side. It is estimated that anywhere from 20 to 25 percent of the electors were actively involved in campaigns. They attended numerous party functions and voted

regularly, with turnout at national elections in these years averaging 70 to 80 percent and state totals not far behind.[15]

Since there was so much campaign activity, newspapers sometimes reserved space or even a regular column for stories about these events. In the *Chicago Tribune*, for example, rallies were listed under the heading "Movements of the People." Newspapers would often have their own reporters cover rallies, but also included a large number of reports from partisan witnesses who sent in descriptions of various political gatherings.

Newspapers did not report on political rallies and the results of straw polls simply because journalists believed these to be good news sources. Dailies during this period typically used reports on campaign rallies to promote their own presidential hopeful and attack the opposition. The *Chicago Tribune*, which supported Lincoln in 1860, reported that

> on the ground where Douglas spoke there were at no time more than 7,000 to 8,000 people—hardly a wigwam full. These were depressed by their failure, shivering with cold and the certainty of a November defeat as the reward for their money and labor. Mr. Douglas' speech was a mean effort even for him, who never has made a good speech in his life. . . . Those who heard him for the first time, went away disappointed and sad. Those to whom his oratory is not new, amused themselves as well as they could while that part of the programme was being performed.[16]

The combination of strong partisanship and widespread grass-roots political activity made the reporting of public opinion crucial in the nineteenth century. Reflection on and description of public sentiment by journalists helped newspapers to make predictions about the election outcome, but most probably attracted readers as well. Interest in the state of public opinion was undoubtedly just as high if not higher in the nineteenth century than it is during contemporary elections, where the press, political consultants, and the public all keep abreast of candidates' poll standings.[17]

The 1850s marked the beginning of the great period of public opinion expression in American politics, so historians of public opinion are drawn to this era: It is fertile ground to begin longitudinal explorations of political participation and discourse. During these years, the partisan daily newspaper was alive and well, but also saw itself as an agent of the people, responsible for reporting the news. [18] Some scholars have argued that the mid-nineteenth century marks a shift in journalism from the editor to the reporter, who actually went out into the field to cover events. Hazel Dicken-Garcia points out, for example, that correspondents' bylines started to appear more frequently during this time, due to their critical news-gathering role in the Civil War. [19] She argues that there was a shift from opinion-based journalism to a more fact- and information-based approach: The news story began to take on its modern form in the 1860s, as journalists used the "inverted pyramid" style to inform readers more quickly and efficiently. Finally, by midcentury the press had achieved a certain self-consciousness about its role as a molder of public opinion. [20] Since the 1850s and 1860s in many ways marked the birth of modern political journalism, I've chosen the 1856 presidential election as a point of departure for this analysis of straw polls in three major newspapers—*The New York Times*, the *Chicago Tribune*, and the *Chicago Times*. [21]

Straw Polls as Partisan Discourse

Straw polling had been conducted since the 1820s, but became extremely popular during the middle decades of the nineteenth century. Straw polls of many types were conducted during the 1860 contest between Lincoln and Douglas, for example. One popular journalistic tactic was to poll people on steamers and passenger trains. The following is an account of "straws" conducted by a *Tribune* reporter:

> They had an excursion from Hillsdale to Goshen, Indiana on Thursday. A vote for President was taken, with the following result: For Lincoln, gentlemen 368, ladies 433—total 796 [*sic*]; for Douglas, gentlemen 156, ladies 60—total 216: for Breckinridge, gentlemen 5, lady 1. Lincoln over all 574. [22]

During the 1876 election, a reporter for the *Tribune* interviewed citizens as they came off a train and headed toward their hotels for the night:

> #### As usual
> An excursion train containing some 200 people from Dayton, O., and neighboring towns, arrived last evening via the Pan-

Handle Road. They are stopping at the Commercial, Gardner's St. James, and Ruhn's Hotel. Coming up, a vote was taken, resulting as follows: Hayes 65, Tilden 13, neutral 3, Cooper 2.[23]

Polling on trains was convenient for journalists, who needed to travel for assignments anyway. Yet newspapers often published straw polls contributed by readers who were themselves traveling on trains. The following *Tribune* report, from 1856, exemplifies this type of straw poll and accompanying editorializing:

> Indicative Straws.—A gentleman just from New York hands us votes taken by him on four of the way trains on the New York Central Railroad. The persons voting were nearly all residents of that State. The votes foot up:

> | | |
> |---|---|
> | Fremont | 129 |
> | Buchanan | 32 |
> | Fillmore | 50 |
> | Fremont majority | 47 |

> This will serve to indicate with considerable accuracy the feeling among the masses of New York upon the slavery question and their preference among candidates.[24]

One man who traveled extensively during the summer of 1856 polled 2,886 people during his trips through the Northeast. All twenty-three of the individual votes taken during his train rides were published by *The New York Times*. Additionally, this gentleman provided commentary on how these statistics were compiled and patterns noticed in the data. For example, he noted that "of literary men, collegiate professors, teachers &c., seven-eighths were Republicans," and that "of forty-two ministers of the Gospel, thirty-nine affirmed they should vote for Fremont; one for Buchanan, and two for Fillmore."[25] Although there were some exceptions, reporters and correspondents rarely attempted to connect the passengers' area of residence, political party, ethnicity, or gender with their choice of candidate: The only important piece of information was the way a particular individual planned to vote.[26] During the 1896 election, a railway employee reported poll data to the *Chicago Tribune*:

> John J. Byrnes, General Passenger Agent and Auditor of the Southern California railroad, reached Chicago yesterday

morning on a Santa Fe train on which, among other passengers, were seventy-five Californians. Some one polled the denizens of the Far West and Bryan got fifteen votes. Just before Mr. Byrnes came East a large manufacturing plant in Los Angeles in which 1000 men are employed was polled, and McKinley was the choice of 997. Mr. Byrnes, who until this campaign has been a Democrat, is confident McKinley will carry California by a big majority.[27]

Potential voters were not the only participants in straw polls, since women's preferences were often tallied by reporters. Even though some women actively campaigned for candidates during elections, they were not permitted to vote in presidential elections during the nineteenth century.[28] Yet some straw poll articles casually report the number of female votes counted on trains, as in the above article about the excursion from Hillsdale to Goshen. It is likely that women were generally included in polls, since journalists implied that *all* riders on a train or steamer were interviewed. Occasionally the number of "ladies" casting straw votes was reported separately from the number of men.

Why would women be included in straw polls when their votes would not be cast in the upcoming election? There are three possible explanations for this. One reason for these inclusions might be that reporters believed women to have an influence on the election *through* their husbands or other males who could cast ballots. Some women did actively participate in campaigns, and, as many scholars have pointed out, they played leading roles in the abolitionist movement, the temperance movement, and the budding feminist movement.[29] Perhaps journalists were recognizing the influence of women in both formal settings and "back channels" of American political life.

The second, more compelling, explanation concerns the role of women as consumers of news. It is possible that reporters felt women should be included in straw polls because they represented part of the paper's readership, and newspapers needed to appeal to women if they were to succeed economically. Writing about economic pressures on newspapers in the 1880s, Michael Schudson points out that nineteenth century merchants had become increasingly interested in luring the female consumer to neighborhood and department stores to buy goods.[30] Advertising was one means of reaching the female audience. In fact, Pulitzer's *New York World* included female-oriented advertising, and also introduced multiple columns on beauty, fashion, cooking, and other traditionally female interests.

Although the *World* was established in 1883, newspapers were probably interested in attracting women readers before that time. Perhaps the inclusion of women in straw polls is a case where women were assumed to be part of a *consumer* public, and their roles as consumers (and not voters) allowed them entry into the quasi-electoral realm of straw polling. Women were not formally part of the polity, yet were permitted to participate at certain times when economic constraints of newspapers and coverage of politics intersected: Straw polls may exemplify this type of convergence.

A third explanation for the inclusion of women in some straw poll counts is rooted in the journalists' partisan and professional motives. It is possible that reporters weren't trying to gauge public opinion through the use of straw polls. Their immediate goals may have been to entertain the reader or use polls as indications of an upcoming victory for their candidate of choice. It is possible that journalists left the serious, systematic head-counting up to local party activists, who were much more concerned with accurate election prediction.

Groups of women, workers, local businessmen, members of social clubs, and those with other group affiliations generally did not wait for journalists to poll their opinions on upcoming elections, however. Citizens often took quantitative techniques into their own hands to assert their voices in the numerical discourse about public opinion found in newspapers. This type of citizen polling is much different than the straw polling conducted on trains or boats: The "people's polls" were not conducted among strangers, but among groups of people who shared a common workplace or community.

"People's Polls"

Until the election campaign of 1936, citizens polled themselves often during presidential contests and reported these findings to the *Chicago Tribune*, the *Chicago Times*, and *The New York Times*. Polls were taken by citizens at drug stores,[31] by students and faculty members at universities,[32] and by workers in factories.[33] One particularly large set of straw votes was published on November 5, 1916, by the *Chicago Tribune*. This collection included scores of polls sent in by readers—printers, trade school students, farmers and livestock feeders, furniture makers, fraternities, traders at a Chicago poultry board meeting, and commercial artists.[34]

The polls favorable to a newspaper's chosen candidate probably had a better chance of being published than those with unfavorable results, although we have no evidence about these private editorial decisions. The most interesting aspect of these polls is that they indicate just how authoritative quantitative discourses had become in American culture. Citizens seemed intent on breaking into political discourse through qualitative means (e.g. letters to the editor, rallies, etc.), but also through quantitative means. Most likely, individuals believed in a bandwagon effect:[35] If they could show their candidate performing well in quasi-elections, perhaps that person *was* the best man for the job. An example from the 1856 *Tribune* captures this thinking:

> The New Haven *Journal of Commerce* has seen a letter from a workman in Samuel Cole's pistol factory, at Hartford, stating the politics of the workmen in one department to be as follows: for Fremont, 109; Buchanan, 37; Fillmore, 3. That, he says, is an immense change of opinion, as Buchanan used to have about 100 majority in these shops.[36]

During the 1856 election, the *New York Times* published a variety of polls conducted not by journalists but by local club leaders and average voters. On September 5, 1856, the following typical "straw" appeared:

> The President of the American Council in Woodstock, Conn., has taken the sense of his brethren respectively on the Presidential question with the following result: Whole number of members in the Council, 230; FILLMORE, 0, BUCHANAN, 3; FREMONT, 227. He says the vote is divided substantially like this throughout eastern Connecticut, and he presumes through western also; but his personal knowledge is confined to the eastern counties.[37]

Although the council president had simply polled the members of his own organization, he had a sense that this "sample" of people was representative of a larger population. The *Times*, like other newspapers of the day, never questioned these results or the president's speculation about the popular sentiment in Connecticut. Many of the citizen polls published in the *Times* and other major city papers were reported first by other regional or local papers. In 1860, for example, the *Tribune* reported the following poll result from the *Indianapolis Sentinel*:

> A BIG STRAW. — Thirty-four Germans in Adams, near the Wells county line, who voted for Buchanan in 1856, now belong to a Lincoln club. How many more there are in that locality who will hereafter vote the Republican ticket we do not know; but certainly enough to make a very considerable change in the returns.[38]

Often newspaper editors would print poll results with much less detail about the participants in the straw, as in this short note which appeared in the *Chicago Times* on September 4, 1860: "A correspondent writes to the Memphis *Appeal*, from Shelby county, that every Democrat in that section, except one, was for [Stephen] Douglas."[39]

Citizens' polls, like those conducted by journalists, were most valued for their rhetorical power: Many polls were published because they projected a clear and decisive victory for the newspaper's favored candidate. Quantitative data from the straws were published, but often with commentary about the validity or compelling nature of the data. The *Tribune* was particularly adept at this sort of writing, and reported this story during the 1856 election:

> OLD DARTMOUTH FOR FREMONT. — Speaking of the exercises of the Commencement at Dartmouth, a writer says:
> One or two of the speakers referred to Fremont and an instant cheer showed the temper of the audience. The change here is wonderful. Six years ago there may have been of the 300 students 26 who didn't swallow Mr. Webster, Fugitive Slave Bill and all. Now there are only 50 who are not Fremonters.
> Despite the deadening influence of Dr. Lord's Middle ageism, the heart of Old Dartmouth is still alive and warm for the Free Men, Free Speech and Fremont.[40]

More than a month later, the *Tribune* reported this piece from a Buffalo paper:

THE OLD PATRIOTS. — The Buffalo *Republic* says that twenty-
four of the survivors of the war of 1812—pensioners—visited
M. Furnham, Esq., of Attica, Pension Agent, on Thursday
when a gentleman who was present inquired their predilec-
tions for the Presidency. The vote stood as follows:

Fremont   21
Buchanan   3

It seems that those who fought and bled for their country still
remain on the side of their country.[41]

Scores of these types of straw polls appear in mid- and late nineteenth century papers, but those which indicated a particularly
large lead for a paper's chosen candidate were especially valued, as
this 1860 *Tribune* poll demonstrates:

PENNSYLVANIA. — A correspondent writes to the New York
Tribune that a thorough canvass of Franklin county, Pennsyl-
vania, shows that it will give more than 800 majority for
Lincoln. Large numbers have changed from the bogus
Democracy to Republicanism. Equally promising accounts
come from other parts of the State.[42]

Straws were reported with partisan commentary, and very often
with a humorous or ironic tone. In 1896, the *New York Times* published this report provided by a reader:

For Bryan and the County Jail.
To the Editor of the New York Times:
    On a south-bound train on the Delaware and Hudson
Railroad last Thursday, in one car an enthusiastic drummer
took the now popular straw vote to determine the political affiliations of the passengers. The poll showed the 23 occupants
divided—18 for McKinley, 5 for Bryan. This was satisfactory,
but more was to come. When the train halted at Ballston,
among those who got off were the five Bryan sympathizers,
and then it was seen that they were handcuffed together, and
were a gang of prisoners on their way to the county jail at that
place.

SOUND MONEY.
Ballston, N.Y., Oct. 5.[43]

Although straws conducted by common citizens were extremely popular from the mid-nineteenth century through the first two decades of the twentieth, they no longer appeared after the 1930s. The publication of "people's polls" diminished considerably as the *Literary Digest*, George Gallup, Elmo Roper, and other pollsters and news agencies began to take over the chore of polling the electorate. After 1936, most polls published in the three newspapers were conducted by professional pollsters or by journalists. The accompanying cartoon from the *Tribune* (figure 4.3) indicates that the polls of interest to candidates, editors, and readers by 1936 were polls conducted by "experts"—political editors, pollsters, and journalists. Only occasionally after 1936 does one see a straw vote conducted by citizens themselves published in these newspapers. [44]

The Decline of "People's Polls"

Straw polling, conducted by average citizens, was of little interest to major newspapers after the introduction of the random sample survey. The ability to accurately predict election outcomes became much more important than collecting the opinions of factory workers and neighbors. Now these groups could be sampled, through the use of statistical procedures, and were represented "scientifically." The new polls were much more accurate than the straw polls had been,[45] and the participation of citizens in the quantitative discourse of public opinion was taken care of "from the top" by the pollster.

With the loss of the "people's polls," one can argue, there was a loss of a particularly interesting type of public opinion discourse. The many straw polls conducted by college students, farmers, and others were attempts at knowing one's own environment. It was probably a quick, enjoyable way to have contact with one's neighbors, engage in social comparison, and participate in a quasi-electoral politics at the same time. Perhaps the shift in polling—from journalists with no particular expertise and average citizens, to those with an expertise in sampling—exemplifies the link Michel Foucault has made between knowledge and power.

Foucault has argued that power can exist only where a supporting, "truthful" discourse exists. In other words, physicians, psychi-

FIGURE 4.3 A cartoon published on the front page of the *Chicago Tribune*, October 6, 1936. (Used with permission of the Chicago Tribune Company.)

atrists, and even scholars have authority because they have also established certain truths and bodies of knowledge that the public accepts as legitimate. Foucault explains:

> In a society such as ours, but basically in any society, there are manifold relations of power which permeate, characterise and constitute the social body, and these relations of power cannot themselves be established, consolidated nor implemented without the production, accumulation, circulation and functioning of a discourse. There can be no possible exercise of power without a certain economy of discourses of truth which operates through and on the basis of this association.[46]

By the nineteenth century, quantification was already an important, "truthful" discourse used to describe the population (e.g., the census). Science, statistics, and quantitative thinking more generally had achieved great legitimacy in the West.[47] The notion that social problems as well as intellectual ones might be solved through systematic analysis of one sort or another was already well entrenched, so it is no wonder that all types of people adopted these discourses.

Until the 1930s, citizens were able to use this legitimated discourse of quantification to assert their own opinions and attitudes through the mass media. Yet as the forces of rationalization and routinization progressed, citizens could no longer perform these calculations as well or as efficiently as the pollster. An inability on the part of the average citizen to randomly select thousands of individuals, poll them on their presidential preferences, perform the necessary calculations, and publish these data made citizens' polling irrelevant. By 1936, newspapers were more interested in the precision of sample survey results than in giving voice to communities and groups wishing to contribute their own versions of public opinion.

The Symbolic Use of Polls

It is nearly impossible to determine the accuracy of the typical nineteenth century straw poll, since the polled areas did not match defined electoral districts. At the time these straws were conducted, they may have helped local party workers, editors, and citizens get a general sense of how residents in their localities would vote in upcoming elections. Conducting, participating in, and reading about the straws was a form of entertainment as well: In the mid-nineteenth century men gained enormous pleasure from political activities and engaging in political discourse. The straw was a popular channel of political participation and communication during election years.

Since straw polls were not scientifically conducted, and were rarely replicated, they could not provide definitive evidence about election outcomes. Papers affiliated with competing parties could always find straws that were favorable to their candidate of choice. As a result, the polls are most interesting for their symbolic value, and not their methodological utility. Straws were viewed as powerful and important rhetorically, since they gave the impression that a favored candidate would win the upcoming election. A straw demonstrating that one's candidate led in popularity (if only among a small group of citizens) served a very specific discursive function: It wasn't only the paper's editors or party officials who supported the prospective president. Polls were *reports from the field* telling readers that they were not alone in their political beliefs. On the contrary, supporters of their favored candidate were everywhere.

Contemporary politicians use similar strategies, attempting to convince the mass public that their constituencies are large and that their support runs deeper than is apparent on the surface. An example is Richard Nixon's notion of the "silent majority"—people dispersed throughout the nation who tend not to express their opinions aloud. As Benjamin Ginsberg observes, Nixon used poll data to argue that most Americans did not agree with the antiwar protesters of the late 1960s and early 1970s: This majority simply chose not to express its opinions in the streets or in the mass media. Ginsberg argues that data and rhetoric about the silent majority were part of a strategy to undermine and delegitimate the claims of protesters.[48]

Just as Nixon used the silent majority idea to indicate widespread support of his ideological position, the nineteenth century straw polls allowed newspapers to speculate on the sentiments of those who didn't necessarily voice their opinions loudly in public. Newspapers had no concrete data about the voting intentions of the *general* public, but they helped their readers to extrapolate from the small amounts of evidence their reporters did have. Much of the typical editorial commentary hinted or directly stated that the straw polls were representations of public opinion.

The disappearance of "people's polls" in the 1930s and the rise of the sample survey were critical developments in the history of public opinion, since the ability to poll shifted away from the public itself. Up until the 1930s common citizens could send polls to a newspaper, but after that time they could no longer participate in this particular form of symbolic communication.[49] Since citizens could not conduct the new sample surveys—which demanded large resources and statistical expertise—any straws they might produce would seem trivial compared to the more authoritative sample surveys of Gallup, Roper, and others.

Polls are used symbolically today by presidents, members of Congress, interest groups, and others wishing to gain political advantage and public support. Yet journalists no longer use polls in this manner, because the norms of journalism have changed so dramatically since the mid-nineteenth century.[50] Today, survey results are quite intentionally treated by reporters and editors as news, although poll data are sometimes used to punctuate a particular theme in a news story. Polls may be used by a paper to set the public agenda or highlight an issue or problem the editors believe to be critical.[51] Yet since most major newspapers—including the ones analyzed in this chapter—now strive to appear impartial and nonpartisan, they no longer engage in the symbolic use of polls so popular in the mid-nineteenth century.

CHAPTER FIVE

Congressmen, Journalists, and Opinion Assessment, 1930–1950

D
URING THE NINETEENTH CENTURY, American journalists, party officials, and legislators discovered the value of public opinion quantification. Straw polls were useful if one sought to understand the seemingly volatile public mood, and poll results had great rhetorical utility as well. In the early decades of the twentieth century, however, the practice of aggregating opinions became increasingly complex and problematic. The *Literary Digest* error of 1936 generated a new brand of skepticism toward opinion quantification, and political elites, who hoped to keep abreast of changing public attitudes, began to doubt the validity of counting opinions. Two parties with a great interest in the public's shifting moods—legislators and journalists—were particularly suspicious of polls. The numerical description of public opinion had proven useful in the past, yet these quantitative endeavors were also potentially hazardous. Many newspaper editors, reporters, and politicians pondered the dependability of polling, given that even the most established pollsters could produce flawed estimates of public opinion.

The 1930s and 1940s represent an important transitional period in the history of public opinion expression and measurement. Three events—the *Digest* misprediction of 1936, George Gallup's success that same year, and the polling errors of 1948—forced those with an interest in the public sentiment to take positions on the issue of measurement. The central questions for policymakers and reporters working during this era were: How should one assess the public mood? And, more important, how can one be sure that estimates of public opinion are valid and reliable? This chapter explores how U.S. congressmen and influential journalists conceptualized and measured public opinion during the years before and after the Second World War. Were these parties, both of whom understood the problems and benefits associated with quantification, drawn to systematic, "rational" techniques of public opinion assessment? Or did they avoid engaging in the numerical description of public opinion? Finally, did either reporters or policymakers working in the 1930s and 1940s use quantitative data in a symbolic fashion, as was the practice in nineteenth century political discourse?

Several scholars have detailed the efforts of survey research pioneers—academics, pollsters, and market researchers—to quantify public opinion after the 1930s.[1] Yet it is not clear how journalists and policymakers, seeking a *working knowledge* of public opinion, thought about the public and evaluated its preferences. In the first part of this chapter, I discuss some social scientific studies from the period of interest which evaluated the attitudes congressmen and journalists held about opinion polls. Congressmen also publicly debated the role of public opinion quantification on the floors of the House and Senate, and their discussion is summarized in this section as well. Next, I present the results of a study which explored how legislators and reporters learned about the public mood in the 1930s and 1940s. Most Americans—whether or not they were directly involved in politics—were confused about the validity of the opinion poll, but congressmen and journalists needed to resolve the issue because their jobs depended on it. I argue that the 1930s and 1940s were critical years for professional pollsters, but also for a variety of individuals not associated with the evolving "science" of survey research. In fact, the methodological practices of nonprofessional opinion assessors are as interesting as those of sophisticated researchers: Congressmen and journalists were quite taken by the authoritative nature of quantitative techniques, but they also remained skeptical of the power of numbers. Finally, I will discuss the infamous 1948 polling debacle, when several respected pollsters predicted that Thomas E. Dewey would win the presidency.

Congressmen, Journalists, and Polls

Two important players on the political scene in the 1930s and 1940s who needed to understand public opinion—policymakers and journalists—were wary of polls. The *Literary Digest* poll of 1936 severely damaged any tentative legitimacy polling might have had in the eyes of political elites or the voting public. Policymakers, on the whole, were reluctant to trust this new means of assessing public opinion because they believed they already possessed effective repertoires for measuring public sentiment. Reporters and editors working during this politically volatile period felt much the same way.

There is a small literature in public opinion research concerning the attitudes of national policymakers and journalists toward polling in the years before and after World War II. Almost all of this research was conducted by social scientists, familiar with polling, who were interested in how quickly the sample survey was diffusing among professionals.

During the 1930s and 1940s very few U.S. congressmen conducted or commissioned public opinion polls in their districts or states. Winston Allard, writing in the *Journalism Quarterly* in 1941, found that U.S. congressmen had mixed feelings about the usefulness of polls.[2] While almost all of the congressmen Allard studied read national Gallup or Fortune polling results at least occasionally, only twenty-one of fifty-six congressmen interviewed believed that national poll results were indicative of attitudes in their own states. When asked if they would consult a "reputable public opinion survey" if they were unsure of how to vote on legislation, only twenty of the congressmen said they would.

By 1953, only 48 of the 438 members of the House of Representatives studied by Carl Hawver employed public opinion polling techniques.[3] Hawver, who worked for Congressman Oakley Hunter in the 1950s, also found that younger members were more likely to use polls than were older representatives, and that use of polls was unrelated to the length of one's tenure in Congress. Few of the polls conducted by members of Congress and their staffs used random sampling techniques, and in many cases, the questions asked on the surveys were rather convoluted, making the results difficult to interpret. Hawver concluded that congressional polls of constituencies during this period were conducted more for public relations purposes than as attempts to measure public opinion. Sending out questionnaires, congressmen believed, helped them to stay in touch with constituents between elections, and highlighted a representative's activities in Washington.

Newspaper editors and executives polled as late as 1953 by a journalism professor named Warren Price were also quite skeptical of the sample survey.[4] Price found that only 6 percent of those editors and executives surveyed conducted scientific polls. The vast majority of editors, he noted, were not influenced by polls as guides for interpreting events. Most newsmen did not believe that the successful polls conducted before the 1952 presidential election "vindicated" polling, which had been disgraced in 1936 and 1948.

These studies of congressmen and journalists were rather limited in scope, but they do indicate a dearth of polls in both professions. The researchers successfully answered the question: Did reporters and legislators use "scientific" polls? Yet they neglected to ask what these professionals *actually did* in order to measure public opinion. Although they failed to use the new sample survey, were congressmen and journalists interested in quantification at all? Even V. O. Key, in his classic book *Public Opinion and American Democracy*, paid little attention to the issue, mentioning only a few methods that congressmen used to assess the public mood. He concluded that these were "unsystematic procedures for the gauging of opinions."[5]

Distrust of the sample survey by politicians was not only evident in the pages of social science journals. Doubts about polls emerged in congressional debates as well, with national legislators expressing three general concerns about survey research. The first was that polls were methodologically flawed. Representative Pierce, author of the first bill to investigate public opinion polls, argued in 1940 that pollsters do not include enough people in their samples to properly gauge public opinion. He also believed that the average citizen might not be completely candid with pollsters, making a poll's results unreliable.[6]

Another objection to polling posed by congressmen echoed Walter Lippmann's doubts about the common citizen's interest in politics. Could the average man or woman assess complex policy matters in a thoughtful manner? Representative Curtis, in a 1941 House debate about polls, argued that

the problems of our Government are not so simple that a man can go down the street and collect so many yeas and so many noes and have the right answer. They are matters to be studied, with long hours of work. I do not believe that polls of public opinion should go unrestrained, and, even granting that at the present time honest, sincere, capable, and truthful men are running them, unless we do something about it they will become a menace in the hands of unscrupulous men.[7]

Also prominent in congressional debate of the 1940s was a fear of a poll-induced "bandwagon effect" that might warp the American voting process. Some worried that the publication of survey results would cause people to support candidates who led in the polls, and disregard their own party loyalties.

Many of the congressional discussions of polls in the 1930s and 1940s made either direct or indirect references to the *Literary Digest* poll of 1936. Senator Nye, who sponsored a Senate bill in 1941 to investigate national polling practices, said

So many people are accepting such [public opinion] polls as being truly indicative of public sentiment that I think the public has every right to know the measure of care that is practiced in taking the polls. All of us have ability to remember that not so many years ago a magazine which had been affording what were accepted as very authentic polls went out of being because it was found on one occasion that one of its polls was far from accurate.[8]

If congressmen and journalists feared the inaccuracy and effects of the new sample survey, how did they measure public opinion during these years? Did interest, on the part of politicians and journalists, in quantifying public opinion wane after the mistakes of 1936? What historians of public opinion need to know about the 1930s and 1940s is not whether policymakers or journalists were polling. The more fundamental issue concerns the authority of numbers: How did these individuals think about and use quantification during a period when the value of numerical approaches was very much in doubt?

The Study

In order to understand how national policymakers and reporters measured public opinion during the 1930s and the 1940s, I conducted a study of U.S. congressmen and prominent American journalists who worked during these years. I obtained a list of retired members of Congress from the United States Association of Former Members of Congress, located in Washington, D.C. From the association's *Directory of Members* it was possible to identify all those congressmen who served part or all of their tenure in Congress before 1950.[9]

Locating journalists for this study was much more difficult because the population of potential respondents is tremendous, and because there are no definitive lists of working journalists. Furthermore, I was primarily searching for journalists and editors who had an interest in the nature of public opinion. In order to obtain a list of journalists who met the criteria for this study I used two bibliographic sources: *Who's Who in America* and *The Encyclopedia of Twentieth-Century Journalists.*[10]

Questionnaires were mailed to 241 congressmen and journalists in order to understand how these individuals assessed public opinion on important issues in the 1930s and 1940s. Respondents were assured that their answers to the survey would be kept confidential—that their names would not be connected to their comments. The survey contained both open and closed question formats so that respondents had the freedom to elaborate on their methods where necessary. Several weeks after the initial questionnaires were sent out, follow-up letters and additional copies of the questionnaire were mailed to nonrespondents. One month after the follow-up questionnaires were mailed, I conducted in-depth telephone interviews with ten of the most interesting respondents. These were congressmen and journalists who, in answer to the survey, described particularly systematic, unsystematic, or idiosyncratic methods for understanding public opinion.

Fifty-three congressmen participated in the study, and forty-four journalists returned completed questionnaires. The average tenure in office for a congressman was seventeen years, and the average length of a journalist's career was forty years. Almost all of the journalist respondents worked for newspapers, although many went on to work in broadcast news or for news magazines after the period of interest. There were only seven women in the total sample and two of these women participated in the study.

Since I asked respondents in this study to report on practices used several decades ago, I was particularly concerned with the accuracy of their long-term memories. Although there is little doubt

that these concerns plague this study and other oral-historical endeavors, I tried to combat the problem by asking informants to describe particular practices in detail for me. I also encouraged them
to send me newspaper clippings or any other records concerning
public opinion assessment that they might have kept in their files.
Many of the study participants obliged, sending additional mate-
rials, providing dates or other details about their strategies, or at-
taching lengthy letters.

The Importance of Public Opinion

Most of the respondents in this study thought that assessing public
opinion was an important part of their work. Seventy-six percent of
the congressmen and 57 percent of the journalists thought that it
was either almost always or always important for them to find out
about the nature of public opinion during the 1930s and 1940s.

The divergence of opinion between the two groups on the importance of the public sentiment can be explained by the different
relationships these professionals had with the public. Congressmen who want to stay in office find themselves perpetually running
for reelection, even in nonelection years. David Mayhew has argued that most communications, either personal or impersonal,
between a member of Congress and his or her constituency stem
from the desire to remain in office.[11] In response to my open-ended
questions, many congressmen said they tried to keep in close touch
with the feelings and opinions of their constituents. One thirty-
eight year veteran of Congress said that he assessed public opinion
by "keeping my nose to the ground whether I had opposition or
not. I always ran as though I did."

TABLE 5.1 Importance of Public Opinion for Congressmen and
Journalists in the 1930s and 1940s

Degree of importance	Congressmen	Journalists
Always important	52.2%	42.9%
Almost always important	23.9	14.3
Sometimes important	15.2	23.8
Rarely important	8.7	19.0
		(N = 97)

Note: All data in this table and the tables which follow are derived from a census of
congressmen and journalists, not a sample.

Many congressmen mentioned that while they used a variety of methods to assess public opinion, they also depended on their own good judgment. In response to my open-ended question asking how they assessed public opinion, 26 percent of the congressmen explained that they were somewhat Burkean in their approach to questions of legislation: They used their instincts as trustees of the people. One congressman wrote:

> I felt that I knew, pretty well, what the "public opinion" was on particular issues certainly in my district. I also knew that it could and did *change* suddenly and frequently. Therefore, I wasn't much concerned about it. Furthermore, I believe (with Edmund Burke) that a Representative's job is to vote the way he thinks is right, rather than to try simply to reflect the momentary opinion of a majority of voters.

One of the few congressmen who claimed he did not use any techniques for trying to assess public opinion saw his job this way:

> Probably I was influenced by my profession—medicine. Doctors assume the patient's relatives and friends want him to get healthy again. One doesn't ask what procedures or treatments they [the patient's family and friends] think will be best. It's *our* job to decide and carry out the proper "treatments" or at least the best possible [ones].

A congressman who served for over thirty years in the House and Senate named several mechanisms for prompting communication from constituents, but also said, "I did not feel that I could make decisions on mail alone, finding that more people wrote when opposed to issues than when approving. I usually cast my votes after very careful study, much reading, listening, and attending committee hearings. I voted my convictions."

Most journalists also thought public opinion was important to them in their work, although 19 percent said it was rarely important. There were three reasons why some of the newspapermen didn't think that assessing public opinion was particularly consequential. Either they believed that assessment of public opinion wasn't part of a reporter's job, they thought public opinion was not an issue in the 1930s and 1940s, or they believed that newspapers were in the business of influencing public opinion and not measuring it. One journalist, who covered presidential and congressional elections for over thirty years, said that while some newsmen pandered to public opinion, he most often tried to influence it. Another journalist noted that in the 1940s, "Too many journalists magnified their own opinions and believed that a majority thought the same. To summarize: We really made judgments by the seat of our pants."

One very well-known journalist argued that newspapers in the 1930s and 1940s were so busy trying to influence public opinion that they had little time for clearheaded assessment of the public sentiment:

It should be borne in mind that during the 1930s and 1940s, most American newspapers regarded themselves as political *leaders* as well as political chronicles. Therefore, most of them looked for signs that public opinion was in step with the publisher's biases. For example, in 1936 the *Chicago Tribune* featured stories on the heavy run on Alf Landon campaign buttons in Chicago (they consisted of felt cut in the shape of a sunflower with a Landon picture on a button in the middle). The *Chicago Daily Times,* on the other hand, featured stories about the number of school children who were looking for the buttons because the felt made an ideal pen wiper—an article which sold for one or two pennies. . . . Newspapers did not really become interested in articles on public opinion until World War II loomed on the horizon (of course there were some exceptions).

He gives another example from Chicago:

I can remember another occasion when the *Chicago Tribune* managed to find a street, this was during the Landon-Roosevelt campaign. . . . The *Chicago Tribune* found a street that was absolutely littered with Roosevelt buttons and so they took a picture of it showing all the buttons on the ground. . . . So the *Chicago Times,* which was pro-Roosevelt, they went ahead and found a street that was littered with Landon buttons and they printed that picture. You see, you have to realize, they weren't lying or anything like that. . . . But nevertheless, you really aren't interested in public opinion when you are trying to lead it.

Most congressmen and journalists in this study, while occasionally noting the role they themselves played in influencing public opinion, were quite serious about assessing the public mood as effectively as possible. We now turn to the methods these individuals used to measure the public sentiment in an era where the sample survey was viewed by many as a rather dubious measurement technique.

Systematic, Quantitative Methods

There were very few congressmen or journalists who did not have multiple methods for assessing public opinion in the World War II era. In terms of polls, my evidence corroborates findings from previous studies, indicating that few of these professionals conducted scientific surveys. As table 5.2 indicates, only 33 percent of the congressmen in this study either conducted or commissioned surveys of any type.

The vast majority of these surveys were actually straw polls, which did not employ the scientific sampling techniques commonly used today. Despite the congressmen's ignorance of the new sampling techniques which Gallup and others were trying to perfect, however, the results of this study indicate that congressmen were making attempts to be as systematic and quantitative as possible, given what they knew about measuring public opinion. One prominent congressman from the Northeast illustrates this point as he describes his greatest attempt at assessing public opinion:

> As [a] ranking Republican member . . . I was invited almost every week to speak on some big radio station on my views against going into war, which naturally became well known throughout the nation. But I did, at my own expense, send out probably over 100,000 postal cards to the enrolled voters in my district . . . asking them whether they favored getting into war or staying out. Much to my surprise the vote was 10 to 1 against going into war both in the small towns and also in the big cities. . . . I presented this to the Congress and it had a good deal of influence on the Democrats who were actually against going to war and were under pressure and propaganda from Roosevelt to favor war. . . . There is no question but that [my] poll had considerable effect on both the Democrats and Republicans in Congress and that President

TABLE 5.2 Percentage of Congressmen Who Conducted or
Commissioned Surveys in the 1930s and 1940s

Conducted and commissioned surveys	8.2%
Conducted surveys only	24.5
Commissioned surveys only	0.0
Neither conducted nor commissioned surveys	67.3
	(N = 53)

Roosevelt knew that he did not have sufficient votes to get us into war unless attacked.

About one-third of the journalists in this study conducted surveys or went door-to-door to assess public opinion during the 1930s and 1940s. Again, while a few of the journalists mentioned that they subscribed to Gallup polling services or actually used the sample survey, my evidence indicates that most journalists were conducting straw polls during this period. One journalist, who worked in the west during the early part of his career and went on to work for the Associated Press, explains that "the method we used was to stop people on street corners or at the post offices. In the thirties and forties, shopping malls had not yet been constructed!" Another man who worked in the United States and in Europe during his thirty-nine years as a journalist describes the survey methodology he used when he worked for a Western periodical in the 1930s. He was hired by the owner to improve the periodical's status and boost its circulation: "Never west of the Hudson, I didn't know one end of an abalone from another. But a door-to-door canvass from Eureka to Encenita convinced me that [the publication's] only hope was to stay and grow as a [specialty] magazine."

Both the congressmen and the journalists used many other systematic, quantitative methods for assessing opinions besides occasional straw polls or commissioned scientific polls. Sixty percent of the congressmen in this study said that they tabulated incoming letters on particular issues in order to assess public sentiment toward those issues. Forty-three percent of the legislators tabulated incoming telephone calls from constituents. Furthermore, 26 percent of the congressmen actually counted editorials from newspapers and magazines to find out how many editorials supported a particular position on an issue or person. One congressman who

TABLE 5.3 Percentage of Congressmen Who Tabulated Letters,
            Telephone Calls, and/or Editorials

Tabulated constituent letters or telegrams	59.6%
Tabulated constituent telephone calls	43.1
Tabulated newspaper or magazine editorials	25.5
	(N = 53)

served in the 1940s said he checked all twenty-seven newspapers in
his district and categorized their positions, pro and con, on topics of
interest in order to get a feel for the nature of public opinion.

The journalists in this study were almost as systematic and
quantitative as the congressmen, which is surprising given that
most of them worked alone, without a staff to help them code or
tabulate readers' communications. Forty-nine percent of the journalists in this sample tabulated letters or telegrams which arrived at
their offices, and 23 percent tabulated incoming phone calls on important issues. Interestingly, 26 percent of the journalists took the
time to analyze editorials from other newspapers and magazines,
categorize the editorials by position, and tabulate them in order to
discover public opinion. One journalist, working for a foreign
newspaper in the years before and during the war, outlines the
elaborate system developed at the paper to quantify public opinion:

RESPONDENT: You see, when the war broke out in England
in 1939 the [paper] started, after a month or so, when it was
a phony war and not much was happening, it started a department headed by, I forget who it was now . . . somebody.
. . . We put in the paper, "Please write to us and tell us what
difficulties you're having" [to] raise questions about how the
war was affecting them. . . . "If you want help, please
write." . . . And you'd be surprised, we got hundreds of letters . . . from readers who were baffled by what was going
on and upset by rationing and all sorts of topics. And so, two
or three of us were dispatched, our ordinary work had
ceased because of the war. . . . I was waiting to go away as a
war correspondent, so they used me and the former tennis
correspondent, I remember, and the former golf correspondent [laughs]. . . . Two or three of us all got into an office
and analyzed these letters and sorted them out and, if we

TABLE 5.4 Percentage of Journalists Who Tabulated
Letters, Telephone Calls, and/or Editorials

Tabulated letters from readers	48.8%
Tabulated telephone calls from readers	23.3
Tabulated newspaper or magazine editorials	25.6
	(N = 44)

could, drafted replies, and if not, forwarded them to the
people that could answer them.

SH: So did you take the letters and put them into general
categories?

RESPONDENT: Oh, yes, we separated them into
styles. . . .

SH: Did you keep a running tab of the kinds of letters you
would get and did you do anything with that data?

RESPONDENT: Oh, yes. Stories were written about what
people were being worried by and . . . it was a daily column.

One reporter, covering the White House for an Eastern newspaper, often asked White House officials for their tabulations of
incoming mail and regularly checked with congressmen on the
nature of their mail. Another journalist, who covered the Senate
and the State Department, said that "favorable and unfavorable
responses to various articles were regularly considered and
tabulated" at his magazine. He also mentioned that he found
these tabulations useful as a "rough check on my editorial judgment."

Besides counting letters, telegrams, telephone calls, and editorials, the legislators and journalists in this study used other systematic methods for assessing public opinion. One congressman
who often visited his district in the Midwest, said that he would
sometimes ask for a show of hands on particular issues when speaking before civic clubs and other groups. Another congressman
maintained a file of individuals in his district and divided them into
groups as to how active and involved in politics they were, so that
he could visit representatives of these groups whenever he went
home:

I had a 3 × 5 card list of about 250 [people] and I classified them in about five or six groups . . . always went to see the editors of the [local newspapers]. And then I had others that were sort of political leaders—leaders in the sense that they supported me very [laughs] heavily and actively and so on down the line to the last group very casually.

Many of the congressmen noted that the margins by which they won or lost elections helped them get a sense of public opinion, although few felt that they could wait two or six years to assess public opinion.

Journalists also had an assortment of quantitative techniques for measuring public opinion besides counting letters, telegrams, and editorials. Two of the journalists said that when the public disagreed with positions taken by them or their editors, the disagreements would show up in cancellations of subscriptions, decreases in circulation, and a drop in coupon returns. Many mentioned that they studied election results to try to understand the nature of public opinion in their region or in the nation. One journalist who worked for a major metropolitan daily during most of his forty-six-year career was the paper's national labor correspondent during the 1940s. He often relied on "unscientific samplings of opinion gleaned through street corner or picket line interviews." He spoke as systematically as possible with individuals involved in labor disputes, in order to assess public and group opinion: "Where a major test of strength between management and labor was developing or where a strike had run for many weeks, preparation of background stories on impact and community attitudes often required such [door-to-door] surveys—sometimes general, sometimes limited to workers and their families."

Qualitative Methods

There were many qualitative methods used by congressmen and journalists to assess public opinion among constituents and readers. Some of these methods were systematic in nature, while others were more haphazard.

Almost all of the respondents (86 percent of congressmen and 82 percent of journalists) read newspapers and magazines to get a sense of the public sentiment. Seventy percent of the journalists in this study said that they would go to coffee shops, bars, and other public places for the express purpose of assessing public opinion.

One of the most useful qualitative means of assessing public opinion for both congressmen (68 percent) and journalists (80 percent) was discussion with colleagues. One congressman was able to meet colleagues from his region often and would discuss public opinion with them:

> We had weekly meetings of the twenty-eight members from Pennsylvania, and the members from Delaware. Both Pennsylvania senators were invited and usually attended. The meetings were exclusively on pending legislation, political discussions of the effect of such legislation, and lack of legislation for various problems. We were all well versed on news articles in the daily papers and weekly magazines.

Journalists too depended on their colleagues when it came to discussing and measuring public opinion. One journalist said:

> When E. W. Scripps was establishing his newspaper chain (later Scripps-Howard) around 1900, he always tried to locate his plant in the red-light district. This was for two reasons: (1) real estate values were cheap; (2) it was close to the business district. . . . That E. W. Scripps bit is not as silly as it sounds. . . . It is a shorthand way of saying that in our times, things were simpler, more human, more coherent. To a great extent, journalists and editors were able to keep "in touch" simply by talking to each other, and to people in the world around them—whores included.

He continues:

> In our time we were in *personal* (not "electronic") touch with each other. Journalists lived nearby and had their communal "watering holes." In New York, for example, we had Bleeck's now-vanished, once-famous "Artists and Writers" bar in the old *Herald Tribune* building . . . the Round Table at the Algonquin Hotel . . . plus clubs: Dutch Treat ("The Literary Kiwanis"), the Coffee House and, for all its stuffiness, the Century. In Boston, the *Globe, Post, Transcript,* and the Hearst papers were side-by-side on "Newspaper Row." . . .

However fierce the competition, journalists were, by and large, "friends and neighbors." They swapped notes. Public opinion was "in the air."

Another veteran reporter agrees that consulting with colleagues and socializing with them was much more prevalent in the 1930s and 1940s than it is today:

> Take a simple thing like the press clubs. The press clubs in most cities are pretty well dead now. Here in [a Midwestern city] they are sustaining one artificially, almost pumping oxygen into it. And the reason why they are having so much difficulty is there is no longer a cluster of newspapers in a given area. There was a time when every city had a newspaper [club]. When I worked in Philadelphia in the thirties, for instance, the *Philadelphia Record*, the *Philadelphia Inquirer*, and the *Philadelphia Bulletin* were all within walking distance of each other. And the Pen and Pencil Club was right in the middle of the affair.

Congressmen and journalists today still find their colleagues valuable sources of information about public opinion. Yet several of the respondents in this study who worked up until the 1970s and early 1980s believed that colleagues were much more important in earlier periods.

Public Opinion "Surrogates"

Most respondents in this study asked individuals who were perceived as somehow "close to public opinion" to assess public opinion for them. These "surrogates" ranged from academics to cabdrivers and train conductors. Often a congressman or journalist would go to one or many of his surrogates on a regular basis, asking them for help in measuring the public sentiment. Sometimes the surrogates themselves were systematic in their methods and were able to supply the legislator or journalist with very accurate head counts on particular issues.

Fifty-three percent of the congressmen in this sample used local party workers, party officials, or others to assess public opinion for them in their home state or district. Most congressmen kept in close touch with party supporters so that they would have strong organizations during election campaigns, and so that they could keep abreast of public opinion. One congressman said that he contacted party people often about the public mood: "I would phone them or write them and ask them to make informal and unscientific surveys of sentiment. You couldn't do this on a regular basis because it would take too much of a constituent's time."

The most common types of surrogates used by congressmen were "official experts"—people whose business it was to be informed about public opinion. These official experts included labor leaders, lobbyists, and educators, among others. In answer to an open-ended question about how they assessed public opinion, 17 percent of the congressmen said that they used official experts to gain an understanding of the climate of opinion. Four percent of the legislators said that they used "unofficial experts"—individuals who understood public opinion well, but did not assess opinion for professional reasons. One example of the use of unofficial experts is illustrated by a congressman from the Midwest:

> I had been in Congress a few years when the question arose as to whether farmers should be included in the social security program. And [a senior congressman] . . . found out that I was a genuine farmer. He accosted me and said that he had on his committee no genuine farmers who were prepared to answer the questions. And he wondered if I would help him to which I replied that I would. And so I became a sort of personal emissary for him and the committee to make that determination and so I used my district in [the Midwest] as a typical example of the problem. And it was a real interesting experience. . . . I called the farmers together, and I had a wide acquaintance of farmers . . . in my district. So I could very readily call a member from each county who was a representative farmer and I just called from my personal knowledge. And they assembled [in a city on three or four occasions] and contrary to all my experiences in asking delegations of that kind to give me their reaction to it, it was almost a negative thing. It puzzled me greatly.

Journalists also mentioned surrogates without prompting in their open-ended answers. Eleven percent asked professionals for help in assessing public opinion and 5 percent used unofficial experts. A journalist who worked for a wire service for over thirty years said that professional politicians often served as public opinion experts:

> In election years, for example, the [wire service] itself took great pains to poll not only newspaper editors and political reporters around the country but also state chairmen and even county and city chairmen. Of course this amounted to a poll of experts rather than a poll of the public. Some of these experts were very astute and uncannily correct in detecting trends in their areas; others were less so, so that the final result was approximate at best.

There were several journalists who successfully used unofficial experts on public opinion to conduct an opinion surveillance for them. One journalist, who covered presidential and congressional elections beginning in the 1930s, said, "I had my own favorite device on gauging elections. I approached Catholic clergy to ask how the vote would go in their area because I knew most priests love politics. I had a favorite bishop who never missed an election."

A few of the journalists in this study noted that city political bosses, who had considerably less power than they had had in the nineteenth century, were still an excellent source of information about public opinion in the cities. One journalist explains:

> RESPONDENT: You had the city machines in places like Chicago, New York, Philadelphia, Pittsburgh, and Boston. The city machines were more complete and had the communities more completely organized than anything else we have ever devised. You would have, at the top, the boss. And he would have a network of people under him responsible for various parts of the city, who would supervise a certain number of wards. The people supervising the wards, the ward leaders, in turn would have precinct captains who would supervise the precincts. The captains in turn would have block captains and sometimes when you had enormous buildings with a lot of people in them, even building captains. And there was a constant flow of information going both up and down.

> SH: Would you say that you used the bosses, as sources of information about public opinion, pretty regularly?

RESPONDENT: Oh, very regularly. Because they were quite reliable. In a way they were more reliable than the polls because the polls can only tell you about current reactions. Now, the bosses had the kind of relationship with their constituencies whereby the bosses could predict what reactions would be under a certain set of circumstances. . . . Today about the best you can do is do some demographic studies and go over some polls. And the trouble is, that's static, you know, it's sort of freezing society in one place. Now the boss understood how society was acting, not just where it stood but how it was acting.

Above all, the bosses were an accurate source for public opinion:

RESPONDENT: And the other thing is that the bosses were remarkably honest . . . about what they would tell you. . . . For one thing, they were not ideological, they were not in politics to carry out a crusade or to advance a cause. They were there because it was the best way to get a square meal. . . . And so therefore they could afford to be very straightforward.

Idiosyncratic Methods

Both congressmen and journalists in this study mentioned several haphazard methods for discovering the nature of public opinion which helped them, along with their other methods, to get a feel for what people were thinking. One journalist said that a friend and invaluable source, Les Biffle, "toured the mid-west in a ramshackle Ford in 1948, and decided that Truman would beat Dewey." Biffle's interest in the farm vote is also recounted in the political science literature: ". . . Leslie Biffle, Secretary of the Senate in the Eighty-first Congress, after making his own cross-country trek disguised as a poultry dealer with a trailer full of chickens in 1948, accurately divined that the farmers were going to vote for Truman despite a showing of the polls to the contrary."[12]

Another journalist, who began his career in New York in 1922, said, "I think we sensed public opinion through everything we saw and heard and read. Political reporters learned much from their sources whose antennae were tuned to their constituents. Any reporter picks up clues from sources, subjects, colleagues, thin air."

One congressman who made it a point to spend time in his

district, attending farm conventions and all of the local county fairs, said, "This might sound odd, but myself and many other members of congress that I knew, used to get a lot of ideas on how the general public felt by reading the walls in bathrooms in towns and cities that we were in. Much of what Americans think is sometimes written privately on bathroom walls."

On Using One's Instincts

In response to open-ended queries, 26 percent of the congressmen in this study noted that they depended on their own instincts and imagination in their work. As noted above, several congressmen approached their work in the House and Senate in a Burkean fashion, acting as trustees rather than representatives. Some journalists felt the same way: Nine percent said that they used their own instincts when it came to public opinion and another 9 percent said they judged the public sentiment "by the seat of their pants." A journalist who spent most of his long career overseas said,

> In the 1930s on [a large newspaper's] staff in New York I tried to envision my average reader and then spoke to him. As [a foreign] bureau chief . . . starting in 1946 I tried to think of the average New York subway goer—why should he care? I tried to understand the mind of the average reader and then set out to tell him what I could about Europe and North Africa. "Public opinion" merely identified the reader and his interests and prejudices; it was a starting point for converse. My source on what readers thought? Just my memory of folks I have known all my life.

Instrumental and Symbolic Uses of Numbers

The combination in the 1930s and 1940s of both traditional methods of assessing public opinion (asking party bosses, frequenting journalistic "watering holes," or interviewing parish priests) and modern, rationalized ones (letter counting, content analysis of newspaper editorials, or polling) marks these decades as a transition period. Here we can see a healthy coexistence of both intuitive techniques for understanding public opinion and the seeds of today's highly routinized conceptions and strategies.

While journalists and political leaders freely wove quantitative data into the fabric of their writings and speeches during the nineteenth century, their mid-twentieth century counterparts were less willing to do so. The advent of the sample survey made the simplistic forms of quantification (e.g., the straw poll) used in the nineteenth century less acceptable in public discourse: After the mistakes of the *Digest* and advances in survey methodology, actors on the national political scene had gained a more sophisticated understanding of public opinion quantification, but were also afraid to use numbers too freely in the public forum. In the 1930s common citizens, political elites, and reporters learned that they lacked the resources to engage in the most scientific forms of polling. Yet legislators and journalists used numbers for their own private purposes nonetheless.

The study summarized in this chapter provides evidence that quantification was alive and well in congressional and newspaper offices. Journalists and congressmen were skeptical of the new opinion poll, but they were also drawn to the instrumental benefits provided by quantification and routinization. First and foremost, numerical descriptions of public opinion helped them to understand the needs and positions of constituents and readers. Only a few of the informants in this study reported using numbers as "ammunition" in *public* debate.

In one sense, mid-twentieth century journalists and legislators had come to respect the power of numbers even more than they had one hundred years before: Quantification could work for you, but there was a chance that these decisive, authoritative figures could hurt you as well. A misprediction ruined the *Literary Digest's* reputation, and a faulty notion of public opinion might destroy a political career.

As political upheaval spread through Europe and as America prepared for war, our conception of public opinion was gradually changing. Professional pollsters began to provide the quantitative data which had always been central to American political discourse, but journalists and congressmen (with some exceptions) refrained from extensive *symbolic* use of opinion statistics. Reporters and policy makers were as interested as ever in numerical reports on public opinion, but were more concerned with the practical use of these data than with their rhetorical value.

Opinion Polling: 1948 and Beyond

Several of the congressmen and journalists in this study referred to the polling errors made by survey organizations before the presidential election of 1948. In the weeks before that election, Gallup, Roper, Crossley, and other major pollsters predicted that Thomas Dewey would defeat Harry Truman on election day. In the October issue of *Fortune* magazine, editors published Roper's estimates indicating that Dewey would capture 44.2 percent of the vote over Truman's 31.4 percent. *Fortune*'s editors were certain that the poll was correct, in part because the major pollsters agreed that Dewey would win the race. They wrote:

> Barring a major political miracle, Governor Thomas E. Dewey will be elected the thirty-fourth President of the United States in November. Such is the overwhelming evidence of Elmo Roper's fifth pre-election Survey in recent months. . . . So decisive are the figures given here this month that *Fortune,* and Mr. Roper, plan no further detailed reports on the change of opinion in the forthcoming presidential campaign unless some development of outstanding importance occurs. [13]

Roper and the other pollsters were wrong about the anticipated Dewey victory, and Truman never let them forget it. Even before the election, on October 29, Truman thought he could win despite the pollster's predictions:

> Sixty million people are going to vote on November the 2nd. That is a conservative estimate in my mind. . . . If that 61 million will vote the Democratic ticket, we will be all right. And when those people vote, they are going to throw the Galluping polls right in the ashcan—you watch 'em. There are going to be more red-faced pollsters on November the 3rd than there were in 1936, when the Literary Digest said that Roosevelt shouldn't be elected. [14]

While in office, Truman joked continually about the dubious value of polling in press conferences and in speeches. Meanwhile, pollsters and the academic survey research community reflected on why the 1948 polls had been wrong. [15] After much discussion and study, pollsters realized that they had stopped polling too soon before election day: There were important "last minute" shifts in public opinion toward Truman. In a 1949 report to the Social Science Research Council, a committee on preelection polls noted that pollsters had failed to examine their data carefully during the preelection period, did not spend enough effort considering the behavior of undecided voters, and made errors in sampling and interviewing as well.[16]

The errors of 1948 were instructive to pollsters, some of whom have worked continuously since that year to improve the predictive ability of election polls. Scores of developments in survey research methodology have made polls better than they were in 1948, and I will discuss some of these changes in chapter 6. Even though today's surveys—those used to predict elections and those employed to measure public attitudes in nonelection periods—are undoubtedly better than they ever were, there is still considerable variance in the quality of polls. As a result, the American Association for Public Opinion Research (AAPOR), a professional organization of academic and nonacademic survey researchers, tries to monitor polling quality as best it can.[17]

Attempts to improve survey research have been successful in many cases, but there are still questions about the accuracy of preelection polls. In a very interesting study of preelection surveys, Irving Crespi explored the ways these polls for national, state, and local elections have changed since 1948. Nonsampling error, he argues, is still a serious problem for pollsters. At times, pollsters create "ad hoc" research designs instead of attending to the guidelines provided in the survey research literature. Often, Crespi believes, pollsters explain errors by "reference to the unique qualities of a particular election rather than by reference to inadequacies in research design."[18] Crespi's concerns with the state of preelection polling are many, and he concludes his book by noting that the "prospects for improvement in the near future must be rated as dim."[19]

Despite these difficulties, which are well known to those who study polls, it is unlikely that a mistake on the scale of the 1948 misprediction will occur again. So many pollsters (with varying degrees of sophistication) conduct surveys prior to a presidential election that there tends to be a fair amount of consensus across their results. Pollsters will always remember the 1948 debacle, and researchers like Crespi hope that these memories will force them to approach election forecasting in a rigorous and cautious manner.

CHAPTER SIX

Contemporary Public
Opinion Research

HROUGHOUT THE NINETEENTH and twentieth centuries, newspaper journalists, party workers, and politicians polled their readers and their constituents. These same groups still conduct or purchase an enormous number of polls and surveys, but in recent decades many others have joined them. Today, political consulting firms, interest groups, market researchers, and television networks conduct and sponsor a myriad of sophisticated surveys each year. With the assistance of computer technology, and some methodological training, individuals and organizations are able to query members of the public about their political views, their buying habits, and their life-styles.

Scores of academics, commercial pollsters, and business writers have published books and articles documenting the changes in polling and survey research since Gallup and others conducted their early polls in the 1930s. In fact, there are so many histories of polling, and so many methodological tracts about survey research, that students and amateur pollsters are often overwhelmed by the sheer size of this literature. It is my intention in this chapter to discuss some of these works, in order to complete the chronicle of opinion assessment initiated in chapter 3. By summarizing recent developments in polling which are recorded in the public opinion literature, I hope to provide a clear picture of modern opinion research.

Up until now, the argument of this book focused primarily on polling—especially preelection polling. During the nineteenth century, the straw polls published in daily newspapers like the *Chicago Tribune* and *The New York Times* were conducted by journalists and party loyalists to predict election outcomes. The surveys conducted or used by journalists and congressmen working in the

years surrounding the Second World War were often election polls
as well. In this chapter I will discuss preelection polling, but I will
also concentrate on survey research. In academe, but also in business, many surveys focus on attitudes, beliefs, and values—not just
on voting preference. Some researchers who are interested in public beliefs or improving survey methodology design very long surveys with open- and closed-ended queries. Many of these surveys
include experimental questions, so that researchers can find better
ways to probe respondents' attitudes. Such surveys are much different than the typical preelection poll, which asks a respondent
how he or she plans to vote, and the likelihood that he or she will
visit the polls on election day. Besides the differences in content
and (often) methodology between the typical opinion poll and the
in-depth survey, brief opinion and preelection polls are often conducted under severe time restrictions. In the days before the Persian Gulf War or during the Clarence Thomas Supreme Court
nomination hearings in 1991, pollsters were forced to conduct their
research quickly—often within a matter of days. Polls on these
sorts of issues must be done in a timely fashion; otherwise they lose
their news value.

The first section of this chapter is devoted to a brief discussion
of organizations that use polls, during and between elections. Although many polls are conducted by commercial pollsters and market researchers, here I will concentrate on the use of polls by the
mass media, political parties, candidates, and political consultants.
After summarizing how polls are used by different organizations, I
will focus on a few major methodological issues in survey research
and polling. I review some of the insights academic survey researchers have gained in the recent past, and the techniques they
have developed to cope with the changing social and political environment. Finally, I'll discuss a small but rather interesting literature in survey research: the attitudes of Americans toward polling,
or the "polls on the polls."

Polling and the Mass Media

Much of this book addresses polling and survey research conducted
by journalists, so my discussion of contemporary polling begins
with news organizations. As James Bryce pointed out in *The American Commonwealth*, journalists help to mold public opinion, but

they also try to assess popular sentiments as best they can. Journalists have always been interested in evaluating public opinion, since in a democracy, public opinion matters—it is news. Rigorous assessment of popular opinion helps editors figure out what the public wants to hear or read about, and therefore shapes news content. Also, people like to read and hear about themselves, and opinion polls enable social comparison on a mass scale.

Journalists have long found polling data provided by others extremely useful. In the nineteenth century, they reported poll results sent to them by like-minded partisan readers. In the twentieth century, news organizations often subscribe to polling services and continually publish or broadcast numbers about the public sentiment collected by others. In the last few decades, however, some news organizations have established their own in-house polling operations. Two journalism professors, David Weaver and Max McCombs, argue that journalists first became interested in social science methodology beginning in the 1930s.[1] After the establishment of the first journalism training programs, housed with the social sciences, many universities created graduate programs in journalism with faculty members trained in social science. By the late 1970s, 61 percent of the seventy-seven journalism master's programs surveyed by researcher Michael Ryan required a course in quantitative research methods.[2]

Philip Meyer, a former reporter who now teaches journalism, popularized the phrase *precision journalism* to describe the ways that social science techniques can be used by reporters and editors.[3] In his influential 1973 book *Precision Journalism*, which is now a widely read text in journalism schools, Meyer argues that reporters should take advantage of developments in the social sciences. Quantitative tools, he posits, can be extremely useful in reporting the news:

> The social sciences can help us . . . in two ways: their findings in many fields provide a continuing check on the conventional wisdom. We can save ourselves some trouble, some inaccuracy, and some lost opportunities by merely paying attention to what the social scientists are doing and finding out. More importantly and of more direct practical value, we can follow their example by abandoning the philosopher's armchair, giving up the notion that a few facts and common sense

will make any problem yield, and make the new, high-powered research techniques our own. [4]

News organizations, like journalism curricula, continue to adopt social scientific methodology in the form of survey research and polling. Daily newspapers and television news programs include a variety of reports about polls and surveys. In 1980, David Paletz and a team of researchers conducted a content analysis to explore how polls are used by the media, and found that during three nonelection years, *The New York Times* published 380 polls. During those same years, the NBC and CBS nightly news programs also contained a large number of polls—83 and 40, respectively. [5] Michael Traugott and Roberta Rusch studied the proliferation of polls in the media by analyzing scores of polls reported by *The New York Times* during the 1980, 1984, and 1988 presidential campaigns. They found that the sheer number of polls reported increased during the course of each campaign, and that references to polls are normally part of articles emphasizing campaign strategy and the "horse-race." [6]

Although there are no definitive reports on the number of political polls conducted each year in the United States, the media are responsible for producing and publicizing much of these data. Some of the national media have joined together to conduct polls (e.g., *The New York Times*/CBS News poll or the ABC News/*Washington Post* poll), and many polls are conducted by regional news organizations. Albert Cantril argues that while there has been a proliferation of polls over the last few decades, polls seemed "ubiquitous" during the 1988 presidential election. Many media outlets used a publication called *Hotline*—a daily report on the campaign that included a compilation of state and local polls. In fact, state and local polls, which are normally overlooked by national media organizations, got attention because of *Hotline*. This dependence of many on *Hotline* was problematic, though, because the publication omitted much methodological data which helps consumers evaluate the reliability of polls. [7]

The large number of polls in the media has shaped the character of contemporary journalism in the United States. Although I discuss the impact of polling and quantification on democratic communication in the concluding chapter, I should note here that many journalists worry about the predominance of polls in the media. In a recent essay, Phil Meyer himself reported on the "uneasiness" felt by many news organizations which depend on polls. On occasion, journalists and editors feel guilty that they may be contributing to public opinion "bandwagons" during elections. In their attempts to lessen the perceived impact of polls, newspapers and television news broadcasts report poll results in such a way that they "seek to conceal" the precision of the data:

> When *The New York Times* reported the final Gallup poll result last November, for example, it deleted the Gallup Organization's basic prediction of a Bush win with 56 per cent of the two-party vote and reported only the less refined numbers showing the undecided portion. *USA Today* used Gordon Black's straightforward prediction of 55 per cent for Bush in a page-one graphic but failed to mention it in the accompanying story which emphasized leaners and the undecided. The three network polls attempted no allocation of the undecided.[8]

Bill Kovach, the Washington editor of *The New York Times*, argues that polling is useful to journalists but is problematic in a number of ways. Polls contribute to "horse-race" reporting, which eliminates many candidates from the contest too early in the campaign. Additionally, since some media organizations have invested so much of their resources in in-house polling, they often ignore other pollsters' results. This can be dangerous, since those other results may differ from a newspaper's own poll findings. Kovach wonders whether the media and their polls *create* issues for public debate: "Is there a danger here," he asks, "that other ideas, other issues or approaches, are squeezed out and an incomplete agenda is being drawn"?[9] In fact, much of the criticism of media poll use, by journalists and by others, focuses on *how* the media report data. The difficulty of communicating complex findings, the lack of proper quantitative training among journalists, and the uncritical reporting of poll data have all received considerable attention.[10] Journalists may on occasion use poll data symbolically, as in the nineteenth century, but the real problem in contemporary poll reporting is misinterpretation of data. I take up these issues in light of democratic theory in the concluding chapter.

Political Parties and Polling

In the nineteenth century, political parties were critical to candidates during elections. Parties asked their loyalists to canvass important areas, and the results of these canvasses were often published in newspapers. Then and now, parties are able to mobilize campaign workers to solicit funds for candidates, encourage people to vote, and persuade them to vote for particular candidates. Candidates often emphasize or deemphasize their affiliation with parties, depending on their personal ideologies or the perceived strength of their party at the national level. Although there is evidence of increasing disassociation of candidates and their parties, and a general weakening of the major parties, these organizations continue to play important roles in elections.[11]

Beyond helping candidates plan their strategies, or furnishing technical assistance, political parties in the United States provide poll data for office seekers. Several party organizations, including the Republican National Committee (RNC), the National Republican Senatorial Committee (NRSC), the National Republican Congressional Committee (NRCC), and the Democratic National Committee (DNC), dispense poll data to candidates. These organizations allow candidates to buy polls at very low cost, so that aspirants can organize strategy around survey results.[12]

Sometimes the major political parties use unscientific polling in combination with direct mail for fund-raising purposes. In his book *Polling and the Public*, Herbert Asher reproduced two such mailings—one from the Republican National Committee, and one from the Democratic Senatorial Campaign Committee. Using data bases which contain the names and addresses of potential contributors, the RNC and the DSCC queried respondents on a variety of issues and asked for donations.[13] These polls, like the ones most citizens receive from their congressmen, senators, and state assemblymen, are not part of a scientific, random sample design. The central goal of the direct mailings is to solicit donations, not to measure public opinion: For assessing popular opinion, the parties engage in the same sorts of scientific polling used by the major pollsters. It is rare that a congressman, senator, or political party releases data collected in concert with a solicitation effort. They fail to release these data either because they never analyze them, or because they understand the unrepresentative nature of the sample.

Unscientific polls conducted by the national party organizations and interest groups are worthy of analysis, even though they do not yield reliable data. It seems, in cases like these, that those responsible for designing the direct mail campaigns have some insight into the place of polls in the current political climate. Asking a citizen to fill out the survey before asking him for money is an involvement technique: There is an assumption that people *enjoy* filling out questionnaires, and that this endeavor makes them feel as though they are participating in the political process. In the examples Asher provides, the potential respondent is told that his or her answers to the survey questions will be made available to the media and to members of Congress. An underlying message of the solicitation is something like this: "We want your money, but your opinions are important to us as well. In fact, your opinions are so important that we ask for them first, before we ask for financial assistance." Even if one cannot give a substantial contribution, he may return *some* amount, and feel better about the party—as if the party cared about his ideas.

Polls have been used symbolically to manipulate voter behavior throughout American political history, but the use of nonscientific polls in direct mail is something very new. Many who write about polling worry about developments such as these, since citizens often mistake unscientific polls for more rigorously conducted ones. Some researchers believe that people have grown increasingly tired of filling out surveys, and they fear that these "fake" polls ruin the chance to conduct scientific surveys. Parties do purchase and conduct a large number of random sample surveys, though, in order to understand the nuances of electoral behavior. These surveys are of much more interest to candidates.

The national party organizations provide two kinds of polling services: They purchase polls from well-known commercial survey research firms, and some have polling capabilities in-house. The parties use poll data to analyze the effectiveness of advertising, to estimate the impact of party initiatives, and to help them decide how to spend funds.[14] These organizations may sell survey data to candidates at low rates, or may advise them on strategy without actually providing the raw data from a relevant survey. Sometimes, candidates are provided with the results of tracking polls—polls done every night or every few days with small samples of respondents.[15] Tracking polls are particularly useful during any given campaign, since they provide time-series data to help strategists evaluate which tactics "work" and which don't.

As many political analysts have noted, the Republican party tends to provide more and better services to its candidates than the Democratic organizations. Paul Herrnson points out that the Republicans help candidates to assess public opinion, but also help them to analyze these data and use them strategically. His study of candidates' relations with the national party organizations reveals that their large assets enable Republicans to provide more survey data to candidates at lower rates. Additionally, the RNC "has given a number of state parties computer systems that can be used to study voting patterns, analyze survey data, and store large compilations of election data."[16]

The national parties, and the candidates they support, find surveys to be of great instrumental value. Polling helps to assess public attitudes on issues, but also enables the evaluation of candidate popularity. Parties have always stood between the public and particular candidates, so it is no wonder that they take opinion measurement seriously. In the nineteenth century, and for much of the twentieth century, party bosses took it upon themselves to assess public opinion. As one of the journalists I interviewed for chapter 5 noted, party bosses were able to report accurately on public opinion in their areas because they had a detailed, textured understanding of their constituents' needs. The fact that parties are now polling demonstrates how rationalization has affected this particular dimension of the electoral process: Party organizations continually search for new ways to use polling, constituent data bases, computer technology, direct mail, and other such strategic tools.

Polling and Political Consulting

Commercial pollsters, parties, and media organizations provide much of the poll data we consume during and between elections. Yet candidates cannot always depend on these data: They often need more specific, local-area surveys revealing their standing and the issues they should address in their campaigns. Very few individuals run for major public office these days without purchasing the services of political consultants, who may assist candidates with strategy and the evaluation of public opinion.

Political consultants are experts who organize campaigns for candidates at the local, state, and national levels. They design campaign strategy, produce advertisements for candidates, place these ads strategically, and supply poll data. Some consultants provide multiple services to candidates, while others concentrate on a few narrow dimensions of campaign strategy.[17] Unlike the national party organizations, which are concerned with multiple races, a consultant is hired to direct and closely monitor a smaller number of individual campaigns. Larry Sabato has studied the ways that political consultants use baseline polls, tracking polls, focus groups, and other such rationalized forms of public opinion measurement. When describing how elite political consultants use polls and surveys, he notes that most major consultants do much more than provide data to candidates:

> The modern national pollster is far more than an objective data collector or a mere engineer or statistician. He is an analytic interpreter, a grand strategist, and to some, a Delphic oracle. All of the prominent national private pollsters are impressively skillful and extraordinarily well versed in the ways and means of politics. Peter Hart [a major consultant who advises Democratic candidates] compares himself and his colleagues to highly trained X-ray technicians: "We look for the bones and where the breaks are, and we learn to get the best angle, to get the best profile, and the best shot."[18]

In recent U.S. presidential campaigns, political consultants have received an extraordinary amount of media attention. Journalists, who have always focused on the horse-race aspects of major campaigns, are particularly interested in how consultants work. These days, the names of major political consultants are almost as familiar (to those who follow electoral politics) as the names of candidates—especially when they help to produce a controversial campaign advertisement. Consultants are often held responsible for the growing number of negative advertisements, and are thought to encourage poll-oriented campaigns: Candidates tend to tailor their policy statements *not* to cohere with their own ideologies, but to fit the most recent poll results. Indeed, consultants encourage this. Some critics believe this to be an ominous development and potentially damaging to democratic campaigning, since polls may discourage candidates from speaking their minds.[19]

Developments in Survey Methodology

Consultants, political parties, mass media outlets, commercial pollsters, market research firms, and others who use survey research normally work quickly. During the typical, fast-paced political campaign, for example, a pollster hired to conduct a survey can rarely take the time to experiment with different research designs. In academic survey research, however, many explore the ways that survey design and administration can affect the nature of the data collected. This work—where researchers manipulate survey design—is valuable to all who conduct polling. Often, developments in survey research which are pioneered by academics are borrowed by commercial pollsters or political consultants looking to improve their own methods. However, in many cases pollsters use their own "rules of thumb" instead of employing more standardized, reliable techniques developed by academics.[20]

Although the literature on survey research methodology is voluminous, it might be instructive to review recent developments in a few important areas. Here, I'll discuss the errors associated with questionnaire design, those errors induced by interviewers who administer surveys in person or over the telephone, and the growing nonresponse rate. One error which I will not discuss is sampling error—the error associated with measuring attitudes of individuals *in a sample* instead of the entire population. This statistic has received considerable attention from those who conduct surveys, and it is often provided by newspapers and television networks when they report poll results. Interestingly, sampling error is one of the few polling errors that *can be estimated* by the researcher.[21] Other errors, which are much more difficult to quantify, are often ignored by journalists, candidates, and others who use polls, although these unmeasured errors can be very significant.

It is very difficult to design a questionnaire that will accurately measure attitudes: Opinions, attitudes, beliefs, and values are nebulous phenomena that can be expressed in a variety of ways. The length of a question on a survey, the words used in the question, and the place of the question on the survey can each affect results. To reveal and diminish these errors, researchers use "split sample" surveys, where they test different versions of a questionnaire. In one study, Tom Smith used the General Social Survey (GSS) to test whether the word *welfare* had more negative connotations for respondents than the word *poor*. He found that individuals were much more likely to support financial assistance for underprivileged individuals when they were labeled "poor." Smith believes that survey researchers must pay close attention to question wording, since policymakers often utilize these results. Using the data from the "welfare" question might

> lead a politician to decide that public assistance programs, lacking public support could (and should?) be cut with impunity. Opposite errors could be made if only the "poor" item was used. An investigator might conclude that concern about ending poverty was the public's top concern, while welfare administrators might think there was strong support for their programs.[22]

As a result of this type of experimentation, survey researchers know how to ask relatively unbiased questions about some issues—like abortion. Yet many pollsters, who must provide data in short periods of time, rarely have the luxury to engage in this sort of experimentation: They must sometimes conduct overnight polls on an issue, or collect data within a week or two. Even though pollsters are sensitive to questionnaire design problems, these problems persist because many opinions are so fluid, weak, or difficult to quantify. These are the very opinions that are influenced most by survey language.

At times, interviewers unknowingly introduce error into a poll or survey. While all reputable pollsters and survey researchers train their interviewers so that they act in a uniform manner, problems remain. In their attempts to explain questions to respondents, interviewers can encourage or discourage certain kinds of responses, or use faulty explanations when attempting to clarify questions. Additionally, the personal characteristics of interviewers may affect the ways that a respondent answers. In one study, published by Howard Schuman and Jean Converse in 1971, researchers found that black respondents' answers to survey questions about "militant protest" and "hostility toward whites" were affected by the race of the interviewer. When blacks spoke to black interviewers, they were more likely to give militant answers. [23]

Some of these "interviewer errors" can be reduced through careful selection of interviewers, rigorous training, close supervision of the questioners, and standardization of the probes that interviewers use to prompt respondents. In recent years, researchers have begun to develop ways to measure errors across interviewers, or to figure out which questions induce the most error. [24]

Perhaps the most serious concern of survey researchers is the growing number of people who refuse to participate in polls. In one study, a researcher evaluated trends in nonresponse from 1952 through 1979. [25] The refusal rates in two major longitudinal surveys climbed steadily since 1952. Some of this increase in nonresponse was due to escalating rates of urbanization. For face-to-face interviews, large cities pose problems for interviewers: Residents are often away from their homes, do not speak English, or live in buildings where there is tight security. Additionally, people in cities tend to be more concerned with privacy, and may fear or avoid interviewers for this reason. [26] In some major social scientific surveys, nonresponse rates have been particularly excessive—often as high as 25 percent. [27]

In a study of nonresponse in telephone surveys, Robert Groves and Lars Lyberg noted several reasons why cooperation of respondents is difficult to achieve. The effect of urbanization on response rates is not a problem with telephone survey research, but there are other sources of nonresponse, such as the elderly, and those with low levels of education. Also, the gender of the interviewer (women interviewers achieve better response rates than males) and a variety of other factors can hurt response rates. [28] In recent years survey researchers have tried to maximize response to their telephone and face-to-face surveys. Among other things, investigators can use persuasive tactics, pay respondents to cooperate, or contact people prior to a survey.

Although the nonresponse rate for most surveys is higher than pollsters and survey researchers would like, the future looks even more grim. Groves and Lyberg worry that new technologies, like answering machines and "caller identification" systems, make it easier for respondents to screen their calls. They often screen out pollsters and survey researchers. Also, recent political debates about how survey data are used could affect response rates, since people may fear the ways that data can be manipulated in the public sphere.[29]

Low response rates are of concern to pollsters and survey researchers because they can greatly affect the validity of a survey. If a large number of people with certain demographic or attitudinal characteristics fail to cooperate with pollsters, the sample is no longer representative of the population. No matter how much effort is made to select a random sample of individuals for a study, a poor response rate can make a survey much less valuable: It is possible that those who fail to respond are *different*, on one or more dimensions, than the rest of the people in the survey.

One last development in survey research methodology is the growing use of computers to assist interviewers. Researchers have long used computers for statistical analysis after they collect survey data, but now computers are used at an earlier phase in the research process. Computer-assisted telephone interviewing (CATI) enables interviewers wearing telephone headsets to sit at computer terminals and conduct interviews while entering respondents' answers. The questionnaire appears on the screen, so interviewers can read the survey items off the screen and enter answers on that same display. There are different types of CATI systems. With some systems, only the questionnaire appears on the screen, and interviewers record respondents' answers. In other systems, though, the computer handles a variety of functions, such as selecting respondents from the sample, keeping records on an interviewer's productivity, and organizing survey responses into the form necessary for data analysis.[30] CATI systems, which were introduced twenty years ago, are now widely used by pollsters and survey researchers, since they help to make the interviewing process much more efficient. For example, before the introduction of CATI systems, it was difficult to conduct interviews with complicated question "branches." In many surveys, a respondent's answer to one question makes an entire set of subsequent questions irrelevant. If an interviewer asks a respondent whether he voted in the last election, and he says he did not vote, ensuing questions about his vote choice are unnecessary. CATI makes this type of questioning easier for the interviewer, since the computer—based upon early interviewer entries—can skip or alter subsequent lines of questioning to match previous responses. This particular CATI option reduces the time it takes to conduct an interview and minimizes the possibility of making errors.

This brief sketch of contemporary survey research outlines some of the developments in the field as well as some of the major issues facing those who conduct opinion polls. All of the problems mentioned—the various errors associated with survey methodology and changes in social life leading to higher nonresponse rates—are subjects of debate among researchers. With changes in communication technology, growing concerns about privacy, and the sheer increase in the number of telemarketing calls, voters are becoming more and more skeptical of the polling process. It is likely that other techniques for assessing public opinion, such as focus groups, will remain popular as polling becomes increasingly more difficult.

Public Perceptions of Surveys and Polls

Survey researchers and pollsters have long been interested in the impressions the general public holds about polls. Some of this interest stems from concerns about the growing nonresponse rate: There is a feeling among researchers that public attitudes about the accuracy of polls may affect willingness to participate in surveys. Others study public perceptions of surveys and *public opinion more generally* in order to understand the way these perceptions can shape attitudes and behavior.

In 1985, the Roper Organization asked the public a variety of questions about opinion polling.[31] They inquired whether respondents believed that polls "worked for the public's best interest," and whether or not polls were influential, accurate, or representative. Additionally, Roper queried respondents about the honesty of pollsters, the honesty of survey respondents, and whether they found participation in polls to be enjoyable or annoying. In general, the study showed that most people had positive feelings about the polling experience: Seventy-five percent of those questioned believed that "most opinion polls work for the best interests of the general public." Most also believed that polls were usually accurate, that pollsters were usually honest, and that survey respondents most often tell the truth in interviews. Among the more interesting findings was that most respondents did not really believe in the representativeness of random sampling. Over half of

Roper's respondents thought that it was impossible to "accurately reflect the views of the nation's population" with 1,500 or 2,000 interviews. Roper's poll about polls raises some interesting questions for students of public opinion. How can it be that a large majority of individuals (75 percent of those polled) believe that polls work for the public interest, and that polls are usually accurate, but also believe that samples are unrepresentative? Part of the problem may be that the representativeness question gets respondents to focus on the small number of people in the typical random sample, when normally they do not. It may be that people generally believe polls when they read poll results in the newspaper or hear them reported on a news broadcast. Yet when asked by a pollster about the number of people in a study, they may feel the need to question sampling procedure—perhaps they hadn't thought of this problem before. There may also be what social scientists call a "social desirability effect" at work here: Respondents may feel as though they are expected to question the size of samples—that a critical answer would be the right answer. If it were scientifically possible to extrapolate national public opinion from 1,500 people, why would Roper be asking them about it?

Besides these "polls on polls" designed to understand public perceptions of survey research, there have been studies of the way media elites view opinion polls. In the previous chapter, we explored the attitudes about opinion methodologies among journalists working in the 1930s and the 1940s. Then, newspaper reporters and editors were skeptical about commercial political polls, although they often devised their own quantitative tactics for assessing the public sentiment. In 1986, the Gallup Organization surveyed editors, journalists, publishers, and management executives to find out how they viewed the 1984 preelection polls.[32] The study revealed that the large majority of media elites believed the polls were generally accurate. Yet these professionals were divided about the effect polling had on the electoral process in 1984. When asked whether the polls "enhanced or interfered with" the process, just over half said the polls interfered. Yet Andrew Kohut, president of Gallup, emphasized the role of partisanship in this survey: "Those [media elites] who voted for Mondale were far more inclined to see polls as interfering with the process than were those who voted for Reagan."[33]

The studies of polls by Roper and Gallup were conducted largely for the professional survey research community. These surveys help pollsters achieve some understanding of the polling environment and why refusal rates have climbed since the 1950s. Social scientists are interested in broader perceptions of polls and public opinion among citizens. For example, Elisabeth Noelle-Neumann argues that one's perception of public opinion (usually garnered through exposure to mass media and polls) can affect one's behavior: If you sense that you hold a minority opinion, you may choose not to express that opinion in public. Her work, based in part on conformity research in social psychology and on her own public opinion studies in Germany, emphasizes the central role of norms in the public expression process. Since people fear isolation, they often conduct a surveillance of public opinion to avoid social quarantine.[34]

In another well-known study, published in 1976, James Fields and Howard Schuman demonstrated that people tend to believe that public opinion reflects their own opinions.[35] When it comes to racial attitudes, the researchers argued, most people engage in "looking glass perception." They explain that respondents, who were residents of Detroit, "simply project on to Detroiters and neighbors their own opinions—*not* because these opinions are disowned or repressed but, quite the contrary, because respondents regard their own opinions as so sensible that they must be held by all other reasonable people."[36] More recently, Carroll Glynn has corroborated these findings to some extent, but has also found a tendency among people to distinguish themselves from others: They believe that their opinions are different from those of their neighbors or other city dwellers.[37] Although Fields and Schuman did not find evidence for a "disowning projection," Glynn did discover some. Respondents in her study projected their own socially undesirable attitudes onto their neighbors:

> When respondents were asked a question about a socially sensitive issue—the possibility of building a home for the mentally retarded in their neighborhood—more than 80% of the respondents stated that they would not mind the home being built in their neighborhood, but just as many also stated that their *neighbors* would indeed mind if the home were built. Soon after the study, members of one of the sample

neighborhoods were faced with the possibility of a home for the mentally retarded being built in the vicinity, and actively fought against the incorporation of the home.[38]

Most of the studies which examine the public's perception of polls or public opinion are conducted by using surveys. This is not surprising, since many of the people who care about public self-perceptions are themselves survey researchers. Few researchers have yet to probe deeply into attitudes about polling as part of the larger political communication process, so many questions remain unanswered. Among these questions are the following: Under what circumstances do people believe polls, and why? How much does context—the way a poll is reported, or the story in which it appears—matter? And finally, do policymakers, media elites, and members of the public view the same polls differently? If so, why is this the case?

Modern Polling and Rationalization

Throughout this book I have used Weber's insights on routinization in order to explain the appearance of particular opinion expression and measurement techniques. The trends delineated in chapter 3 indicate that our tools for assessing popular attitudes have become more rational: They now efficiently provide a certain type of public opinion data in a relatively short period of time. As long as an individual or institution can pay for polling, it can purchase the services of well-trained survey researchers. In this day and age, where numerical expressions of public opinion are so highly valued, polling has become indispensable to many groups—PACS, candidates, journalists, and political parties.

In the period since the 1948 polling debacle, changing technology and a new professionalism have helped to accelerate the rationalization of public opinion measurement. Computers are now employed by most organizations that poll the public. In fact, the changes in data collection technology are an ideal-typical case of Weberian rationalization: CATI systems allow the survey researcher to conduct interviews more efficiently *and* gain more control over interviewer behavior. Furthermore, computers enable the storage of large data sets that can be easily accessed, if a political party or interest group wants to see whether issue attitudes have changed over the course of time. The diffusion of the telephone has also made survey research and polling less time-consuming and less expensive. When fewer families owned telephones, interviewers were often forced to travel and visit people in their homes. Now, within a matter of seconds, interviewers stationed behind computer terminals can call anyone in the country and ask a battery of questions. It is much easier to contact people over the telephone, since calling them repeatedly will eventually yield a high rate of contact. Going back to a respondent's house repeatedly, on the other hand, is a rather expensive endeavor.

Although many major pollsters are drawn to surveys administered over the telephone, surveys are often mailed to individuals. In general, researchers risk getting a lower response rate when they use this method of administration, but computer technology has made mail surveying somewhat easier than in the past. One can use computers to compile a sample of individual names and addresses, and also print mailing labels. In combination with laser printers, computers enable the survey director to design attractive questionnaires or to personalize the questionnaire form by neatly inserting the respondent's name, address, or other information.

Beyond the technological changes, the gradual expansion of academic survey research institutions has made it possible to train large numbers of students in the techniques of survey research and polling. At many universities, students can receive training as survey interviewers, supervisors, or directors. This well-documented growth of academic survey research institutes at universities[39] has yielded several studies—such as the National Election Study and the General Social Survey—which are conducted every few years. The data these surveys yield are often available (via computer) to academics and nonacademics outside of the universities where the studies are based, so researchers, journalists, and policymakers have access to an enormous amount of attitudinal and behavioral information.

The growth of rationalization in public opinion research has not, at this point, replaced other, less routinized forms of data collection. Politicians, consultants, journalists, and citizens themselves will always use other techniques to understand the public, but polls are now widely cited by the media and viewed as critical to the political process. The growth of polling is important from a variety of perspectives, and in chapter 8 I take a normative view of survey research. The central questions are, first, whether or not polling dampens public expression, and second, whether the steady rationalization of the public sphere strengthens democracy.

Before exploring these general issues, however, there is one more important narrative about the quantification of public opinion that has received very little scrutiny from academics—computing crowd size at political rallies and demonstrations. The history of this practice, since the mid-nineteenth century, is the subject of the next chapter. Techniques for quantifying crowds have not changed dramatically over time, as did the tools for aggregating individual opinions. Yet the fact that American journalists, party workers, police, and others have always estimated crowd size, and still attend to these figures, makes an examination of this phenomenon important to any chronicle of opinion quantification. In the last few chapters, I documented continuity and change in attitude expression and measurement. With crowd counting, there is also continuity and change, though the practice has yet to achieve anything near the "scientific" status of survey research.

CHAPTER SEVEN

Crowd Estimation
and Public Opinion

The *[Chicago Times] and Herald* a few days since contained a flaming account of a Douglas demonstration at Quincy on the 2d inst., wherein the numbers present were stated at from 60,000 to 80,000. A friend writes us . . . that the number present, by actual count as they passed under the "triumphal arch," was just *eleven hundred and sixty-six*, including men, women and children, and of that number not more than three hundred were voters. . . . And this miserable failure is trumpeted in the *T. and Herald* as one of the immense meetings of the campaign.

Chicago Tribune
October 6, 1860

Reporters traveling with [Candidate George] Bush on his jet believed the crowd [at a rally in Portland, Maine] numbered about 1,200 and was split about evenly between Republican and Democratic forces. . . . "Fifty-fifty? Give me a break," Bush said. ". . . Come on. If you can't count. . ."

Chicago Tribune
October 27, 1988

E stimates of crowd size at rallies and demonstrations are a staple of American political journalism. Since the heyday of the political meeting in the mid-nineteenth century, reporters have noted the number of people in attendance at rallies because readers and candidates believe these data to be meaningful. In our day, complaints from political activists about media or police crowd estimates abound.[1] Most often, individuals who participate in rallies, or groups which organize these events, claim that the size of the demonstration has been underestimated by journalists, police commanders, or the National Park Service.[2] Those who protest American domestic and foreign policies have argued that reporters and police both have an interest in maintaining the political status quo. As a result, activists say, these parties continually underestimate the size of protest demonstrations.[3]

As the excerpts above demonstrate, disputes over the size of crowds are traditional. In the nineteenth century, partisan journalists spent considerable effort trying to discredit the crowd estimates published in other newspapers. These conflicts were often intense ones, with papers taunting each other and exchanging vicious insults. Although journalists working for contemporary newspapers no longer engage in this type of discourse, political activists, campaign managers, and the occasional candidate sustain these quantitative debates.

This chapter concerns the changing nature of crowd estimation practices during political campaigns, beginning with the presidential race of 1856. Counts of demonstration participants have been largely ignored by students of political history, who have analyzed the content of speeches given at rallies instead of the discourse *about* the rallies themselves. Yet this discourse about crowds is fascinating, since it reveals much about the practice of journalism, the relationship between social control and quantification, and the problematics of public opinion rationalization.

There has been some academic discussion of contemporary crowd estimation. Much of this work was published in the late 1960s and early 1970s, when scholars began to study protests associated with the civil rights and anti-Vietnam War movements. Leon Mann, an Australian psychologist, analyzed estimates of crowds at two antiwar rallies in Washington during the mid-1960s. He found that "hawk" newspapers tended to publish smaller estimates of these crowds than "dove" papers. Mann argued that conservative editors were most likely to use estimates from official sources—the police or National Park Service—instead of the much higher figures provided by rally sponsors.[4]

A more widely cited article on crowd estimation was published by ex-newspaperman Herbert Jacobs in 1967.[5] Jacobs, who went on to teach journalism at the University of California, was disturbed by a lack of precision in crowd counting among reporters. His conversations with several prominent newspapermen indicated that none had reliable systems for crowd estimation. Samuel Blackman, editor for the Associated Press, told Jacobs that the AP would like to buy an "IBM crowd-estimator any time they invent one."[6] By studying a variety of political rallies staged in Berkeley's Sproul Plaza, Jacobs was able to devise a simple estimation procedure for journalists. He checked the accuracy of his procedure, which was based on the determination of crowd density, using aerial photographs of the demonstrations.

Systematic techniques for estimating crowd size did not become part of the curriculum of journalism schools, however. Journalists who cover politics tend to gain experience in crowd estimation over time, and work with other reporters at a demonstration to arrive at a consensus about crowd size. Reporters and editors often depend on police estimates, so the police usually count the crowd as they patrol a demonstration area. Like reporters, police also believe that they become accurate estimators through experience. One Chicago police commander said that city police have reliable "rules of thumb" for counting the crowd at popular rally sites such as Daley Plaza.[7]

Trends in Crowd Estimation

Methods for determining crowd size, and the manner in which these figures are used, have both changed considerably over time. Yet there are also many continuities in the quantitative discourse about crowds since the mid-nineteenth century. In order to study these changes, I systematically collected articles on political rallies from three newspapers—*The New York Times*, the *Chicago Sun-Times*, and the *Chicago Tribune*—from the presidential election of 1856 through the 1976 election at twenty-year intervals.[8] I also gathered articles on demonstrations from the 1860 campaign, since a tremendous number of rallies were organized that year. In addition, coverage of rallies during a recent election—the 1988 race between George Bush and Michael Dukakis—was included in the sample of articles. Each of the three newspapers published scores of crowd counts during the last few months of each campaign. As a result, over 550 articles in my sample included quantitative estimates.[9]

American newspapers have traditionally published numerical crowd estimates, and during most election years, provided these statistics for over half of the rallies they reported. Moreover, the most common source for these estimates was the journalist who covered the event for his or her newspaper. Occasionally, in the nineteenth and early twentieth centuries, an unidentified "witness" or "observer" was cited as the source of an estimate. In the twentieth century, police and Park Service estimates began to appear, although journalists continued to provide their own estimates as well. It is likely that, in many cases, journalists conferred with police in order to calculate the number of participants at a given event.

Despite these continuities in the history of crowd estimation, there was a significant change in the practice as America moved from gemeinschaft to gesellschaft. While crowd counts were useful from instrumental and symbolic perspectives in the nineteenth century, they became largely symbolic by the mid-twentieth century. The reasons for this change are threefold—the diffusion of the sample survey, the rise of campaign management, and a gradual ascent of objectivity norms in journalism. In the nineteenth century, numerical crowd estimates were thought to be reliable indicators of the public sentiment, and were also viewed as useful rhetorical weapons by partisan journalists. When a small number of people attended a rally for a Democratic candidate, it was almost certain that Republican newspapers would report this poor showing the next day. By the mid-twentieth century, quantitative estimates of crowds were no longer used by newspapers to measure public opinion or to discredit opposing candidates and parties. After the widespread diffusion of scientific (and nonscientific) opinion polling, these estimates were useful only from a symbolic standpoint, since they could no longer be construed as measurements of national public opinion. Beginning in the mid-twentieth century, more precise methods for opinion assessment made crowd size irrelevant for predicting election outcomes, though these estimates still play a rhetorical role in a variety of public debates.

Counting the Crowd: 1856–1896

Crowd estimation at campaign rallies was an integral part of mid-nineteenth century political discourse. Since partisanship was intense, and political involvement was heavy, reports of parades, public meetings, and other such gatherings were of great interest to citizens. In general, men viewed politics as an arena for serious discussion and action, but also saw politics as a source of amusement and entertainment.[10] As a result, newspaper reports on political events were replete with irony, satire, and the occasional exchange of juvenile insults. Since interest in politics ran high, rallies were often highlighted on the front pages of major daily newspapers, and were usually described in vivid detail. Quantitative crowd estimates were central to reports on rallies, and these attendance figures—like straw polls—were woven into the ideological fabric of the newspaper itself. Unlike straw polls, however, crowd estimates were debatable: Often two or more reporters or witnesses attended the same rally, so they were able to argue about the size and nature of the crowd.

Quantitative descriptions of rally crowds were so popular that they were often a source of humor in the daily paper. During the 1860 campaign, for example, reporters published attendance figures, yet also made jokes about these numerical estimates. The pro-Lincoln *Chicago Tribune* was particularly adept at quantitative jesting, as this conversation—supposedly overheard at a procession for Douglas in Chicago—demonstrates:

> *Tally man at the Times and Herald* — Here Jim you count the procession coming up, and I'll count the one coming down—count all between the side-walks.
>
> *Jim* — I've counted both of them when they went by before.
>
> *Tallyman* — Well, count 'em again; ain't that the Governor's orders, to count everything that passes, from 6 o'clock till midnight?[11]

The Republican *Tribune* often questioned the arithmetic skills of the Democrats that year, claiming that crowds at Douglas rallies were invariably overestimated. The paper published the following piece from the *Concord Democrat* on August 27:

> The 20,000 Lie. — The *Patriot* and Boston *Herald* multiplied the 2,000 actually present at the Douglas reception in Concord by 10 and made it 20,000. This is a fair specimen of Democratic arithmetic. Douglas was at Portland the other day, and out went the report in Democratic figures and fancies again, that there were 20,000 people present and that there was a general illumination of the city. The *fact* is, there were not more than 6,000 people in all and just *eight* houses were illuminated.[12]

Since *Tribune* reporters could not travel to every Douglas rally to check Democratic turnout estimates, they often relied on papers like the *Concord Democrat*. In late September of 1860, the *Tribune* printed this piece from the *Buffalo Express:*

> "ARITHMETICAL PROGRESSION." — The fellow with the india rubber conscience, who travels with Douglas and "does" the reports for the Associated Press, also writes letters to the Albany *Argus*. It will be remembered that he telegraphed all over the State that Douglas addressed from 15,000 to 20,000 people in this city. In his letter to the *Argus*, in which he speaks of the same gathering, he puts the number at 30,000 to 40,000! If Lucifer is "the father of lies," what must this fellow be![13]

During the elections of the mid- and late nineteenth century, a large number of journalists reported on rallies where people gathered to hear candidates or their supporters speak. The reporters described the content of speeches, but almost always described the crowd as well. Sometimes a quantitative estimate of the crowd was published by itself, but more often, these data were part of a larger, detailed description of the event. In an 1876 article from the *Chicago Times*, a pro-Tilden rally in Indianapolis was described this way:

> The event was looked forward to with great expectation. . . .
> By 7 o'clock the streets were crowded in the neighborhood of

the hotel and Grand opera-house. The distinguished speaker [George W. Julian] was met at the Grand hotel by a uniformed escort of 1,200 Tilden guards, the line extending fully half a mile, and presenting a grand appearance. The streets were ablaze with reform torches. At the opera-house a vast and intelligent audience was gathered, and it was estimated that the overflow not able to find accommodations was fully 1,500 strong.[14]

Journalists thought it important to give readers a sense of how large the rally crowd was, and they often described the character of the group in attendance. In an 1856 article titled "Fremont Fever in Indiana" and subtitled "Tremendous Movements of the People," the editors of the *Chicago Tribune* described a Republican rally held in Andersonville, Indiana. The editors noted that Andersonville was a "small, out-of-the-way town" eleven or twelve miles from the nearest railroad station. Public opinion in Andersonville was behind Fremont:

> We anticipated a respectable neighborhood meeting, of three or four thousand people, but to the astonishment of every body present, there were not less than *fifteen thousand* in attendance—men, women, and children—pervaded by an enthusiasm which throws all former campaigns in the shade! The heat and the dust were almost insupportable; yet the sturdy farmers, their wives, sons and daughters, in carriages, wagons, and on horse back, came to the meeting in processions of thousands in a body, covered with dust, but animated by an enthusiasm which no ordinary obstacle can dampen. They came with drums beating and banners flying, and cannons roaring.[15]

Although there were a tremendous number of rallies and meetings held during presidential campaigns throughout the nineteenth century, the number of rallies covered by daily newspapers soared in 1896. The campaign between William McKinley and William Jennings Bryan drew more Americans to the polls than any previous election, since the issues—free silver, the tariff, and law and order, among others—were particularly salient ones. The depression of 1893, and violent clashes between labor and management in a variety of cities throughout the country, caused voters to look to government for relief.[16]

There were other reasons why the 1896 campaign was such a lively one. That year the Republicans had raised an enormous amount of money, so McKinley's campaign organization was strong. Due in part to the strategic genius of campaign director Mark Hanna, scores of events were planned to promote McKinley and enable him to meet the voters. Although he was unable to compete with the fund-raising success of the Republicans, Bryan engaged in intense, emotionally charged campaigning during the summer and early fall of 1896. The energy of the candidates and a heightened interest in the issues were reflected in the extensive space devoted to election events in newspapers.

Newspapers often included quantitative estimates of the crowds at McKinley and Bryan rallies. In the *Chicago Tribune* that year 54 percent of the reports on political rallies gave at least one numerical crowd statistic. When Bryan was traveling through Ohio in August of 1896, thousands appeared to greet him. The *Tribune*, which did not support Bryan but sensed his enormous appeal and popularity, reported this:

> As the train drew away from the platform [at Bucyrus] hundreds ran along with it, grabbing at Mr. Bryan's hand, until some one fell, and those behind, pressing forward, piled up a mass of writhing humanity, involving twenty or thirty people. Over 8,000 people were surging around the depot when the Bryan train pulled into Crestline, O. Mr. Bryan was escorted through the noisy crowd to a decorated platform near the depot, where amid the wildest cheering, he spoke.[17]

Unlike its practice in previous campaigns, the Republican *Tribune* usually reported that the crowds turning out for Democratic rallies in 1896 were large. Yet when the paper's editors had evidence that the crowds were smaller than reported by Bryan supporters, they emphasized these numerical discrepancies:

> Canton [Ohio] was credited with 1,000 [rally attendees], and similar exaggeration with a partisan object was applied to the exhibition at every point. . . . A procession was announced to start from in front of the City Hall to proceed to the station to meet Mr. Bryan. This procession actually consisted of fifty-

three individuals when it took up its line of march, and when the railway was reached it numbered by actual count 107 marchers.[18]

In this same piece, the *Tribune* also made much of Bryan's neat and "studied appearance," constructed in order to "please the masses." He seemed, to the *Tribune* reporter, to look "like a Methodist preacher with a good-paying parish."[19]

The *New York Times*, less blatantly partisan than the *Chicago Tribune*, reported crowd estimates in 43 percent of its stories on rallies in 1896. The *Times*, more than the *Tribune* or *Chicago Times*, was more likely to describe the composition of crowds as well as their size. In a September 29 article about a rally in Canton, the *Times* reporter described a delegation of "200 or 300 colored people" who came to hear McKinley that day.[20] On that same day the *Times* reported on the crowd present during Bryan's arrival at Grand Central Station in Manhattan, "A crowd of about 600 persons greeted him, including principally persons employed about the station, commuters who were waiting for their trains, a number of newspaper men, and a scattering of Tammany politicians."[21] All three daily papers studied here used quantitative estimates gathered at rallies as indicators of public opinion. Straw polls, which were reported in different articles, were also used for this purpose, but rallies allowed reporters to judge the *intensity* of public opinion. Straws could give a reporter or partisan observer a good sense of voting intentions, but gave no clue about the passion of the electorate. At rallies, on the other hand, people demonstrated their support through attendance and through emotional displays. Straw polls may have provided "objective" predictions about election outcomes, but rallies made for a better story: Demonstrations yielded numerical and qualitative data about public opinion.

Crowd Estimation and Rationalization, 1916–1988

Although the sample survey was not used to anticipate a presidential election outcome until 1936, when Gallup predicted that Roosevelt would defeat Landon, signs of increasing rationalization were present in the 1916 campaign.[22] Campaign management, which Hanna had mastered in 1896, accelerated in the early decades of the twentieth century. Also during this era, many individuals sought new, systematic approaches to public opinion measurement. Academics, for example, urged their colleagues to pay more attention to attitude measurement, even if they could not agree on the meaning of "public opinion."[23] In the political sphere, the *Literary Digest* drew considerable attention and respect for its supposedly "scientific" opinion prediction methods.

The growing desire for precision, then, had begun years before sampling was applied to the assessment of popular sentiment. Not surprisingly, those who counted crowds at political rallies began to question the meaning of their statistics.

During the 1916 presidential election campaign, news of the contest was overshadowed by news of the war in Europe. The progress of the war was reported in great detail, so little space remained for descriptions of campaign events. In August of 1916, President Wilson announced that he would not launch an extensive speaking tour, and would instead give only six or eight speeches at different locations before election day. He said he would, however, receive delegations at his summer home.[24]

There may have been fewer rally reports in 1916 than in previous years, but there was more attention to the tactics of campaigning. It was becoming increasingly clear that a well-organized campaign manager could plan campaign events which appeared spontaneous. There were hints of this as early as 1896, when *The New York Times* reported on the illusion of spontaneity at a Bryan rally: "A feature of the occasion was one interruption of the speaker [Bryan] by questions which seemed to have been formulated to meet Mr. Bryan's 'ready answers.'"[25] Reporters and campaign managers looked for new ways to scrutinize the rallies as performances—by the candidates and by the crowd. Part of this scrutiny involved getting better measures of attendance. At one Chicago parade for Republican Charles E. Hughes in 1916, for example, a counting machine was employed to get a more accurate estimate of crowd size. Use of such a device was not mentioned before 1916 in newspaper reports on rallies and parades studied here. Until 1916, reporters usually rounded off their estimates to the nearest tenth or hundredth. By using the counting machine, though, the *Tribune* reporter at the Hughes parade was able to give a precise count of marchers, who totaled 7,849.[26] Despite the impressive turnout and the seemingly objective measurement of crowd size, though, the reporter still described the passionate feeling among the marchers and the crowds along the parade route.

Up until the 1930s, crowd estimates were thought to be important indicators of public opinion. Large crowds who demonstrated wildly were evidence that a candidate's chances of victory were great. But by the 1936 election between Roosevelt and Landon, estimates of crowd size had become less useful to reporters. Journalists still reported attendance at rallies, but placed much less emphasis on those figures. The central reason for this diminishing interest in crowd estimates is tied directly to the rising popularity of the opinion poll. Since the *Literary Digest* had not yet been wrong about any election outcome, its prediction of a Landon victory in 1936 received enormous attention from major metropolitan dailies. The ordinarily cautious *New York Times* consistently reported *Digest* poll results under headlines like "3 Cities for Roosevelt"[27] or "Landon Leads in 7 Cities."[28]

Crowd estimates were not a source of controversy as they so often were during mid- and late nineteenth century elections. In this sample of articles from the 1936 campaign, there were *no* disputes over crowd size. Newspapers were still blatantly partisan, so the lack of disputes was not the result of diminishing party loyalty of the papers. It is more likely that disputes over crowd size disappeared because journalists no longer believed these estimates indicated public opinion: They could consult the traditionally dependable *Digest* poll if they sought an accurate sense of public sentiment. Rallies were interesting displays of emotion, and speeches at rallies were news, but crowd counts were no longer the source of debate among partisan papers.

Although there is no definitive turning point in journalistic portrayals of crowd composition, there is a distinct, gradual change in the way participants have been described over time. In the nineteenth century, extensive description of the crowd's mood and character was central to most stories about political meetings. It was common for journalists to infer the feelings of individuals in the crowd simply by observing behavior. Crowds were most often described as "enthusiastic," but were also labeled "eager and truth-hungry,"[29] "earnest and keen-witted,"[30] or "vast and intelligent."[31]

By the mid-twentieth century, though, increased attention to norms of objectivity on the part of journalists,[32] and increased re-

liance on poll data, made these descriptions inappropriate and unnecessary. Both the size and the nature of crowds in twentieth
century campaigns became part of the journalistic narrative about a
rally, instead of a central focus. In a sense the crowd *was* the story in
the nineteenth century: Partisan feeling was strong and participation in politics was much more enthusiastic, so the crowd was
viewed as an important component of the campaign. Voting turnout
among eligible voters was very high in the nineteenth century, and
it was likely that the crowd at any given rally was composed of
people who would cast ballots.

In the decades following the First World War, however, journalistic interest shifted away from rally crowds. It had become increasingly clear that crowds could be manufactured by campaign
strategists, and that high attendance at rallies was not necessarily
an indicator of national public opinion. Since contemporary candidates rarely conduct "whistle-stop" tours, most of the political gatherings reported by journalists are not public rallies open to all, but
well-planned speaking engagements by candidates. In the 1976
election, for example, the candidates' agendas were usually the focus of the typical rally account, even if there was a mention of the
size of the crowd. During a rare whistle-stop tour, which *The New
York Times* described as a "950-mile media event," a reporter
briefly described crowd size and behavior in passing. The journalist
highlighted Carter's tactics—the message he was trying to send to
the public: "At every stop along the way, [Carter] focused on Presidents past—an honor roll of Democrats, a rogues gallery of
Republicans—and offered himself to cordial crowds as a candidate
steeped in and evolved from the finest tradition of his own party."[33]
During the 1988 campaign between Michael Dukakis and George
Bush, crowds were barely mentioned, as reporters concentrated on
the strategies of the candidates. As many journalists and academics
have pointed out, the dominant theme of reporting during 1988 was
the tactics of candidates and their managers.[34] This journalistic focus, together with the increasing reliability of polls and the exclusive nature of most political gatherings, meant that little attention
was paid to crowds. In fact, public opinion polls occasionally appeared in articles about political gatherings, as indicators of public
opinion. In these pieces, it seemed that the rally and crowd were
evaluated by the journalist *in light of a candidate's standing in the
polls*. In a November 1988 article, the *Chicago Sun-Times* outlined

the candidates' last-minute activities, including Bush rallies in California and several Midwestern states. In the middle of this report, the journalist noted that "Although Bush aides said their own polls showed Bush's lead holding steady at 9 points for five days, the vice president's effort to beef up his speeches and his decision to return Monday to the Midwest for appearances in Michigan, Missouri and Ohio pointed to an edginess over the surveys."[35] In contemporary presidential election campaigns, poll standings determine when election rallies will be held and where they will take place.

Who Cares about Crowd Size?

Despite a decline in journalistic interest in crowd size during presidential election campaigns, disputes about crowds can still be located in contemporary political discourse. Since polls can tell us, with a fair degree of accuracy, who will win the presidency, turnout at public political rallies is no longer indicative of public opinion. Yet there are other places where one finds debates about crowd size. On issues where public opinion is divided and intense, and where political activists organize public demonstrations, one often finds disputes about crowd size. One of these issues is abortion.

Opinions about abortion, compared to those expressed on other social and political issues, are passionate ones.[36] As a result, there have been an extraordinary number of pro- and antiabortion rallies since before the Supreme Court legalized the practice in 1973. In a 1989 article, published the day before a scheduled pro-abortion rally, *The New York Times* actually anticipated a dispute about attendance estimates. Beside an article on the plans for the rally, a smaller article, titled "Crowd Counts Differ Greatly," reviewed disputes about crowd estimates after a variety of rallies—a 1971 antiwar rally, a 1987 rally for Soviet Jewry, a gay rights rally that same year, and a 1989 antiabortion rally.[37]

As the *Times* predicted, there were debates about crowd size following the 1989 proabortion rally in Washington. A prominently positioned article in the *Washington Post* a few days later was titled "Size of Abortion-Rights March Disputed." The reporter noted a 300,000-person discrepancy between the estimate provided by the police and the one provided by rally organizers. Although the journalist wrote that these disputes are "nothing new in the nation's capital," she interviewed abortion-rights activists about crowd estimation. Eleanor Smeal, then with the Fund for the Feminist Majority, argued, "We think [the police] are wrong. . . . We were marching so close together we were taking each other's shoes off. U.S. Park Police . . . have low-balled us in the past."[38] Each party in this dispute—police and activists—used what it believed were systematic methods for estimating the crowds: grid measurements, subway ridership figures, aerial estimates of crowd density from helicopters, and the like. In response to charges of "low-balling," a police captain said that politics did not affect police estimates, since police are apolitical.[39] A few days after this article appeared, an antiabortion reader wrote to the editor of the *Chicago Tribune* that the media give prominent coverage to proabortion events, but fail to cover antiabortion or "prolife" rallies: "We have sent several buses from Illinois [to Washington] every year—only to have the story buried in the last pages of the papers and a deflated attendance number reported."[40]

The interest in crowd estimates at abortion rallies, and the absence of interest in these figures during campaigns, indicate several changes in the nature of public opinion expression and the structure of American politics. First, major abortion rallies tend to be public ones, widely advertised in advance. This is not the case for rallies during presidential campaigns, since these rallies are often speaking engagements closed to the public. Public rallies for candidates are rarely announced far in advance, since rally locations tend to be chosen on the basis of current poll results, with candidates appearing in particular areas for immediate, strategic reasons. Second, the debate concerning abortion has lasted for over two decades, so proabortion and antiabortion activists have been able to build huge, effective organizations. As a result, they can mobilize extremely large crowds. They care deeply about coverage of these events, believing that a "show of strength" may affect public opinion about abortion. Campaign managers, on the other hand, often schedule several rallies for one day. Whether a crowd is large or enthusiastic matters, but the moment is a fleeting one which may or may not be covered by the mass media.

A third reason why crowd estimation disputes occur in the debate over abortion concerns polls. Abortion activists, on both sides of the issue, are largely unaffected by survey results. When a poll supports them, they cite it. When a poll doesn't support their position, it is usually ignored. [41] Since proabortion groups view the issue as a matter of personal choice, and the antiabortion groups frame their position in terms of morality, the public opinion garnered from scientific polls seems irrelevant to them: One can be right and still be in the minority, so the backing of public opinion may not affect one's desire to take action. This is not the case in electoral politics, where standing in the polls matters immensely: Polls indicate the probable outcome on election day, and the next presidential contest is four years away.

Police and Crowd Estimation

Police appeared in articles about political rallies as early as 1896, although they were probably present at rallies throughout the nineteenth century. In the 1896 election reporters mentioned the number of police present as part of their description of the event. Often these events were lively and the crowd was wild, so police were viewed as necessary for crowd control. During a Pittsburgh rally for Bryan, "A corps of about 100 policemen was on duty at the various entrances [of the Grand Opera House], and in the course of the early evening there was an incipient riot, in which one person was severely beaten and some of the officers had their brass buttons torn off."[42] Police were a presence at large campaign rallies, but they did not always count the attendees. It wasn't until the midtwentieth century that police began to calculate the size of crowds. Beginning in 1936, journalists credited local police or the National Park Service with crowd estimates.

Transformations in the criminal justice system and in local government organization changed the real and perceived roles of police at political demonstrations. In the late nineteenth century, urban police forces became increasingly rationalized: Police began to take on more responsibilities and established themselves as critical components of local government. It was during this time that many informal patrol systems evolved into highly structured ones, with uniformed officers and hierarchical chains of command.[43] Until the antiwar, civil rights, and student demonstrations of the 1960s, the police were generally viewed as impartial observers who were interested in order and not politics.

After the 1960s, though, activists began to distrust police and their crowd estimates, because they often viewed police as fun-

damentally conservative and hostile toward progressive movements.[44] Despite these claims of bias, reporters still ask for crowd
statistics from police, and police still count crowds. Since police
tend to stay at a rally for its duration, and deal with crowds as part of
their routine duties, they are still viewed as somewhat reliable by
journalists.

The control and counting functions of police at rallies are related, since the number of people at a rally determines how many
police are sent to the scene. At political rallies, police engage in
observation on two levels: They look in order to assess the size and
nature of the crowd, and they look for potential problems (e.g.,
fights or harassment). Police observation is not a disciplinary technology in the sense of the Panopticon, but it does represent an interesting form of social control. Beyond their routine control
responsibilities, police are also asked to conduct a *surveillance of
public opinion.* Nineteenth-century journalists often used accounts of witnesses in their reports on political rallies, yet they did
not report police estimates.

Benjamin Ginsberg has argued that governments assess public
opinion for purposes of social control: They need to understand the
extent of particular opinions so that they can better persuade or manipulate those opinions. On a smaller scale, and in a more sporadic
manner, police need to assess public opinion as well. If they can get
a sense of a crowd's size and intensity of feeling, they can also think
more carefully about techniques for controlling that crowd should it
turn unreasonable or violent.

Instrumental and Symbolic Dimensions of Crowd Estimation

In the nineteenth century, quantitative crowd estimates served
both instrumental and symbolic functions, but in the twentieth, the
instrumental value of these statistics began to fade. With the advent of scientific polling and a change in journalistic norms, disputes over rally attendance figures became the domain of political
activists, not journalists.

The instrumental uses of crowd estimates in the mid- and late
nineteenth century were many. The size of a political demonstration gave candidates a sense of their chances for victory in that
locale, helped them to determine where they needed to campaign,
and enabled them to experiment with different rhetorical styles.[45]

As the typical nineteenth century presidential candidate made his way across the nation, he would stop several times a day to give a speech or simply to shake hands with local supporters. The press believed that most of these stops were news, and would cover them in great detail when they could. Both the size of crowds and the character of their responses to candidates were regularly included in news articles.

Quantitative estimates of crowd size were also critical on a symbolic level during the nineteenth century. Disputes arose over these numbers because they were believed to be reliable indications of popularity. Crowd figures were very flexible symbols: They could be used selectively to demonstrate the strength of a newspaper's favorite candidate or to illustrate the lack of support for his opponent. Attendance estimates, paired with descriptions of the crowd itself, provided extremely vivid images of political strength. If a candidate could draw an enthusiastic crowd of 10,000 or 20,000 in a politically hostile region of the country, for example, he suddenly seemed an important contender, worthy of the presidency.

In the twentieth century, the instrumental functions of crowd estimates gradually began to evaporate. Opinion polls, such as the famous *Literary Digest* survey, began to replace the seemingly unreliable, and easily manipulated, crowd figures. Even though polling suffered a temporary loss of legitimacy after the *Digest*'s 1936 error, polling became indispensable by the mid-1950s: As pollsters refined their methods and formed professional organizations to ensure quality control, politicians, journalists, members of Congress, activists, and others began to depend on these instruments.[46]

In Weberian terms, it became clear that reliance on polls was more *rational* than reliance on crowd estimates. Crowds do not represent the population demographically, and are usually composed of individuals who hold uniform political beliefs. Through the use of sampling, pollsters are now able to assess the opinions of many types of people—whether they attend political rallies or not. In our day, polls serve all of the functions that crowd estimates did in the past. Surveys indicate strength of public opinion in particular regions of the country, and they provide evidence about a candidate's chances of victory. Candidates no longer need to "try out" their speeches during cross-national tours, because polls help them to determine the issues of greatest interest to their constituencies.[47] Poll data have become critical tools for modern political consultants, who attempt to design effective and efficient campaign strategies.

People still argue about the size of crowds at political rallies, although these are typically not campaign rallies. After antiwar rallies, abortion rallies, anti-nuclear power demonstrations, and other such events, there are often disputes over the size of the crowd in attendance. Even though activists who organize these events sometimes have the resources to commission scientific opinion polls, the vivid display of an immense, lively demonstration often receives serious attention from national news networks and major newspapers. After rallies, activists carefully monitor news reports in order to challenge estimates of crowd magnitude: For activists, crowd size and significance are highly correlated. As the sociologist Neil Smelser puts it, "Telling the size of a crowd is in the same category as uttering an effective slogan. As a measure of public sentiment, it's not very precise. But as rhetoric and symbolism, it matters very much."[48]

Political activists understand the importance of this type of rhetoric, and many believe that crowd estimates affect the character of media coverage they receive. After the outbreak of the Persian Gulf War, scores of antiwar demonstrations were held throughout the nation. Protest organizers complained that the media either ignored their demonstrations or underestimated the number of protesters in attendance. One such organizer in San Francisco said that some papers tried to "trivialize" the antiwar sentiment by publishing low estimates of a rally in that city. Estimates of the crowd ranged from 20,000 (in the *Los Angeles Times*) to 40,000 (in the *San Francisco Examiner*) to 200,000 (the organizers' estimate).[49]

In response to charges of "low-balling" made by activists, newspaper editors downplay the importance of crowd estimates. Editors interviewed on the subject by a *Los Angeles Times* correspondent said that the identity of activists and the importance of their cause determined coverage by newspapers. A *Washington Post* editor said, "You can say you got a kazillion people . . . but that doesn't necessarily mean you're going to get on Page 1. It depends on what the issue is and whether there's a real sense that it's something that means a whole lot to other people."[50]

In electoral politics, crowd estimates have been practically replaced by polls, but crowds still serve functions on the campaign trail. On television a large crowd makes an impressive backdrop for a candidate's speech, and the media do occasionally report crowd size at campaign rallies. Yet in this age of political consultants, polls, and campaign management, the size of a crowd is merely another pliable item: Voters, journalists, and consultants all know that crowds can be manufactured very quickly for a "media event." The magnitude of a crowd no longer resonates with meaning as it did during election campaigns of the nineteenth century.

CHAPTER EIGHT

Opinion Quantification
and Democracy

LTHOUGH THE QUANTIFICATION of public opinion began long ago, techniques for counting opinions have become increasingly sophisticated over the course of time. By using numbers to describe the public mood, we have also begun to alter the form and content of public expression itself. In the past, public opinion was conceptualized in a variety of ways: Rousseau believed public opinion to be commensurate with the general will, Locke likened opinion to social norms, and a variety of others believed it to be the conversation in salons or the content of newspapers. In contemporary politics, however, public opinion is most often thought to be the aggregation of individual opinions, compiled by pollsters. As we've seen, shifts in the meaning of public opinion are closely tied to the development of new tools for expressing and measuring the popular sentiment. Today, the most authoritative tools are quantitative ones.

Now that we can efficiently condense political sentiment into numerical symbols, public opinion has become a commodity: News organizations, politicians, pressure groups, and others with an interest in public opinion purchase data in hopes of gaining power, attention, or profits. At times, the use of these data is almost entirely instrumental, as when a legislator seeks to understand the mood of his or her district concerning a particular policy issue. At other times, quantitative public opinion data are used as rhetorical weapons to denigrate the views of a political foe or to preempt attacks on one's own position. In a democracy such as ours, to possess "objective" evidence of the public will is to control a very valuable asset indeed.

This book began with the introduction of several powerful

notions—rationality, surveillance, symbolic communication, and social control—each of which has been a focus of intense academic scrutiny. Application of these concepts to the complex history of public opinion illuminated important aspects of that chronicle, although a tremendous amount of research on the topic remains to be done. My intention in this concluding chapter is to address some of the larger questions about political communication posed earlier. Here I underscore the many queries and issues that remain unresolved, and also advance several arguments about current public opinion processes in hopes of provoking new types of research in this area.

Two central questions revolve around the effects of increasingly rationalized expression. First, how does the quantification of public opinion affect the ways we express ourselves and the substance of these communications? And second, does the quantification of public opinion—in the form of crowd counts, straw polls, or scientific polls—enhance public discourse in a modern democracy or diminish the quality of that discourse? To answer these questions, we must reevaluate the case studies and theoretical notions from previous chapters in a normative light: Should we strive to rationalize the expression and measurement of public opinion even further, or should we pause to reassess its quality?

Formal Rationality Versus Ideology

Max Weber, as I noted early in this study, feared the growth of routinization. Throughout his life, he worried about the rise of instrumental thinking and the effects of rationality on our practices. Although Weber knew that rationalization progressed in an uneven fashion in different spheres of social action, he believed this trend to be a linear one. On occasion, a charismatic leader with new ideas might reverse trends toward systematization, but this is a rare and temporary occurrence. For Weber, scientific thinking exemplified instrumental reason, while affective or ideologically motivated thought and action were characteristic of substantive rationality.

Instrumental reason or "formal" rationality competes directly with substantive rationality. Weber believed that when we use a means/ends or cost/benefit analysis to understand a phenomenon, something is invariably lost. With a concentration on goals to be reached, and the means for achieving them, we tend to lose sight of unmeasurable values and the feelings evoked by our actions. While Weber most certainly believed that instrumental reason—in the form of the faceless, heartless bureaucrat—would come to dominate our world, rationalization is usually a much more subtle process. In fact, the introduction of rationalized procedures in an organization usually appears to be a positive, constructive process. In the academy, for example, the introduction of standardized tests helps admissions committees decide among multitudes of prospective students, since assessing grades from very different high schools is a formidable task. And in many businesses, routinized training programs, standardized employee evaluations, and methodical exit interviews create a sense of fairness and equity: If everyone is to be treated in the same manner, deviations from these standard practices can be located and corrected in a prompt fashion. Most people have had negative encounters with rationalization— when dealing with an agency or bureaucrat who will not bend a seemingly absurd rule, for example. Yet many of these same individuals have probably benefited from the existence of standard practices as well.

It has always been difficult to understand exactly what is lost when a practice is routinized. In banking, for example, the introduction of the automated teller machine has replaced much of our interaction with human tellers. But how valuable was the interaction with tellers? How shall we measure the loss of human contact, when we have gained so much in the way of convenience?

In the realm of public opinion communication, the introduction of standard, quantitative expression and measurement practices also poses difficult questions. The public opinion poll does allow for equality of expression, since all opinions are treated as equivalent in the typical survey. Yet these polls, which are so abundant in the mass media, have probably replaced other types of expression.

Unfortunately, we cannot address this issue as rigorously as we might like to. The diffusion of straw polls, and then sample surveys, was a gradual process so we cannot analyze a narrow historical period and focus on forms of expression that disappeared. Indeed, it would be difficult to locate *definitive* evidence indicating a decrease in particular types of opinion communication. Even when we find clear declines in certain categories of opinion expression (e.g., voting), these might be attributable to a growing political alienation or feelings of helplessness, and not due to replacement by another form of expression.[1] In fact, it may be that rising political alienation is one key to understanding the success of the public opinion poll.

Political scientists have found that scores on two variables—citizen trust in government and feelings that leaders are responsive to public needs ("external political efficacy")—have both declined steadily since the early 1950s.[2] Events such as the Watergate scandal and the Vietnam War contributed to these declines. Yet so did other factors, such as an inability of the major political parties to mobilize their constituencies.[3] Opinion polling has become pervasive in this context of increasing political cynicism, a lack of trust in public officials, and a general political alienation. One could argue that these are the *ideal* conditions for the acceleration of rationalized public opinion measurement and expression techniques. First, responding to polls is a *reactive* form of political expression. Answering a pollster's queries does not necessarily demand thoughtful analysis, ideological commitment, or actual involvement. Second, participation in polling is quick and easy, because of its routinized procedures, and does not demand the same level of emotional (and physical) intensity as does striking, demonstrating, door-to-door canvassing, or attending meetings. In fact, the efficient (and fairly painless) interviewing procedures used by pollsters seem appropriate in a country where partisanship and ideology have become increasingly displaced by political "independence" and skepticism.

Some individuals who participate in polls do have very strong feelings about particular issues, write to their congressmen, or take part in political demonstrations. I am simply arguing that aggregate data, which indicate increasing political alienation in America, may be associated with the escalating rationalization of public opinion expression. Definitive evidence that the opinion poll, or other forms of opinion quantification, has replaced more intense, emotional, and value-driven forms of public expression is not available to us. Yet it is likely that rationalized techniques flourish where ideology and interest in politics are dormant.

To put this argument in terms of the Weberian trade-off between formal and substantive rationality, opinion polling has thrived because many Americans are unwilling or unable to express themselves in more ideological and emotional ways. Although straw polling was used throughout the latter half of the nineteenth century—a time when partisanship and political involvement ran high—polls were a *part of* emotionally charged, ideological discourse, not a substitute for it. A recent case study of polling during the 1990 Nicaraguan presidential election clarifies the relationship between instrumental and substantive rationality in public expression. The election, in which the incumbent Sandinista party (FSLN) headed by Daniel Ortega competed with the American-backed UNO party led by Violetta Chamorro, was an emotionally charged contest: In fact, the ideological battle was reminiscent of nineteenth century American elections where partisanship and emotion were critical components of the campaign. In this environment, as survey researcher Peter V. Miller discovered, polls were not viewed as authoritative evidence about the public mood. In fact, poll results about the upcoming election were viewed as one type of political rhetoric, to be used for partisan purposes. Miller notes that polls conducted by a variety of organizations were woven into ideological arguments during the campaign. As a result, polls could not be discussed in a "neutral" fashion by those with a stake in the election outcome:

> Observations of the polls were made in an epistemological "twilight zone" where one's political position was all-important and polls were propaganda weapons. Neutral observation was virtually impossible; observers were branded with a political label by default—"If you're not on my side, you must be the enemy."[4]

Perhaps instrumentally rational means for expressing opinion (e.g., polls) have approximately the same value as more substantively rational communicative actions (e.g., demonstrating, letter writing, etc.) in intensely ideological political conflicts or periods.

Polling and ideology are closely connected, since quantitative data seem to matter most when other, ideologically motivated forms of political expression are lacking.[5] Similarly, campaign management—another instrumentally rational element in elections—has become increasingly important as political alienation grows: Campaign consultants are now viewed as critical by candidates wishing to mobilize a seemingly uninterested populace.[6]

Symbols, Polls, and Power

Throughout this book I have highlighted the interplay between symbolic and instrumental functions of numbers—the ways that quantitative data are gathered for specified purposes, but also become public property in political discourse. In the past, straw polls or crowd counts sent to newspapers were often referred to by competing newspapers during campaigns. Today, poll data are collected and publicized by survey or news organizations, but are used by a variety of parties for their own rhetorical purposes. In a conversation a few years ago with a political activist who was working against U.S. involvement in Central America, I asked whether she made use of public opinion polls. Like other activists, she did, explaining that "we use [poll data] when it's to our advantage. I think all groups do. If [polls] say 60 to 70 percent of the people are against support to the Contras we will quote that, and use that."[7] These sorts of uses of quantitative data are not new phenomena, but they have been largely ignored by those who study political expression.

Symbolic uses of opinion data are particularly interesting to students of power, because this sort of communication upsets standard beliefs about the power of polls. Polls are thought to direct political discourse,[8] stimulate voting "bandwagons,"[9] and oppress poor, marginalized interest groups.[10] Each of these hypotheses has some empirical support, although each is still the subject of ongoing research in the social sciences. All of these theories are intuitively appealing as well, since polls do seem to have an enormous amount of influence during elections. Yet if we are attuned to the symbolic uses of polls—the ways they can be used by a variety of parties in the course of public debate—the extent of their power becomes a complicated issue. While it is true that not every group has the resources to collect opinions and broadcast the results of a poll, it is also true that results from publicized surveys may be exploited by activists or interest groups. The ability to conduct polls and use them privately (instrumental uses) *and* the ability to manipulate these data once they are publicized (symbolic uses) should both be evaluated if one is to understand the alleged power of polls.

Earlier I explored Foucault's ideas about power, knowledge, and how the two merge in the forms of discourse and symbolic communication. Although it is clear that quantitative data produced through "scientific" means are often believed to be authoritative, these data *are not always* viewed as legitimated discourses. As in the debates over crowd size, numerical estimates—no matter how carefully they are calculated—are not necessarily the most respected form of discourse about the public. When we think about polls in terms of discursive power, it seems that these surveys cannot be viewed simply as instruments or techniques of domination. The ideological environment and historical context in which polls are used are critical. Yet the simple notion that we must examine the contexts in which polls are used has not influenced the many academics, journalists, and citizens who believe that polls are inherently powerful.

The power of polls becomes even more complex when we evaluate cases where numbers were used solely for instrumental purposes. An example is the group of congressmen and journalists studied in this book. During the 1930s and the 1940s, public opinion quantification was thought to be a dubious practice, since the *Literary Digest* had failed so miserably in predicting the outcome of the 1936 election. As a result, legislators, editors, and reporters—who continually sought the views of their constituencies—did not look to polling as a rhetorical asset. For these individuals, counting opinions was a useful practice, but the statistics they collected were rarely used in the context of public argument. Are polls really "powerful" when they are used for private purposes? They are probably helpful, but to say they are tools for domination may be an overstatement.

Instrumental and symbolic uses of polls are tightly intertwined in many instances, but the connection between the two functions is most obvious in national politics. When running for office, poll results tell prospective candidates how hard they should run, which issues they should emphasize, and whether their campaign strategies have had an impact on the attitudes of the electorate.[11] As V. O. Key, Ginsberg and others have pointed out, those already in office use private poll data to "test the waters" of public opinion before introducing new policies. On the symbolic level, politicians, candidates, and campaign workers often release private poll data when they believe these data will positively affect public perceptions of them. Although John F. Kennedy often turned to pollsters for information, Lyndon Johnson was even more attuned to the rhetorical value of private polls. Bruce Altschuler, in a study of Johnson's poll use, notes that Johnson commissioned a variety of surveys for his own purposes. The president would make special efforts to publicize these private polls when they seemed useful symbolically:

> Because Johnson had so many private polls available, it was a simple matter to leak any that were more favorable than the public polls to the media. Johnson's main pollster was Oliver Quayle, who regularly took polls, usually of individual states or parts of states between 1964 and 1968. Because Gallup and Harris used national samples, there was considerable material which could be made available to the press as "contradicting" unfavorable results. While such leaks were useful when the public polls were unfavorable, they were not used during the early stages of the administration when ratings were high. [12]

Interestingly, polls are used instrumentally and symbolically despite the widely held belief that they do not provide a "true" picture of the public mood. Pollsters themselves are well aware of the scores of errors one can make in the course of conducting a national opinion survey. [13] There is also considerable sophistication among candidates, interest group leaders, and citizens about the methodological problems associated with polling. [14] For example, many people know that the way a poll question is phrased can affect the distribution of opinion. Many also understand that the timing of a poll can affect the results. Yet these doubts about polling error, which have been with us since the sample survey was first introduced, are linked to ideology: People tend to be more critical of polling methodology when the poll results are inconsistent with their beliefs. In the nineteenth century, journalists doubted straw polls and crowd estimates when these numbers ran counter to their own interests and positions. And in the twentieth century, experimental work on cognitive processing of poll results indicates that individuals discount a poll's methodology when results of that poll are inconsistent with their ideologies. [15] People are more likely to critique the sample size, question wording, and reliability of a poll when that poll challenges their own attitudes.

Numbers and Conflict

One reason why people quantify public opinion is to resolve conflicting arguments about the nature of popular attitudes. In *The*

Pulse of Democracy, George Gallup and Saul Rae argued that elections, newspapers, and other such indicators of public opinion were not precise enough to assess the public mood. The results of elections, they believed, did not necessarily provide solid data on public opinion, since one could vote for a candidate and still oppose his platform. Furthermore, they noted, voters could agree with a candidate on a few issues, but disagree with him or her on a variety of others. Given these simple truths, how, the authors ask, can we sense popular sentiment on individual issues from election results? Newspapers, the early pollsters argued, were useful measures of opinion, but also not particularly reliable. Referring to James Bryce's description of newspapers as "weathercocks," Gallup and Rae explained that

> because newspapers mold, as well as reflect, public opinion, and because their influence is often exerted in quite opposite and contradictory directions, they sometimes make very confusing "weathercocks." The busy legislator who scans the day's editorial columns drawn from a wide geographical area, or even from within the confines of a single city, is instantly struck by the divergent interpretations and conflicting courses which are urged upon him. One editorial insists that the people call for a firm stand in support of the embargo on arms and munitions; another solemnly announces that public opinion demands immediate revision. Which is he to believe?[16]

After arguing that both elections and newspapers provide mixed cues about the nature of public opinion, Gallup and Rae made their case for opinion polls. Although still in the "experimental stage," they contended, public opinion polling yields better information than do older assessment techniques. Polls answer questions about the popular mood.

This simple notion, that rigorous sampling and counting of opinions might clarify the nature of public feeling, does not seem to describe the various functions of today's surveys. Although unsystematic straw polling and crowd estimation were always a source of conflict, even contemporary "scientific" polls can create confusion about the public mood instead of understanding. In fact, though criticism of opinion polls is not uncommon in academic and popular discourses, only occasionally do journalists try to assess the meaning and value of the poll data they use so often. When criticism is offered in the context of presenting poll data, it is usually superficial because journalists may not have the time, space, or inclination to develop an informed critique. An example is a recent article titled "Numbers Serve to Prove You Can't Quantify Life," published in the *Chicago Tribune*. The article reported on a 1991 Chicago area survey, and its author questioned some of the poll findings about city life. He philosophically noted:

> Survey statistics can be just as enlightening and just as frustrating [as sifting through a stranger's wallet]. . . . [Do these survey results] mean, then, that the suburbs are better than the city? That all suburbs are safe and prosperous? . . . Not necessarily. That's sort of like asking whether the cup is half-full or half-empty. It depends on your point of view.[17]

Although many journalists do have an intuitive grasp of the methodological problems associated with polls, these problems are usually overlooked in reports containing poll data. Part of the problem is that many journalists simply do not understand polling procedures or the meaning of poll results.[18] As Richard Morin, director of polling for the *Washington Post*, puts it, polling techniques have become increasingly sophisticated, but journalists have not always kept up with these changes: "Those of us who don't have some appreciation for numbers, demographics, polling, computers, informational graphics . . . and the science behind political science, are not serving our readers or viewers well."[19] Yet to blame journalists for the flaws in polls or the misuse of results is unfair, since many use the techniques as responsibly as they can. Hundreds of people—from the anonymous survey respondent who may or may not be candid with an interviewer, to the journalist who writes about poll results—contribute to the problems of surveys. Polling, it should be remembered, is a social and not an individual practice.

Despite advances in survey methodology, poll results still do conflict, although not to the extent that they did in the nineteenth century.[20] And polls usually provide only a superficial glimpse of the public mood, not a textured, complex account of popular beliefs. Regardless of how well a poll has been conducted, it furnishes only a fragment of evidence about public opinion.[21] Since this is the case, it might be best to treat these data as points of departure—as places to inaugurate debate and not to terminate it. If we think of these data as useful—although not definitive—sorts of evidence, we will feel far less oppressed by polls. During the 1988 presidential campaign and during the 1992 primary season, complaints about the polls were plentiful: Citizens, activists, and even journalists felt as though the polls were deciding the election outcomes and displacing sincere, unstandardized expression. Yet polls need not supplant less rationalized forms of political discussion or reporting. A lesson from the nineteenth century use of straw polls: Quantitative data should force us to engage in argument, not avoid it.

Opinion Quantification and Democratic Theory

One question that theorists of public opinion have asked repeatedly for the last few decades concerns the impact of polls on democracy. In books and articles about the dominance of opinion polls, many authors pause to question the effects of this type of quantification on political participation and on the nature of discourse.[22] Since Americans have always quantified public opinion—especially during presidential election campaigns—these queries may seem odd: Why pose such questions about late twentieth century numerical public expression, when opinion quantification has such a long history? There are, in fact, many good reasons to engage in this line of inquiry, since the numerical description of opinion has accelerated and changed with the introduction of the sample survey.

One way to evaluate the impact of polls is to view them as part of a trend toward increasing rationalization of public opinion. As I argued in chapter 3, techniques of the expression and assessment of public opinion have become more routinized and systematized over time. How can we make sense of these trends in the context of democratic theory? In the spirit of Weber, it seems that this question can best be answered by the use of *ideal types*. If we employ classical democracy as a standard, or an ideal model introduced for the purpose of theorizing, the consequences of increased opinion rationalization become apparent.

In an age when the "trustee" model of government is widely accepted,[23] and where the sheer size of most democracies makes any type of substantial, direct participation in government seemingly impossible, the ideal of Athenian democracy seems somewhat irrelevant—a quaint, impractical notion from the past. Yet dimensions of classical democracy—open debate, direct par-

ticipation, and the majority principle—have always been useful to
political philosophers. By "mapping" the form of our democratic
system onto the classical one, we can understand how our own practices are similar and how they deviate.[24]

To summarize the tenets of classical democratic theory is a difficult task because the theory has been formulated in so many different ways. Writers who are placed in the category of "classical
theorist" comprise an eclectic group, including such thinkers
as Jean-Jacques Rousseau, Charles de Secondat Montesquieu,
Jeremy Bentham, John Dewey, and Raymond Williams.[25] Yet
there are enough broad commonalities among these different versions of the theory that students of political philosophy are able to
consider classical democratic theory without too much confusion as
to its meaning.[26]

Classical democratic theory has been used by many scholars as
a normative standard which we can apply to our contemporary gov-
erning process. Three outstanding features of classical democracy
are the centrality of the "common good" or "general will," maximum participation in government by the populace, and rational
discussion and debate about politics.[27]

The debate among political theorists about what the common
good is, and how it is determined, has been pivotal to discussions of
political participation for centuries. Many writers with an interest
in public opinion, including Locke, Rousseau, and Bentham, believed that public opinion and the common good were almost
interchangeable—that public opinion was most simply a societal
consensus about values and goals. Although these and other writers
equated public opinion with the common good, that particular
definition never became a convention. I will leave aside, in this discussion, the debate on how the general will is (or is not) articulated,
in order to concentrate on two features of classical democracy
which are more directly relevant to the arguments that follow—the
degree of participation by citizens in government and the quality of
that participation.

Central to classical democratic theory is the value placed on
participation by members of the populace.[28] Plato and Aristotle
both preferred a polity small in size so that citizens could come to
know each other and have ample opportunity for engaging in political debate and decision making.[29] Much later, Bentham and some
of his contemporaries argued that maximum participation in gov-

erning was in the best interests of both individual citizens and society as a whole.[30]

Although citizen participation was said to improve political decision-making processes and create the foundations for a just society, the personal benefits of participation were at the core of many classical theories. Lane Davis noted that in these democratic theories, people can develop morally only through political action.[31] Maximum participation of individuals in the political process produced a rational, free-flowing discourse about the issues facing the polity and the common good.[32] Alexis de Tocqueville's portrait of nineteenth century American political participation and debate comes close to describing the discursive component of classical democratic theory: "To take a hand in the regulation of society and to discuss it is his biggest concern and, so to speak, the only pleasure an American knows. This feeling pervades the most trifling habits of life."[33]

These elements of classical democratic theory—maximum participation of citizens in political debate and wide-ranging discourse—have become increasingly irrelevant in contemporary empirical political theory. Joseph Schumpeter was one of the first to note, referring to studies of political apathy and alienation, how badly the model described modern political activity.[34] Carole Pateman, after reviewing the classical theory debate, concluded that the "classical democracy" exists only as a myth.[35]

Despite the debate over which theorists might be labeled "classical" and which were not, or arguments concerning particular details of each theoretical variation, two essential elements of classical democracy—broad participation and free-flowing discourse—are widely agreed-upon dimensions of the normative theory. The question for scholars of public opinion is not whether democratic societies exhibit all characteristics of classical models (they clearly do not), but whether these societies move closer to or farther away from these ideals. Do our contemporary public opinion expression and measurement techniques capture some of the principles of Athenian democracy? Or does the historical development of techniques for expressing public opinion indicate a movement away from these classical ideals?

It seems clear that opinion polls have not single-handedly moved us away from classical democratic models. Their presence in national politics is, however, symptomatic of this move, and they may be accelerating these trends: Polls encourage a structured, re-active sort of participation, making it unnecessary to generate our own forms of public expression, our own questions, and our own critiques. There is some evidence that polling may discourage cer-tain forms of political participation by instigating voting and opin-ion bandwagons.[36] At this point, though, these studies are far from definitive. It is more likely that polls (in addition to other forces) inhibit political discussion and debate. *Conversation,* as theorists from Tarde to Habermas have argued, is fundamental to the con-struction of a democratic public sphere, and polls do not seem to generate interpersonal communication. In a way, polls make many political discussions superfluous, since they give the illusion that the public has already spoken in a definitive manner. When the polls are published, and presidents and policymakers claim that they will heed these polls, what more is there to say?[37]

My argument is not that opinion polls are useless, or that they are detrimental to voting. Instead, I contend that the rigid, struc-tured nature of polling may narrow the range of public discourse by defining the boundaries for public debate, and by influencing the ways that journalists report on politics. These are not new argu-ments; Michael Robinson, Margaret Sheehan, Charles Atkin, and others have already written about these effects. They have not, however, linked the problem of polling to the general increasing rationalization of the public sphere.[38]

Public opinion polls and surveys are, in fact, quite useful. As we have seen, American politicians and journalists have long recog-nized the methodological utility and instrumental value of these ag-gregation techniques. Modern survey techniques enable the pollster to draw a representative sample of Americans, and this can be a valuable and worthwhile endeavor. The public expression tech-niques of the past—such as coffeehouses, salons, and petitions—did not allow for such comprehensive representations of the entire public's views. The question for students of democratic theory, though, is whether polls dampen other forms of political expression and thereby change the shape of the public sphere. Since polls are so authoritative, we have a tendency to find them believable. Yet surveys are far from perfect, as so many have pointed out. Shall we let them dictate the contours of public debate?

Survey researchers have worked diligently to improve the character of polls, but they cannot control how polls are used in public debate. Polls are very valuable, from a rhetorical standpoint, and politicians and interest groups are well aware of this power. No matter how careful some survey researchers are, quantitative data are often misconstrued or misrepresented by journalists, pressure groups, and the public. Because polls can be decontextualized and distorted, we should always question their value. In the past, as we have seen, Americans questioned the worth of numbers that supposedly represented public opinion. The simple fact that our techniques for quantifying political sentiment have improved, however, does not mean that this questioning must cease.

In the nineteenth century, partisan journalists used straw polls and crowd counts to promote their ideological positions and mobilize their constituents. In the twentieth century, reporters and editors treat the sample survey as a tool for gathering information, and tend not to use it rhetorically. This is not to say, however, that polls don't shape the news. One need only think about the most recent presidential election campaign to realize that preelection polls help journalists to develop stereotypes of candidates. Some are seen as front-runners and others as underdogs, and journalists often slant the news around these observations. On one level, this is not at all problematic, since one candidate usually *is* the front-runner. On another, it is dangerous: Many actions of candidates are misconstrued, reported, or ignored because of journalists' poll-based preconceptions.

Although critics of modern democracy abound,[39] some recent books in political science have explored the ways that democracy works—in particular, instances of successful communication between the public and policymakers.[40] For example, Benjamin Page and Robert Shapiro, in their comprehensive book *The Rational Public*, contend that American policy preferences (on many political issues) are rather stable over the course of time. And policymakers, they demonstrate, often heed these preferences. Furthermore, Page and Shapiro argue, opinion surveys are excellent tools for revealing the public mood.[41]

These sorts of arguments about the usefulness of polls are compelling ones, and I do not take issue with them. Polls do capture a narrow dimension of the public's preferences. But the influence of polls is complex, and sometimes troubling, since survey data are so readily used as symbols in policy debate. Page and Shapiro themselves argue that policymakers are "out of step" with public preferences in a third of all issue debates. In discussing this, the authors posit that the lack of congruence is due to a lack of proper information: On some issues, members of the public are misinformed by policymakers or media, so their attention to those issues is low. In these cases, policy elites can "manage" public opinion instead of heeding it.

It is during these periods, I believe, that the symbolic and rhetorical value of polls becomes critical. Policymakers can use polls (in addition to other symbols) to manipulate public preferences. Quantitative data are especially useful to elites, since they are so authoritative: If a policymaker can show that the public is behind him or her, it becomes easier to continue on that course.

Page and Shapiro also make the point that although there is much congruence between public preferences and public policy activity, American political discourse is not quite a "marketplace of ideas." They argue that political information available to citizens through the mass media often reflects the desires of wealthy individuals, powerful institutions, or the government. It seems that polls are often used to legitimate or delegitimate particular opinions in this so-called marketplace. In the nineteenth century, as we've seen, political parties were constantly engaged in numerical battles. Today the situation is somewhat different. Since it costs much more to design and implement a sample survey than it did to conduct a straw poll, those without resources cannot easily conduct polls. Ironically, surveys which may help policymakers to judge public needs may on occasion be used to manipulate that same public.

The public, as so many political scientists have argued, needs better information and more avenues for direct participation in policymaking. Yet until citizens use the information available to them and exhibit more interest in politics, public opinion polls—with their narrow foci—will shape political debate.

Polls may discourage political discussion, but some new, experimental forms of rationalized public opinion expression clash even more obviously with models of classical democracy. An example is the QUBE experiment in Columbus, Ohio, several years ago.[42] Warner-Amex introduced the QUBE system, which allowed cable television subscribers to respond to questions asked during political programming. Viewers could use a "push-button console" to vote, and QUBE aggregated their responses in a matter of seconds. In one instance, a local city planning commission held a meeting on the air, posing questions for viewers, who could register their opinions immediately using their consoles. Although this experiment in "teledemocracy" was impracticable in a number of respects, it is very interesting when treated as an extreme example of opinion rationalization.

The QUBE system, and others like it, was in part designed to boost direct participation in politics. Whether large-scale introduction of these technologies might increase political involvement over the long term is unknown, but these schemes represent a new sort of opinion quantification—one that takes polling to an even more sophisticated level. Consistent with methods for aggregating opinion like the sample survey, these computer networks enable only the most minimal form of political expression. Systems like QUBE are innovative in their use of interactive technology, but do not enhance the *quality* of public discussion. As in polls, the opinion expression enabled is structured, private, and anonymous. That this sort of expression is far from models of political discussion outlined in classical democratic theory is obvious. In a way, these instrumentally rational schemes seem inappropriate for smaller communities wishing to enhance meaningful political dialogue and involvement. Sustained, interpersonal communication enlarges the public sphere in ways that polling or certain teledemocracy schemes never can: When people must take responsibility for their opinions, and argue in public, political discourse becomes interesting and exciting. Communities wishing to augment political dialogue should implement communications technologies which allow for direct, *unstructured* participation.[43]

Reconceptualizing Public Opinion Processes: Toward a New Research Agenda

Since the early days of the sample survey, students of public opinion have learned much about the measurement of popular attitudes. The sheer number of polls conducted has increased dramatically, and more and more news organizations, candidates, and corporations want to commission surveys. The data derived from these surveys are believed to be authoritative, or are at least viewed as the most objective means for understanding the volatile public mood. In the course of this study, I have tried to evaluate the role of opinion quantification in culture and at the same time question this role. It seems as though public opinion researchers themselves—no matter how much they value theory—have not offered many thorough, historically informed critiques of their practices. In fact, opinion researchers are still grappling with sociologist Herbert Blumer's attack on survey research and polling, which is now over forty years old.[44]

Blumer's critique has stood the test of time because he understood the methodologies of polling and foresaw the legitimacy poll data would achieve in the public arena. He noted that opinion researchers were misguided in part because they decontextualized opinions: Instead of studying public opinion formation and change as part of a larger social process, opinion researchers avoided the study of status groups and the power relationships among them. Blumer believed that a concentration on the refinement of measurement tools was problematic, and not particularly useful to social theorists:

> Those trying to study public opinion by polling are so wedded to their technique and so preoccupied with the improvement of their technique that they shunt aside the vital question of whether their technique is suited to the study of what they are ostensibly seeking to study. Their work is largely merely making application of their technique. They are not concerned with independent analysis of the nature of public opinion in order to judge whether the application of their technique fits that nature.[45]

Contemporary survey researchers are aware of the deficiencies of public opinion polling, and their concerns are readily found in the pages of academic journals. Even though some social theorists have good reasons for distrusting survey research as a tool for understanding opinion, the *uses* of surveys should be of great value to them. The instrumental rationality that drives the development of quantitative opinion techniques, and the many ways these techniques are used, have not yet attracted significant scholarly attention.

In this study, I have tried to explore some of these issues in the context of American political history. Of greatest interest were the dual roles of numerical opinion descriptions—their instrumental and symbolic functions in the public sphere. In closing, I would like to offer some ideas toward further theorizing and research in the area of public opinion.

The Uneven Pace of Rationalization

Even though public opinion expression and measurement techniques have become increasingly systematized, this trend is not a smooth one. At times, public opinion expression may actually become *less* rationalized. For example, some contemporary journalists have argued that polls should be supplemented with qualitative data about the public mood during presidential election campaigns. As a result, several prominent network journalists (e.g., Peter Jennings of ABC News) made special efforts to speak with citizens about the candidates and issues during the 1988 campaign. Occasionally, several minutes of a nightly national newscast were devoted to interviews with "ordinary Americans" in bars, cafeterias, and workplaces in smaller cities and towns. Although polling will most likely play a large (or even larger) role in campaign coverage in the future, we may also see more alternatives to rationalized opinion.[46]

Among political elites and citizens, resistance to polls may be far more significant than we think. To study the ways polls *fail* to help elites, and the moments when these actors actually ignore opinion polls, might prove to be extremely instructive. Under what conditions do policymakers, reporters, interest group leaders, and other such politically involved individuals neglect to use polls? In which circumstances are these data given less attention than qualitative indicators of public opinion? Interviews with elites would be a critical part of this research endeavor, but one could also analyze congressional hearings, speeches, news articles and editorials, position papers, and other such documents with attention to the use of poll data.

Studies of citizens who have little interest or involvement in politics may reveal challenges to opinion rationalization as well. During campaigns, people complain about the flood of polls in the media, but how do they process this information? Researchers with an expertise in the analysis of political cognition could explore how people use or think about quantitative opinion data in the context of their political beliefs and actions.[47] I have conducted some exploratory interviews with well-educated voters, and have found that some are extremely cynical about the usefulness of polling data. Many say they do not trust polls, and others do not pay attention to results of surveys reported by the media.[48] These attitudes toward poll data may be indicative of a larger political alienation and cynicism, or they may represent a unique distaste for polls themselves. In-depth interviews with individual citizens would most probably reveal these beliefs, but there are possibilities for laboratory experimentation and survey research as well. Some researchers in communications and journalism have already begun conducting studies on the perceived credibility of polls.[49]

In trying to understand citizen resistance or distrust of polls, evidence from recent mass communication research is particularly instructive. Over the last decade a variety of researchers have conducted ethnographies of television audiences in an attempt to understand the meanings people derive from programming.[50] Several of these scholars have found that consumers of mass culture (e.g., television audiences, romance novel readers, soap opera viewers, etc.) often resist the messages encoded in these texts, treat them critically, or reconstruct meaning according to their own belief systems.[51] The interpretive methodologies employed by these researchers, and their interest in the relationship between reader/viewer and text, are models for understanding how people process opinion poll data in the context of ideology.[52]

Meanings and Techniques of Public Opinion

The meaning of public opinion, as we have seen, has changed dramatically over time. In the past, the popular sentiment was thought to be the product of group interaction, or encoded in public action of one sort or another. With the advent of the opinion poll, the essence of public opinion has been transformed: We are now most likely to think of public opinion as the result of a confidential, scientifically conducted survey of unconnected individuals. Along with these semantic and methodological changes has come a metamorphosis in the perceived role of public opinion. It is difficult, however, to judge whether public opinion has become more or less important to presidents, legislators, journalists, or citizens themselves. Since the meaning of public opinion has changed, we know that eighteenth or nineteenth century statements about the value of public opinion cannot be compared to contemporary ones. An example of this comparability problem is Abraham Lincoln's meditations on his "public opinion baths."

During 1863, while the Civil War raged, a journalist from New York named Charles Halpine called on the president at the White House.[53] Halpine was surprised that Lincoln actually met with the sizable group of men and women, "representing all ranks and classes," who stood in a grand waiting room. Halpine thought that Lincoln could manage the crowd more effectively by screening them, and suggested he do so. Lincoln responded by saying that he valued these visits by common citizens. His explanation to Halpine is worth quoting at length:

> I feel—though the tax on my time is heavy—that no hours of my day are better employed than those which thus bring me again within the direct contact and atmosphere of the average of our whole people. Men moving only in an official circle are apt to become merely official—not to say arbitrary—in their ideas, and are apter and apter, with each passing day, to forget that they only hold power in a representative capacity. Now this is all wrong. I go into these promiscuous receptions of all who claim to have business with me twice each week, and every applicant for audience has to take his turn, as if waiting to be shaved in a barber's shop. Many of the matters brought to my notice are utterly frivolous, but others are of more or less importance, and all serve to renew in me a clearer and more vivid image of that great popular assemblage out of which I sprung, and to which at the end of two years I must return. I tell you . . . that I call these receptions my *"public opinion baths,"* for I have but little time to read the papers and gather public opinion that way; and though they may not be pleasant in all their particulars, the effect, as a whole, is renovating and invigorating to my perceptions of responsibility and duty.[54]

It is clear, from this quotation and others from Lincoln, that he viewed public opinion, at least in part, as a product of discourse and communication. These conversations with common citizens are much more reminiscent of the coffeehouse conversations discussed in chapter 3 than of the quantitative opinion data widely available today. Lincoln, like most nineteenth century politicians, used a variety of means to assess public opinion—conversations in his opinion "baths," newspaper editorials, voting totals, reports from party officials, and the like. Yet it is doubtful that an American president of the late twentieth century would hold these sorts of meetings twice a week, or that he would think of these gatherings *as representing public opinion.* Citizens do still visit the White House, and are still greeted by the president or his staff. Leaders have conversations with constituents. But it is unlikely that these discussions are identified as "public opinion": Public opinion is thought to be measured most reliably by polls, and presidents since Kennedy have made extensive use of survey research.

If we are to achieve a better understanding of how the meaning of public opinion has changed over time, and why, we need to concentrate more seriously on these issues. Harwood Child's collection of public opinion definitions was useful, but they were definitions proposed by theoreticians and philosophers. We still know very little about the ways that political actors—statesmen, journalists, and voters—discussed and thought about "public opinion." Clearly, scholars need to engage in more fine-tuned discursive and historical analyses of the phrase. This could be done systematically, using continuously published texts such as the *Congressional Record,* presidential inaugural addresses, or newspaper editorials. How are phrases like *public opinion* or *public sentiment* used, and at which historical moments do these usages begin to change? Another approach might involve the analysis of significant texts during periods of great political upheaval or ideological transformation. How were phases like *public opinion* used in public discourse or in private correspondence during the Civil War, the Great Depression, or the late 1960s? These projects are daunting ones, but they are critical if we are to conceptualize trends in the history of public opinion. In this book, I presented one analysis of changing opinion techniques using theories of rationality. Ultimately, scholars should combine the study of changing techniques with the semantic study of public opinion, "mapping" both types of history onto trends in American politics.

Thinking about Public Opinion

Theorizing about public opinion has always been a part of meditations about democratic process. With changes in the nature of measurement and expression techniques, we have more and more books and journals devoted to the study of popular sentiment. Yet the time has come to think anew about the way we study public opinion and its role in the political sphere. There are scores of fresh, important questions that should dominate our thinking about public opinion.

Political scientists are committed to studying the relationship between polling and public policy, but we know much less about the effects of polls on political discourse and political action. For instance, are people debilitated by polls, as some activists would have us believe? Do people fail to demonstrate, write letters to public officials, or talk to their neighbors about issues because public opinion "speaks" through the pollsters? Have opinion polls replaced political action, or would involvement in politics remain low even without the presence of so many polls in the media during and between elections?

The study of public opinion is an ancient area of inquiry. Beginning with Plato and Aristotle, hundreds of writers and philosophers have focused their attention on the nature and importance of the popular will. This enormous body of literature is still of great interest to scholars, who often return to Tocqueville's insights on the "tyranny of the majority" or Machiavelli's writings on manipulating the popular mood. Yet since the great periods of opinion rationalization and quantification in the nineteenth and twentieth centuries, the fundamental questions we must ask about public opinion are considerably different than they once were. Quantitative opinion data are everywhere, but have they made political discourse more "democratic" or more *substantively* "rational"? It seems, from this discussion, that the use of numbers to describe popular feeling has not encouraged political involvement or enhanced political discourse in any significant way. Even though opinion polls are valuable to political candidates, journalists, and presidents—both instrumentally and symbolically—their impact on political expression has not been as dramatic as early pollsters once hoped.

NOTES

Chapter One

1. W. J. M. Mackenzie, "The Function of Elections," in David Sills, ed., *The International Encyclopedia of the Social Sciences* (New York: Macmillan, 1968), pp. 1–6.

2. On the history of statistics, see William Alonso and Paul Starr, *The Politics of Numbers* (New York: Russell Sage, 1987); Patricia Cline Cohen, *A Calculating People: The Spread of Numeracy in Early America* (Chicago: University of Chicago Press, 1982); B. Lécuyer and A. Oberschall, "The Early History of Social Research," in David Sills, ed., *The International Encyclopedia of the Social Sciences* (New York: Macmillan, 1968), pp. 35–50; Theodore Porter, *The Rise of Statistical Thinking: 1820–1900* (Princeton, N.J.: Princeton University Press, 1986); and Stephen M. Stigler, *The History of Statistics: The Measurement of Uncertainty Before 1900* (Cambridge, Mass.: Harvard University Press, 1986).

3. The term *statistical thinking* is Porter's.

4. Cohen, *A Calculating People*, p. 43.

5. See Porter, *The Rise of Statistical Thinking*, pp. 18–20.

6. Lécuyer and Oberschall, "The Early History of Social Research," p. 38.

7. Ibid., p. 36.

8. John Sinclair, *The Statistical Account of Scotland*, vol. 20 (Edinburgh: William Creech, 1798), p. xiii. On early surveys also see Martin Blumer, Kevin Bales, and Kathryn Kish Sklar, eds., *The Social Survey in Historical Perspective 1880–1940* (Cambridge: Cambridge University Press, 1991).

9. Porter, *The Rise of Statistical Thinking*, pp. 5–6.

10. Ibid., pp. 52–55.

11. Lécuyer and Oberschall, p. 43.

12. Dorothy Ross, *The Origins of American Social Science* (Cambridge: Cambridge University Press, 1991), pp. 53–97.

13. Ibid., p. 429.

14. See Leo Bogart, *Polls and the Awareness of Public Opinion* (New Brunswick, N.J.: Transaction, 1988); Jean Converse, *Survey Research in the United States: Roots and Emergence, 1890–1960* (Berkeley: University

of California Press, 1987); Tom Smith, "The First Straw?' A Study of the Origins of Election Polls," *Public Opinion Quarterly* 54 (1990): 21–36; Michael Wheeler, *Lies, Damn Lies, and Statistics: The Manipulation of Public Opinion in America* (New York: Liveright, 1976).

15. Albert E. Gollin, "Polling and the News Media," *Public Opinion Quarterly* 51 (1987): S86–S94.

16. See Converse, *Survey Research in the United States*; Jack Honomichl, "How Much Spent on Research? Follow Me," *Advertising Age* (June 21, 1982); Seymour Sudman and Norman Bradburn, "The Organizational Growth of Public Opinion Research in the United States," *Public Opinion Quarterly* 51 (1987): S67–S78.

17. *Rationalization* is Weber's term, although others, including the members of the Frankfurt School, have used it extensively in their work.

18. Guenther Roth, "Rationalization in Max Weber's Developmental History," in Scott Lash and Sam Whimster, eds., *Max Weber, Rationality, and Modernity* (London: Allen and Unwin, 1987), pp. 77–78.

19. Donald N. Levine, "Rationality and Freedom: Weber and Beyond," *Social Inquiry* 51 (1981): 5–25.

20. Reinhard Bendix, *Max Weber: An Intellectual Portrait* (Garden City, N.Y.: Anchor, 1962), p. 9.

21. The secondary literature on *The Protestant Ethic and the Spirit of Capitalism* is rather extensive. A good introduction may be found in Bendix, *Max Weber*, or in Rogers Brubaker's excellent study, *The Limits of Rationality: An Essay on the Social and Moral Thought of Max Weber* (London: George Allen & Unwin, 1984). Also see Dirk Käsler's *Max Weber: An Introduction to His Life and Work* (Chicago: University of Chicago Press, 1988), pp. 74–141.

22. Martin Albrow, "The Application of the Weberian Concept of Rationalization to Contemporary Conditions," in S. Lash and S. Whimster, eds., *Max Weber, Rationality, and Modernity*, pp. 164–66. On rationality at the individual level of analysis, see Barry Hindess, "Rationality and the Characterization of Modern Society," in S. Lash and S. Whimster, eds., *Max Weber, Rationality, and Modernity*, pp. 137–53.

23. Max Weber, *Economy and Society: An Outline of Interpretive Sociology*, ed. Guenther Roth and Claus Wittich (Berkeley: University of California Press, 1978), p. 85.

24. For a more complex, fourfold typology of rationality, see D. Levine, "Rationality and Freedom."

25. Brubaker, *The Limits of Rationality*, p. 35.

26. Weber, *Economy and Society*, p. 585.

27. Talcott Parsons, introduction to Max Weber, *The Sociology of Religion*, trans. Ephraim Fischoff (Boston: Beacon Press, 1964), pp. xxxii.

28. Weber, *Economy and Society*, p. 656.

29. Ibid., p. 433.

30. Ibid., pp. 606–7.

31. Max Weber, *The Protestant Ethic and the Spirit of Capitalism*, trans. Talcott Parsons (New York: Charles Scribner's Sons, 1958).

32. Ibid., p. 26; pp. 76–77.

33. Weber, *Economy and Society*, p. 1156.

34. Ibid.

35. Max Weber, "Science as a Vocation," in *From Max Weber: Essays in Sociology*, ed. and trans. H. H. Gerth and C. Wright Mills (New York: Oxford University Press, 1946), p. 139.

36. Max Weber, quoted in J. P. Mayer, *Max Weber and German Politics* (London: Faber & Faber, 1943), pp. 127–28.

37. Barry Smart, *Foucault, Marxism, and Critique* (London: Routledge & Kegan Paul, 1985), p. 124.

38. Weber, *Economy and Society*, p. 247. Also see Luciano Cavalli, "Charisma and Twentieth-Century Politics," in S. Lash and S. Whimster, eds., *Max Weber, Rationality, and Modernity*, pp. 317–33. Several Marxist and neo-Marxist critics use Weber's insights on rationalization in their theorizing, but have disagreed with Weber's conclusions. See, for example, Georg Lukács, *History and Class Consciousness*, trans. Rodney Livingstone (Cambridge, Mass.: M.I.T. Press, 1971), or Jürgen Habermas, "New Social Movements," *Telos* 49 (1981): 33–37. Also see Jean Cohen's discussion of Marx and Weber on rationalization, "Max Weber and the Dynamics of Rationalized Domination," *Telos* 14 (1972): 63–86.

39. Herbert Marcuse, "Industrialization and Capitalism," in Otto Stammer, ed., *Max Weber and Sociology Today* (New York: Harper & Row, 1972), p. 135.

40. See Max Horkheimer and Theodor Adorno, *Dialectic of Enlightenment*, trans. John Cumming (New York: Continuum, 1987); Jürgen Habermas, *The Theory of Communicative Action*, trans. Thomas McCarthy (Boston: Beacon Press, 1984).

41. Weber believed socialism was doomed to failure, because rationalization would accelerate in a planned, centralized economy. See *Economy and Society*, pp. 109–18.

42. Herbert Marcuse, "Some Social Implications of Modern Technology," in Andrew Arato and Eike Gebhardt, eds., *The Essential Frankfurt School Reader* (New York: Continuum, 1982), p. 143.

43. Michel Foucault's work is complex, and this chapter provides only a brief introduction to some of his ideas. There are several fine introductions to Foucault. See, for example, Barry Smart, *Foucault, Marxism, and Critique*. Also see Smart's *Michel Foucault* (London: Tavistock, 1985) and Hubert L. Dreyfus and Paul Rabinow, *Michel Foucault: Beyond Structuralism and Hermeneutics* (Chicago: University of Chicago Press, 1983).

44. Michel Foucault, *Discipline and Punish: The Birth of the Prison*, trans. Alan Sheridan (New York: Vintage, 1979), p. 26.

45. Michel Foucault, *The History of Sexuality*, vol. 1, trans. R. Hurley (New York: Vintage, 1990), p. 92.

46. See Dreyfus and Rabinow, or David Couzens Hoy, "Power, Repression, Progress: Foucault, Lukes, and the Frankfurt School," in Hoy, ed., *Foucault: A Critical Reader* (New York: Basil Blackwell, 1986), pp. 123–48.

47. Foucault, *History of Sexuality*, p. 94.

48. Foucault, *Discipline and Punish*, p. 224.

49. Ibid., p. 27.

50. Dreyfus and Rabinow, p. 5.

51. Michel Foucault, *Madness and Civilization: A History of Insanity in the Age of Reason*, trans. Richard Howard (New York: Vintage, 1973).

52. Heteroglossia is Bakhtin's notion that every language is composed of a multitude of sublanguages. He argued that language is "heteroglot from top to bottom: it represents the co-existence of socio-ideological contradictions between the present and the past, between differing epochs of the past, between different socio-ideological groups in the present, between tendencies, schools, circles and so forth." See his essay "Discourse in the Novel," in *The Dialogic Imagination*, ed. Michael Holquist, trans. Caryl Emerson and M. Holquist (Austin: University of Texas Press, 1981), p. 291.

53. Foucault, *History of Sexuality*, pp. 100–101.

54. Ibid., p. 101.

55. Foucault, *Discipline and Punish*, pp. 200–228.

56. Ibid., p. 217.

57. Dreyfus and Rabinow, p. 192.

58. Weber and Foucault do have different perspectives on the rationalization process. Although Weber did not *always* see rationalization as a linear, global process (despite what some scholars assume), he did make macrohistorical arguments. Foucault, on the other hand, made great efforts to emphasize the *local* nature of rationalization. He argued that scholars must concentrate on particular instances of rationalization if they

are to understand it properly. See his essay, "The Subject and Power," in Dreyfus and Rabinow, p. 210. Also see Colin Gordon, "The Soul of the Citizen: Max Weber and Michel Foucault on Rationality and Government," in S. Lash and S. Whimster, eds., *Max Weber, Rationality, and Modernity*, pp. 293–316.

59. Foucault, *History of Sexuality*, pp. 95–96.

60. See Robin Toner, "Dukakis Nears the Wire in 9-State, 48-Hour Dash," *The New York Times*, November 8, 1988, p. A10.

61. The general rationalization of American politics is beyond the scope of this book, yet there is much evidence for increasing rationalization. In electoral politics, for example, political consultants, PACs, and pollsters wield more and more influence during and between contests. See Larry J. Sabato, *The Rise of Political Consultants* (New York: Basic, 1981).

62. Benjamin Ginsberg, *The Captive Public: How Mass Opinion Promotes State Power* (New York: Basic, 1986).

63. On the problems of survey research, see Robert M. Groves, *Survey Costs and Survey Errors* (New York: John Wiley & Sons, 1989).

Chapter Two

1. For an excellent study of instrumental and symbolic social action, see Joseph Gusfield, *Symbolic Crusade: Status Politics and the American Temperance Movement* (Urbana: University of Illinois Press, 1986).

2. Sigmund Freud, *A General Introduction to Psychoanalysis* (New York: Simon & Schuster, 1972), p. 158.

3. Raymond Firth, *Symbols: Public and Private* (London: George Allen & Unwin, 1973), pp. 148–49. Contemporary cognitive psychologists are interested in symbols, but most often discuss them in the context of metaphors or "schemas." On the role of metaphor in cognition, see George Lakoff, *Women, Fire, and Dangerous Things: What Categories Reveal about the Mind* (Chicago: University of Chicago Press, 1987).

4. Firth, p. 130.

5. Émile Durkheim, *The Elementary Forms of the Religious Life: A Study in Religious Sociology*, trans. Joseph Swain (London: George Allen & Unwin, 1915), pp. 219–20.

6. Edward Sapir, "Symbolism," in E. Seligman, ed., *Encyclopaedia of the Social Sciences*, vol. 14 (New York: Macmillan, 1934), pp. 492–95.

7. See Murray Edelman's criticism of Sapir's categories in his afterword to *The Symbolic Uses of Politics* (Urbana: University of Illinois Press, 1985), p. 198.

8. On the relationship between political events and presidential popularity, see Richard Brody and Benjamin Page, "The Impact of Events on Presidential Popularity: The Johnson and Nixon Administrations," in A. Wildavsky, ed., *Perspectives on the Presidency* (Boston: Little, Brown, 1975), pp. 136–48.

9. George Herbert Mead, *Mind, Self, and Society: From the Standpoint of a Social Behaviorist* (Chicago: University of Chicago Press, 1962), p. 147.

10. Kenneth Burke, *On Symbols and Society* (Chicago: University of Chicago Press, 1989), p. 109.

11. Ibid., p. 110.

12. Firth, p. 75.

13. See, for example, Fred Greenstein, *Children and Politics* (New Haven, Conn.: Yale University Press, 1965).

14. See D. Easton, *A Systems Analysis of Political Life* (New York: Wiley, 1965); and D. Easton and J. Dennis, *Children in the Political System: Origins of Political Legitimacy* (New York: McGraw-Hill, 1969).

15. On media events as rituals, see Eric Rothenbuhler, "Media Events, Civil Religion, and Social Solidarity: The Living Room Celebration of the Olympic Games" (Ph.D. diss., University of Southern California, 1985).

16. C. Wright Mills, *The Sociological Imagination* (New York: Grove Press, 1961), pp. 36–38.

17. Hans Gerth and C. Wright Mills, *Character and Social Structure: The Psychology of Social Institutions* (New York: Harcourt, Brace, 1953), p. 275.

18. Peter Berger and Thomas Luckmann, *The Social Construction of Reality: A Treatise in the Sociology of Knowledge* (Garden City, N.Y.: Anchor Books, 1967), p. 92.

19. For an analysis of the flag, bald eagle, and other American symbols, see Wilbur Zelinsky, *Nation into State: The Shifting Symbolic Foundations of American Nationalism* (Chapel Hill: University of North Carolina Press, 1988), pp. 196–208.

20. Quoted in Zelinsky, p. 243.

21. Gerth and Mills, p. 384.

22. On Reagan's policy toward Nicaragua and its relationship to public opinion, see Barry Sussman, *What Americans Really Think and Why Our Politicians Pay No Attention* (New York: Pantheon, 1988).

23. Todd Gitlin, *The Whole World Is Watching* (Berkeley: University of California Press, 1980).

24. See Edelman, *The Symbolic Uses of Politics.*

25. On the use of advertising to manipulate consumer preferences, see Mark Crispin Miller, *Boxed In: The Culture of TV* (Evanston, Ill.: Northwestern University Press, 1988).

26. Zelinsky, p. 244.

27. For an opposing view on numbers, see the critiques of positivism by members of the Frankfurt School. Among these are Max Horkheimer, *Critical Theory: Selected Essays* (New York: Herder & Herder, 1972); and Herbert Marcuse, *Reason and Revolution: Hegel and the Rise of Social Theory* (New York: Oxford University Press, 1981).

28. On the use of polls by the news media, see David L. Paletz et al., "Polls in the Media: Content, Credibility, and Consequences," *Public Opinion Quarterly* 44 (1980): 495–513.

29. On the public's understanding of polling procedures, see Burns W. Roper, "Some Things That Concern Me," *Public Opinion Quarterly* 47 (1983): 303–9. For a discussion of how polls are reported in the mass media, and the types of survey details that should be reported, see Peter V. Miller, Daniel M. Merkle, and Paul Wang, "Journalism with Footnotes: Reporting the 'Technical Details' of Polls," in Paul J. Lavrakas and Jack K. Holley, eds., *Polling and Presidential Election Coverage* (Newbury Park, Calif.: Sage Publications, 1991), pp. 200–214.

30. Benjamin Ginsberg, *The Captive Public: How Mass Opinion Promotes State Power* (New York: Basic, 1986).

31. Stephen J. Gould, *The Mismeasure of Man* (New York: W. W. Norton, 1981).

32. David I. Kertzer, *Ritual, Politics, and Power* (New Haven, Conn.: Yale University Press, 1988), p. 12.

33. For a history of survey research, see Jean Converse, *Survey Research in the United States: Roots and Emergence, 1890–1960* (Berkeley: University of California Press, 1987).

34. Irving Crespi, "Surveys as Legal Evidence," *Public Opinion Quarterly* 51 (1987): 84–91.

35. William Alonso and Paul Starr, *The Politics of Numbers* (New York: Russell Sage Foundation, 1987).

36. On the use of television rating and survey data in business, see Peter V. Miller, "The Folklore of Audience Measurement," paper presented at the annual meeting of the Midwest Association for Public Opinion Research, Chicago, Ill., 1985; and Solomon Dutka, "Misuses of Statistics in Marketing and Media Research: What Will Happen to Research Quality in the '90s?", transcript of proceedings of the ARF seventh

annual Research Quality Workshop (New York: Advertising Research Foundation, 1989), pp. 129–44.

Chapter Three

1. Harwood Childs, *Public Opinion: Nature, Formation, and Role* (Princeton, N.J.: D. Van Nostrand, 1965).

2. These definitional categories are not mutually exclusive. Some public opinion researchers have articulated definitions that could fit into two or more of the categories.

3. During the Persian Gulf War, for example, journalists and other commentators made continual reference to the "fact" that public opinion supported President Bush's policy. When making these types of statements, journalists were most often referring to public opinion data indicating widespread support. Opinions of war protesters were not referred to as "public opinion."

4. George Gallup and Saul Rae, *The Pulse of Democracy: The Public Opinion Poll and How It Works* (New York: Greenwood, 1968), p. 6. Ben Ginsberg, in his book *The Captive Public* (New York: Basic, 1986), has argued that polls and public opinion have become synonymous in American politics. He notes that other forms of public expression (e.g., opinions of interest groups, parties, or grass-roots organizations) are no longer considered "public opinion," because they have been displaced by the sample survey.

5. Cited in Childs, *Public Opinion*, p. 17.

6. Jean-Jacques Rousseau, *The Social Contract and the Discourses*, ed. and trans. G. D. Cole (New York: E. P. Dutton, 1950).

7. John Locke, *An Essay Concerning Human Understanding*, ed. Alexander Campbell Fraser (Oxford: Clarendon Press, 1894).

8. Elisabeth Noelle-Neumann, *The Spiral of Silence: Public Opinion— Our Social Skin* (Chicago: University of Chicago Press, 1984). One might place Habermas in this category of theorists, since he argues for the importance of communication in opinion formation. Yet since his work is concerned with the development of the public sphere as a whole, and since his discussions of "public opinion" are embedded in a rather complex argument about positivism and history, I hesitate to group him with theorists specifically concerned with definitions of public opinion. See Chapter 7 of his 1989 book, *The Structural Transformation of the Public Sphere: An Inquiry into a Category of Bourgeois Society* (Cambridge, Mass.: M.I.T. Press). Also see Benjamin Nathans, "Habermas's 'Public Sphere' in the Era of the French Revolution," *French Historical Studies* 16 (1990): 620–44,

and Craig Calhoun's recent edited volume, *Habermas and the Public Sphere* (Cambridge, Mass.: M.I.T. Press, 1992).

9. See Walter Lippmann, *The Phantom Public* (New York: Harcourt, Brace, 1925) and *Public Opinion* (New York: Free Press, 1965).

10. Pierre Bourdieu, "Public Opinion Does Not Exist," in A. Mattelart and S. Siegelaub, eds., *Communication and Class Struggle* (New York: International General, 1979), pp. 124–30.

11. Jürgen Habermas, "The Public Sphere: An Encyclopedia Article," *New German Critique* 1 (1974): 50. Also see his *Structural Transformation of the Public Sphere*.

12. See Langdon Winner, *Autonomous Technology: Technics-Out-of-Control as a Theme in Political Thought* (Cambridge, Mass.: M.I.T. Press, 1983), pp. 2–12.

13. Cited in Winner, p. 9. See Jacques Ellul, *The Technological Society*, trans. John Wilkinson (New York: Alfred A. Knopf, 1964).

14. Aristotle, *The Politics*, ed. and trans. T. A. Sinclair (Baltimore, Md.: Penguin Books, 1962), p. 123.

15. David Minar, "Public Opinion in the Perspective of Political Theory," *Western Political Quarterly* 13 (1960): 39.

16. See Minar or Paul Palmer, "The Concept of Public Opinion in Political Theory," in *Essays in History and Political Theory in Honor of Charles Howard McIlwain* (New York: Russell & Russell, 1964), pp. 130–57.

17. Wilhelm Bauer, "Public Opinion," in E. Seligman, ed., *Encyclopaedia of the Social Sciences* (New York: Macmillan, 1930), p. 671. Also see Kurt Back, "Metaphors for Public Opinion in Literature," *Public Opinion Quarterly* 52 (1988): 278–88.

18. Bauer, p. 672.

19. Palmer, p. 232.

20. Little has been written about public opinion expression in non-Western nations during this period, since historians have concentrated on Western Europe and America. The phrase "public opinion" was coined in prerevolutionary France, and it is likely that the expression did not diffuse outside of the West until after the late nineteenth or early twentieth century.

21. Niccolò Machiavelli, *The Prince*, trans. N. H. Thompson (Buffalo, N.Y.: Prometheus, 1986), p. 59. In this discussion of Machiavelli I refer only to *The Prince*.

22. Ibid., p. 63.

23. Elizabeth Eisenstein, *The Printing Press as an Agent of Change:*

Communications and Cultural Transformations in Early-Modern Europe (Cambridge: Cambridge University Press, 1979), p. 132.

24. Charles Tilly, "Speaking Your Mind without Elections, Surveys, or Social Movements," *Public Opinion Quarterly* 47 (1984): 465.

25. Robert Darnton, *The Great Cat Massacre and Other Episodes in French Cultural History* (New York: Vintage, 1985), p. 77. A more comprehensive, although less literary, work on eighteenth century and early nineteenth century crowds is E. P. Thompson's classic article, "The Moral Economy of the English Crowd in the Eighteenth Century," *Past and Present* 50 (1971): 76–136. Thompson argues that eighteenth century English rioters were not *challenging* the status quo, but believed they were "defending *traditional* rights or customs; and, in general, that they were supported by the wider consensus of the community" (p.78; emphasis mine). On European crowds during this period, see also George Rudé, *The Crowd in History: A Study of Popular Disturbances in France and England, 1730–1848* (London: Lawrence and Wishart, 1981).

26. C. S. Emden, *The People and the Constitution* (London: Oxford, 1956), pp. 74–75. Interestingly, much petitioning in Britain during this time was initiated by women. See P. Higgins, "The Reactions of Women, with Special Reference to Women Petitioners," in B. Manning, ed., *Politics, Religion and the English Civil War* (London: Edward Arnold, 1973), pp. 179–224.

27. Emden, p. 75.

28. See Dena Goodman, "Enlightenment Salons: The Convergence of Female and Philosophic Ambitions," *Eighteenth Century Studies* 22 (Spring 1989): 329–350; Joan Landes, *Women and the Public Sphere in the Age of the French Revolution* (Ithaca, N.Y.: Cornell University Press, 1988); Carolyn Lougee, *La Paradis des Femmes: Women, Salons, and Stratification in Seventeenth Century France* (Princeton, N.J.: Princeton University Press, 1976); Kingsley Martin, *The Rise of French Liberal Thought: A Study of Political Ideas from Bayle to Condorcet* (New York: New York University Press, 1954); Peter Quenell, *Affairs of the Mind: The Salon in Europe and America from the Eighteenth to the Twentieth Century* (Washington, D.C.: New Republic Books, 1980); and Chauncey Brewster Tinker, *The Salon and English Letters* (New York: Macmillan, 1915).

29. M. Roustan, *The Pioneers of the French Revolution* (Boston: Little, Brown, 1926).

30. Helen Clergue, *The Salon: A Study of French Society and Personalities in the Eighteenth Century* (New York: Burt Franklin, 1971).

31. Palmer, p. 238.

32. Mona Ozouf, "'Public Opinion' at the End of the Old Regime," *Journal of Modern History* 60 (1988): S1–S21.

33. Lewis Coser, *Men of Ideas* (New York: Free Press, 1970), pp. 13–14.

34. Jürgen Habermas, *The Structural Transformation of the Public Sphere: An Inquiry into a Category of Bourgeois Society* (Cambridge, Mass.: M.I.T. Press, 1989). See especially pp. 32–34 and pp. 67–70.

35. Bauer, "Public Opinion."

36. Keith Baker, "Politics and Public Opinion under the Old Regime," in J. Censer and J. Popkin, eds., *Press and Politics in Pre-Revolutionary France* (Berkeley: University of California Press, 1987), pp. 233–34. Baker argues that the notion of a French "public" emerged during the last decades of the Old Regime, when a variety of political elites began to appeal to the public as an "abstract authority," in the face of growing political conflict and a faltering monarchy.

37. Coser, p. 20. Also see Harold Routh, "Steele and Addison," in A. Ward and A. Waller, eds., *The Cambridge History of English Literature, Volume 9* (Cambridge: Cambridge University Press, 1932), pp. 26–65. For a critique of coffeehouses, see Alvin Gouldner, *The Dialectic of Ideology and Technology: The Origins, Grammar, and Future of Ideology* (New York: Oxford University Press, 1976).

38. For a history of elections, see W. Mackenzie, "The Function of Elections," in D. Sills, ed., *The Encyclopedia of the Social Sciences*, vol. 5 (New York: Macmillan, 1968), pp. 1–6.

39. Harold Gosnell, "Ballot," in E. Seligman, ed., *Encyclopaedia of the Social Sciences*, vol. 2 (New York: Macmillan, 1930).

40. James Bryce, *The American Commonwealth* (New York: Macmillan, 1891), p. 251.

41. Ibid., p. 263.

42. Ginsberg, *The Captive Public.*

43. For a review reception theory applied to mass media, see Robert Allen, "Reader-oriented Criticism and Television," in R. Allen, ed., *Channels of Discourse: Television and Contemporary Criticism* (Chapel Hill: University of North Carolina Press, 1987).

44. James R. Beniger, "The Popular Symbolic Repertoire and Mass Communication," *Public Opinion Quarterly* 47 (1983): 483.

45. Jane Mansbridge, *Beyond Adversary Democracy* (Chicago: University of Chicago Press, 1983).

46. See T. Bender, *Community and Social Change in America* (New Brunswick, N.J.: Rutgers University Press, 1978); Christopher Lasch,

"The Family as a Haven in a Heartless World," *Salmagundi* 35 (1976): 42–55; or Richard Sennett, *Families Against the City: Middle Class Homes of Industrial Chicago, 1872–1890* (Cambridge, Mass.: Harvard University Press, 1970).

47. An exception is the open-ended question, which is occasionally used by professional pollsters.

48. On nineteenth-century political involvement, see Michael McGerr, *The Decline of Popular Politics: The American North, 1865–1928* (New York: Oxford University Press, 1986).

Chapter Four

1. On the history of straw polls, see Tom Smith, "The First Straw? A Study of the Origins of Election Polls," *Public Opinion Quarterly* 54 (1990): 21–36; and Claude Robinson, *Straw Votes: A Study of Political Prediction* (New York: Columbia University Press, 1932).

2. There is a large methodological literature on sampling. For an introduction, see Charles Backstrom and Gerald Hursh-Cesar, *Survey Research* (New York: J. Wiley, 1981); Seymour Sudman, *Applied Sampling* (New York: Academic Press, 1978); and Leslie Kish, *Survey Sampling* (New York: J. Wiley, 1967). For more recent information about advances in survey research techniques, consult the *Public Opinion Quarterly*, a publication of the American Association for Public Opinion Research.

3. George Gallup and Saul Rae, *The Pulse of Democracy: The Public-Opinion Poll and How it Works* (New York: Greenwood, 1940), p. 35.

4. Smith, "The First Straw?" p. 27.

5. Michael Wheeler, *Lies, Damn Lies, and Statistics: The Manipulation of Public Opinion in America* (New York: Liveright, 1976), p. 69.

6. For a history of modern survey research, see Jean Converse, *Survey Research in the United States: Roots and Emergence, 1890–1960* (Berkeley: University of California Press, 1987).

7. Alexis de Tocqueville, *Democracy in America*, ed. J. P. Mayer (New York: Anchor, 1969), p. 254.

8. James Bryce, *The American Commonwealth* (New York: Macmillan, 1894), p. 265.

9. On nineteenth century changes in transportation, manufacturing, and distribution of goods, see James R. Beniger, *The Control Revolution: Technological and Economic Origins of the Information Society* (Cambridge, Mass.: Harvard University Press, 1986); for a description of changes in family life, see Mary Ryan, *Cradle of the Middle Class: The*

Family in Oneida County, New York, 1790–1865 (New York: Cambridge University Press, 1981).

10. There are numerous histories of journalism; see Frank Mott, *American Journalism, A History: 1690–1960* (New York: Macmillan, 1968); E. Emery and M. Emery, *The Press and America: An Interpretive History of the Mass Media* (Englewood Cliffs, N.J.: Prentice-Hall, 1984); Michael Schudson, *Discovering the News: A Social History of American Newspapers* (New York: Basic, 1978).

11. Morton Keller, *Affairs of State: Public Life in Late Nineteenth Century America* (Cambridge, Mass.: Harvard University Press, 1977), p. 566.

12. Frank Mott, *American Journalism, A History: 1690–1960*, p. 216. Although contemporary journalists are socialized to avoid obvious affiliation with political parties and causes, one might still argue that modern news reporters have recognizable political biases. For a discussion of news bias or "slant," see Robert Entman, *Democracy without Citizens: Media and the Decay of American Politics* (New York: Oxford University Press, 1989).

13. Michael Schudson, *Discovering the News: A Social History of American Newspapers*, p. 122.

14. On the fanfare of nineteenth century election campaigns, see Michael McGerr, *The Decline of Popular Politics: The American North, 1865–1928* (New York: Oxford University Press, 1986).

15. Robert Dinkin, *Campaigning in America: A History of Election Practices* (Westport, Conn.: Greenwood, 1989), p. 62.

16. *Chicago Tribune*, 6 October 1860, p. 1.

17. On the role of polls in contemporary American politics, see chapter 6.

18. Schudson, *Discovering the News*, p. 17.

19. Hazel Dicken-Garcia, *Journalistic Standards in Nineteenth-Century America* (Madison: University of Wisconsin Press, 1989), p. 53.

20. Ibid., p. 48.

21. In order to evaluate the straw polls in a comprehensive manner, I gathered election reports from three newspapers of varying types. I chose *The New York Times* because of its reputation, since its inception, as a thorough, serious, and "well balanced" publication (Mott, p. 280). As Emery and Emery put it, "There was a minimum of personal invective in the *Times*. It was invariably fair in tone, if not in content, and no rival equaled it in developing the technique of careful reporting" (p. 153). The two Chicago papers—the *Tribune* and the *Times*—were chosen because they

stood at opposing poles on the ideological spectrum. Both were critical organs of public opinion in the Midwest and had large readerships during the years covered in this study. The three papers tended to take different ideological perspectives on the issues during presidential campaigns and provide a range of political discourses.

The *Chicago Times* was not a continuously published paper. In 1896, the paper became the *Times-Herald.* For coverage of the 1936 election, I studied the *Chicago Daily Times.* For the 1956, 1976, and 1988 elections, I read the *Chicago Sun-Times.* The *Sun-Times* and the *Tribune* are currently the two major Chicago newspapers.

I chose to study elections at twenty-year intervals in order to analyze long-term trends in the reporting of public opinion. The 1860 campaign was included because it was a critical turning point in American political history. The 1988 campaign was included so that I could compare past election campaigns to a recent one.

For each newspaper, I randomly selected fifteen sample days between July 1 and election day. Only scattered issues of the *Chicago Times* could be located for 1860, so I used the eight issues available from the Illinois State Historical Library. Issues of the 1856 *Chicago Times* could not be located. Additionally, only scattered issues of the 1856 *Chicago Tribune* were available. All reports on campaign rallies, meetings, parades, demonstrations, election betting pools, and straw polls were collected from the sample newspapers.

22. *Chicago Tribune,* 7 October 1860, p. 2.

23. *Chicago Tribune,* 25 August 1876, p. 2.

24. *Chicago Tribune,* 15 August 1856, p. 3.

25. *The New York Times,* 13 September 1856, p. 4.

26. It should be noted that journalists were not the only people conducting straw polls during election campaigns. As Smith and others have pointed out, party workers and leaders conducted numerous polls to get a sense of where their candidates stood. As America moved into the twentieth century, and as party membership began to decline, political consultants began to assume many of the campaign management responsibilities, including polling and canvassing. On nineteenth century party straws in the Midwest, see Richard Jensen, *The Winning of the Midwest: Social and Political Conflict, 1888–96* (Chicago: University of Chicago Press, 1971). For a history of political consulting, polling, and campaign management, see Larry Sabato, *The Rise of Political Consultants: New Ways of Winning Elections* (New York: Basic, 1981). The election of 1908 is thought by some to be one of the first highly systematized election campaigns. On how Taft's campaign was organized, see Walter Wellman, "The Management of the Taft Campaign," *Review of Reviews* 38 (1908): 432–38.

27. *Chicago Tribune*, 11 August 1896, p. 4.

28. On women in partisan politics, see Dinkin, *Campaigning in America*, p. 67; Mary Ryan, *Women in Public* (Baltimore, Md.: Johns Hopkins University Press, 1990).

29. See Ellen Carol DuBois, *Feminism and Suffrage: The Emergence of an Independent Women's Movement in America, 1848–1869* (Ithaca, N.Y.: Cornell University Press, 1978); Sara M. Evans, *Born for Liberty: A History of Women in America* (New York: Free Press, 1989); Mary P. Ryan, *Cradle of the Middle Class*.

30. Schudson, *Discovering the News*, pp. 99–100.

31. *The New York Times*, 6 November 1876, p. 8.

32. *The New York Times*, 17 August 1916, p. 10; *Chicago Tribune*, 22 October 1896, p. 3; *Chicago Tribune*, 14 October 1936, p. 3.

33. *Chicago Tribune*, 15 August 1956, p. 2; *Chicago Tribune*, 20 September 1896, p. 11.

34. *Chicago Tribune*, 5 November 1916, p. 3.

35. See Dan Merkle, "The Effects of Opinion Poll Results on Public Opinion: A Review and Synthesis of Bandwagon and Underdog Research," paper presented at the meeting of the International Communication Association, Chicago, 1991.

36. *Chicago Tribune*, 15 August 1856, p. 2.

37. *The New York Times*, 5 September 1856, p. 3.

38. *Chicago Tribune*, 28 September 1860, p. 2.

39. *Chicago Tribune*, 4 September 1860, p. 2.

40. *Chicago Tribune*, 7 August 1856, p. 2.

41. *Chicago Tribune*, 17 September 1856, p. 2.

42. *Chicago Tribune*, 26 July 1860, p. 2.

43. *The New York Times*, 7 October 1896, p. 4.

44. The *Chicago Sun-Times* printed the results of a poll of visitors at the 1976 Notre Dame–South Carolina football game. The fans favored Gerald Ford by a margin of 3,133 votes. Ford is quoted as saying, "I like those odds" (24 October 1976, p. 2).

45. On the accuracy of straws, see Claude Robinson, *Straw Votes: A Study of Political Prediction* (New York: Columbia University Press, 1932). For a review of polls that failed to predict the winners of presidential contests, see Michael Wheeler, *Lies, Damn Lies, and Statistics*.

46. Michel Foucault, "Two Lectures," in *Power/Knowledge: Selected Interviews and Other Writings, 1972–1977*, ed. Colin Gordon (New York: Pantheon, 1980), p. 93.

47. See Theodore Porter, *The Rise of Statistical Thinking: 1820–1900* (Princeton, N.J.: Princeton University Press, 1986).

48. Benjamin Ginsberg, *The Captive Public: How Mass Opinion Promotes State Power* (New York: Basic, 1986), pp. 66–67.

49. It is important to note that citizens' voices are still published in major newspapers. "Man on the street" interviews are often found in papers, for example. In these stories, several pictures of individuals are published alongside their opinions. Perhaps the "people's polls," although no longer considered "public opinion," evolved into this "man on the street" genre of reporting.

50. See Schudson, *Discovering the News.*

51. On the use of polls by media organizations, see David L. Paletz et al., "Polls in the Media: Content, Credibility, and Consequences," *Public Opinion Quarterly* 44 (1980): 495–513.

Chapter Five

1. See, for example, Jean Converse, *Survey Research in the United States: Roots and Emergence, 1890–1960* (Berkeley: University of California Press, 1987).

2. Winston Allard, "Congressional Attitudes toward Public Opinion Polls," *Journalism Quarterly* 18 (1941): 47–50.

3. Carl Hawver, "The Congressman and His Public Opinion Poll," *Public Opinion Quarterly* 18 (1954): 123–29.

4. Warren Price, "What Daily News Executives Think of Public Opinion Polls," *Journalism Quarterly* 30 (1953): 287–99.

5. V. O. Key, *Public Opinion and American Democracy* (New York: Alfred A. Knopf, 1961), p. 421.

6. W. Pierce, *Congressional Record.* 77th Cong., 1st sess., 1941. Vol. 87.

7. C. Curtis, *Congressional Record.* 77th Cong., 1st sess., 1941. Vol. 87, 3945.

8. G. Nye, *Congressional Record.* 77th Cong., 1st sess., 1941. Vol. 87, 4865.

9. Seventy-seven members who served during the 1930s or 1940s were listed in this directory. Not all former members belong to the association, but the organization was able to provide an unpublished list of 59 additional former members of Congress. In 1988, the year this study was conducted, there were 7 members of Congress who served during the 1930s or 1940s. Of the 143 members and former members of Congress who served during

the period of interest, 13 could not be located. The final sample consisted of 130 former and current congressmen.

10. William H. Taft, *Encyclopedia of Twentieth-Century Journalists* (New York: Garland, 1986). Using the computerized data base of *Who's Who*, I was able to locate 21 journalists or editors who worked during the 1930s and 1940s. I obtained 90 names of journalists and editors who worked during this period from the *Encyclopedia*. Journalists who specialized in subjects where public opinion was not particularly important (science writers, advice columnists, etc.), those who never worked for American newspapers or magazines, and several whose addresses were unavailable were excluded from the study. The final sample of journalists and editors included 111 individuals. (Copies of the questionnaires sent to congressmen and journalists are available from the author.)

While the list of congressmen I compiled was a census of those members who served during the period of interest, the sample of journalists is somewhat biased. I was most concerned with the practices of influential journalists, so the group included very few lesser-known journalists or journalists with short careers.

11. David Mayhew, *Congress: The Electoral Connection* (New Haven, Conn.: Yale University Press, 1974).

12. W. E. Binkley and M. C. Moos, *A Grammar of American Politics* (New York: Knopf, 1958).

13. "The Fortune Survey," *Fortune*, October 1948, pp. 29–32.

14. Harry S. Truman, *Public Papers of the Presidents of the United States* (Washington, D.C.: General Services Administration, 1956), p. 920.

15. On why the 1948 polls failed, see Lindsay Rogers, *The Pollsters: Public Opinion, Politics, and Democratic Leadership* (New York: Alfred A. Knopf, 1949); Frederick Mosteller et al., *The Pre-Election Polls of 1948: Report to the Committee on Analysis of Pre-Election Polls and Forecasts* (New York: Social Science Research Council, 1949); Norman Meier and Harold Saunders, eds., *The Polls and Public Opinion* (New York: Henry Holt, 1949); or, more recently, Hugh Hardy, ed., *The Politz Papers: Science and Truth in Marketing Research* (Chicago: American Marketing Association, 1990).

16. Mosteller, *The Pre-Election Polls of 1948*, pp. 290–315.

17. For the AAPOR standards for disclosing poll methodology and results, see the organization's *Certificate of Incorporation and By-Laws* (Princeton, N.J.: AAPOR, 1986).

18. Irving Crespi, *Pre-Election Polling: Sources of Accuracy and Error* (New York: Russell Sage, 1988), p. 171.

19. Ibid., p. 184.

Chapter Six

1. David Weaver and Maxwell McCombs, "Journalism and Social Science: A New Relationship," *Public Opinion Quarterly* 44 (1980): 477–94.

2. Michael Ryan, "Journalism Education at the Master's Level," *Journalism Monographs* 66 (1980): 13.

3. Phil Meyer claims that Everette Dennis coined the term *precision journalism*. See Meyer, "Precision Journalism and the 1988 U.S. Elections," *International Journal of Public Opinion Research* 1 (1989): 195–205.

4. Philip Meyer, *Precision Journalism: A Reporter's Introduction to Social Science Methods* (Bloomington: Indiana University Press, 1973), p. 13.

5. David L. Paletz et al., "Polls in the Media: Content, Credibility, and Consequences," *Public Opinion Quarterly* 44 (1980): 495–513.

6. Michael Traugott and Roberta Rusch, "Understanding the Proliferation of Media Polls in Presidential Campaigns," paper presented at the annual meeting of the Midwest Association for Public Opinion Research, Chicago, November 17–18, 1989.

7. Albert Cantril, *The Opinion Connection: Polling, Politics, and the Press* (Washington, D.C.: Congressional Quarterly Press, 1991), pp. 33–37.

8. Philip Meyer, "Precision Journalism and the 1988 U.S. Elections," p. 203.

9. Bill Kovach, "A User's View of the Polls," *Public Opinion Quarterly* 44 (1980): 571.

10. See Burns Roper, "Some Things That Concern Me," *Public Opinion Quarterly* 47 (1983): 303–9; or Ronald Elving, "Proliferation of Opinion Data Sparks Debate over Use," *Congressional Quarterly* (August 19, 1989): 2187–92.

11. See Martin Wattenberg, *The Decline of American Political Parties, 1952–1984* (Cambridge, Mass.: Harvard University Press, 1986).

12. Cantril, *The Opinion Connection*, p. 16.

13. Herbert Asher, *Polling and the Public: What Every Citizen Should Know* (Washington, D.C.: Congressional Quarterly Press, 1988).

14. Paul Herrnson, *Party Campaigning in the 1980s* (Cambridge, Mass.: Harvard University Press, 1988), p. 78.

15. Ibid., p. 79.

16. Ibid., p. 101.

17. Larry J. Sabato, *The Rise of Political Consultants: New Ways of Winning Elections* (New York: Basic, 1981), p. 9.

18. Ibid., p. 73.

19. See Sabato, p. 321. On candidates' use of polls see also Michael Kagay, "As Candidates Hunt the Big Issue, Polls Can Give Them a Few Cues," *The New York Times,* 20 October 1991, section 4, p. 3.

20. Irving Crespi, *Pre-Election Polling: Sources of Accuracy and Error* (New York: Russell Sage Foundation, 1988). As part of his comprehensive study of preelection polling, Crespi conducted a series of in-depth interviews with thirty national and state-level polling organizations. He queried pollsters in order to map out areas of methodological consensus and disagreement.

21. On sampling error, see Robert Groves, *Survey Costs and Survey Errors* (New York: John Wiley & Sons, 1989).

22. Tom Smith, "That Which We Call Welfare by Any Other Name Would Smell Sweeter: An Analysis of the Impact of Question Wording on Response Patterns," in Eleanor Singer and Stanley Presser, eds., *Survey Research Methods* (Chicago: University of Chicago Press, 1989), p. 107.

23. Howard Schuman and Jean Converse, "The Effects of Black and White Interviewers on Black Responses," in Singer and Presser, eds., *Survey Research Methods,* pp. 247–71.

24. See Groves, *Survey Costs and Errors,* chapter 8, and also Peter Miller and Charles Cannell, "A Study of Experimental Techniques for Telephone Interviewing," in Singer and Presser, eds., *Survey Research Methods,* pp. 304–23.

25. Charlotte Steeh, "Trends in Nonresponse Rates, 1952–1979," in Singer and Presser, eds., *Survey Research Methods,* pp. 32–49.

26. Ibid., p. 45.

27. Tom Smith, "The Hidden 25 Percent: An Analysis of Nonresponse on the 1980 General Social Survey," in Singer and Presser, eds., *Survey Research Methods,* pp. 50–68. Not all of the "nonresponses" to the 1980 GSS were refusals: Out of a sample of 1,931, 1,468 interviews were conducted, 315 people refused to participate, 66 could not be reached at their homes, and 84 cases were eliminated for other reasons (p. 56).

28. Robert Groves and Lars Lyberg, "An Overview of Nonresponse Issues in Telephone Surveys," in Robert Groves et al., eds., *Telephone Survey Methodology* (New York: John Wiley & Sons, 1988), pp. 191–212.

29. Ibid., pp. 210–11.

30. William Nicholls, "Computer-Assisted Telephone Interviewing: A

General Introduction," in Robert Groves et al., eds., *Telephone Survey Methodology,* p. 378. Also see the other essays on CATI systems in this same volume.

31. Burns Roper, "Evaluating Polls with Poll Data," *Public Opinion Quarterly* 50 (1986): 10–16.

32. Andrew Kohut, "Rating the Polls: The Views of Media Elites and the General Public," *Public Opinion Quarterly* 50 (1986): 1–9.

33. Ibid., p. 6.

34. Elisabeth Noelle-Neumann, *The Spiral of Silence: Public Opinion—Our Social Skin* (Chicago: University of Chicago Press, 1984). Noelle-Neumann's theory is a controversial one. For critical comments about the "spiral of silence," see K. Sanders, L. Kaid, and D. Nimmo, *Political Communication Yearbook 1984* (Carbondale: Southern Illinois University Press, 1985).

35. James Fields and Howard Schuman, "Public Beliefs about the Beliefs of the Public," *Public Opinion Quarterly* 40 (1976): 427–48.

36. Ibid., p. 438.

37. Carroll Glynn, "Perceptions of Others' Opinions as a Component of Public Opinion," *Social Science Research* 18 (1989): 53–69.

38. Ibid., p. 67.

39. See Jean Converse, *Survey Research in the United States: Roots and Emergence, 1890–1960* (Berkeley: University of California Press, 1987).

Chapter Seven

1. See *The New York Times,* 9 April 1989, p. 28.

2. See *Chicago Tribune,* 17 April 1989, p. 16.

3. See Leon Mann, "Counting the Crowd: Effects of Editorial Policy on Estimates," *Journalism Quarterly* 51 (1974): 278–85.

4. Ibid. Although there is not much academic literature on crowd estimation, a variety of scholars have studied crowd behavior itself. In history see, for example, both of George Rudé's books, *The Crowd in the French Revolution* (London: Oxford University Press, 1959) and *The Crowd in History: A Study of Popular Disturbances in France and England, 1730–1848* (London: Lawrence and Wishart, 1981). Also see J. S. McClelland, *The Crowd and the Mob* (London: Unwin Hyman, 1989). In social psychology, see S. D. Reicher, "Social Influence in the Crowd: Attitudinal and Behavioral Effects of Deindividuation in Conditions of High and Low Group Salience," *British Journal of Social Psychology* 23 (1984): 341–50,

and "The St. Paul's Riot: An Explanation of the Limits of Crowd Action in Terms of a Social Identity Model," *European Journal of Social Psychology* 14 (1984): 1–21. Also see Le Bon's famous essay on mass psychology, first published in 1895, *The Crowd: A Study of the Popular Mind* (New York: Penguin Books, 1977).

5. Herbert Jacobs, "To Count a Crowd," *Columbia Journalism Review* (Spring 1967): 37–40.

6. Ibid., p. 37.

7. Commander Peter Schurla, Special Events, Chicago Police Department. Interview with author, January 23, 1990.

8. Any article which mentioned a political meeting, demonstration, parade, or other gathering was included in the sample. Only articles which included the name of at least one presidential or vice-presidential candidate were chosen for the sample.

For each of the nine election campaigns, I randomly selected fifteen sample days between July 1 and election day. All articles about rallies which appeared on a sample day were included in the analysis. This procedure could not be followed for the *Chicago Times* and the *Chicago Tribune* for 1856 and 1860, since many issues from those years could not be located. Instead, I analyzed those issues available in the Chicago Public Library and the Illinois State Historical Society in Springfield.

9. The actual number of estimates is much higher, however, since many articles contained multiple attendance figures. Sometimes journalists reported on three or four different rallies in one campaign article, and gave an estimate of the crowd for each of these gatherings.

10. See Michael McGerr, *The Decline of Popular Politics: The American North, 1865–1928* (New York: Oxford University Press, 1986), and Robert Dinkin, *Campaigning in America: A History of Election Practices* (Westport, Conn.: Greenwood Press, 1989).

11. *Chicago Tribune*, 6 October 1860, p. 1.

12. *Chicago Tribune*, 27 August 1860, p. 4.

13. *Chicago Tribune*, 28 September 1860, p. 2.

14. *Chicago Times*, 27 August 1876, p. 3.

15. *Chicago Tribune*, 1 August 1856, p. 2.

16. Gilbert Fite, "Election of 1896," in Arthur M. Schlesinger, Jr., ed., *History of American Presidential Elections, 1789–1968* (New York: Chelsea House, 1971).

17. *Chicago Tribune*, 11 August 1896, p. 3.

18. Ibid., p. 1.

19. Ibid.

20. *The New York Times,* 29 September 1896, p. 2.

21. Ibid., p. 3.

22. Gallup had used the sample survey before the 1936 election. In 1932 he experimented with the technique, predicting that his mother-in-law would win her bid to become Iowa's next secretary of state.

23. See A. Holcombe, "Round Table on Political Statistics: The Measurement of Public Opinion," *American Political Science Review* 19 (1925): 123–26.

24. *Chicago Tribune,* 16 August 1916, p. 4.

25. *The New York Times,* 29 September 1896, p. 3.

26. *Chicago Tribune,* 5 November 1916, p. 1.

27. *The New York Times,* 15 October 1936, p. 17.

28. *The New York Times,* 7 October 1936, p. 4.

29. *Chicago Tribune,* 5 September 1856, p. 2.

30. *Chicago Tribune,* 5 November 1876, p. 1.

31. *Chicago Times,* 27 August 1876, p. 3.

32. See Michael Schudson, *Discovering the News: A Social History of American Newspapers* (New York: Free Press, 1978).

33. *The New York Times,* 21 September 1976, p. 26.

34. See Paul Abramson, John Aldrich, and David Rohde, *Change and Continuity in the 1988 Election* (Washington, D.C.: Congressional Quarterly Press, 1990), p. 13.

35. *Chicago Sun-Times,* 7 November 1988, p. 1.

36. See Barry Sussman, *What Americans Really Think and Why Our Politicians Pay No Attention* (New York: Pantheon, 1988), pp. 192–99.

37. *The New York Times,* 9 April 1989, p. 28.

38. *Washington Post,* 11 April 1989, p. 1.

39. Ibid.

40. *Chicago Tribune,* 17 April 1989, p. 16.

41. Abortion activists are not the only ones who use opinion data selectively. I have interviewed individuals concerned with U.S. policy in Central America, and they readily admit that they use poll data when it supports their arguments.

42. *Chicago Tribune,* 11 August 1896, p. 1.

43. See Eric H. Monkkonen, *Police in Urban America, 1860–1920* (Cambridge: Cambridge University Press, 1981).

44. See Anthony Platt and Lynn Cooper, *Policing America* (Englewood Cliffs, N.J.: Prentice-Hall, 1974).

45. See Robert G. Meadow, "Televised Campaign Debates as Whistle-Stop Speeches," in William C. Adams, ed., *Television Coverage of the 1980 Presidential Campaign* (Norwood, N.J.: Ablex, 1983).

46. The professional organization for pollsters—the American Association for Public Opinion Research—was established in the 1930s.

47. See Larry J. Sabato, *The Rise of Political Consultants* (New York: Basic, 1981).

48. *Los Angeles Times*, 22 October 1991, p. A27.

49. Ibid.

50. Ibid.

Chapter Eight

1. On the decline of voting in America, see Frances Fox Piven and Richard A. Cloward, *Why Americans Don't Vote* (New York: Pantheon, 1988).

2. See Paul Abramson, *Political Attitudes in America: Formation and Change* (San Francisco, Calif.: W. H. Freeman, 1983).

3. Martin P. Wattenberg, *The Decline of American Political Parties, 1952–1984* (Cambridge, Mass.: Harvard University Press, 1986).

4. Peter V. Miller, "Which Side Are You On? The 1990 Nicaraguan Poll 'Debacle,'" *Public Opinion Quarterly* 55 (1991): 281–302.

5. Survey researchers themselves try to avoid ideological bias when designing poll questions. Although Ben Ginsberg has argued eloquently that governments were drawn to polling and to general elections because they sought control over the populace, those who conduct polls are probably not desirous of this sort of control: Polling the public is simply an interesting job, and a service that many organizations are willing to pay for.

6. On the ways that candidates and prospective candidates rely on political consultants, see Larry J. Sabato, *The Rise of Political Consultants* (New York: Basic, 1981).

7. This interview is from an exploratory study I conducted in the spring of 1990, "Mass Media and Public Opinion: Citizens' Constructions of Political Reality," *Media, Culture, and Society* (in press).

8. Pierre Bourdieu, "Public Opinion Does Not Exist," in A. Mattelart and S. Siegelaub, eds., *Communication and Class Struggle* (New York: International General, 1979), pp. 124–30.

9. Daniel M. Merkle, "The Effects of Opinion Poll Results on Public

Opinion: A Review and Synthesis of Bandwagon and Underdog Research," paper delivered at the forty-first annual conference of the International Communication Association, Chicago, 1991.

10. Ginsberg, *The Captive Public*.

11. Sabato, *The Rise of Political Consultants*; James R. Beniger and Robert Giuffra, "Public Opinion Polling: Command and Control in Presidential Campaigns," in A. Heard and M. Nelson, eds., *Presidential Selection* (Durham, N.C.: Duke University Press, 1987).

12. Bruce E. Altschuler, "Lyndon Johnson and the Public Polls," *Public Opinion Quarterly* 50 (1986): 285–99; the quote is on p. 291.

13. See Sabato, *The Rise of Political Consultants*, or Richard Morin, "Do You Agree or Disagree That Election Polling Needs Improving"? *Washington Post National Weekly Edition*, 20–26 May, 1991, p. 37.

14. Although my evidence is not definitive, the political activists and nonactivists I have interviewed were extremely critical of polling methodology. Only a few of them understood the mechanics of sampling and the error associated with it, but many understood how the placement and phrasing of questions can affect poll results.

15. See Daniel M. Merkle, "The Impact of Prior Belief and Disclosure of Methods on Perceptions of Poll Data Quality and Methodological Discounting," paper presented at the annual meeting of the Association of Education in Journalism and Mass Communication, Boston, August, 1991.

16. George Gallup and Saul Rae, *The Pulse of Democracy* (New York: Greenwood, 1940), p. 23.

17. George Papajohn, "Numbers Serve to Prove You Can't Quantify Life," *Chicago Tribune*, 1 May, 1991, p. 18.

18. See David L. Paletz et al., "Polls in the Media: Content, Credibility, and Consequences," *Public Opinion Quarterly* 44 (1980): 495–513, and Peter V. Miller, Daniel M. Merkle, and Paul Wang, "Journalism with Footnotes: Reporting the 'Technical Details' of Polls," in Paul J. Lavrakas and Jack K. Holley, eds., *Polling and Presidential Election Coverage* (Newbury Park, Calif.: Sage Publications, 1991), pp. 200–214.

19. Morin, p. 37.

20. John P. Robinson and Robert Meadow, *Polls Apart* (N.Y.: Seven Locks Press, 1982).

21. For an insightful discussion of the problematics of opinion polling, see Irving Crespi, *Public Opinion, Polls, and Democracy* (Boulder, Colo.: Westview, 1989). Crespi demonstrates how a reliance on a few polls, or a failure to understand the complexity and volatility of public opinion, can lead to a flawed understanding of popular moods.

22. See Crespi, *Public Opinion, Polls, and Democracy,* or Barry Sussman, *What Americans Really Think and Why Our Politicians Pay No Attention* (New York: Pantheon, 1988).

23. On representative versus direct democracy, see F. Christopher Arterton, *Teledemocracy: Can Technology Protect Democracy?* (Newbury Park, Calif.: Sage, 1987); Benjamin Barber, *Strong Democracy: Participatory Politics for a New Age* (Berkeley: University of California Press, 1984); and Jane Mansbridge, *Beyond Adversary Democracy* (Chicago: University of Chicago Press, 1983).

24. J. Roland Pennock, *Democratic Political Theory* (Princeton, N.J.: Princeton University Press, 1979); Joseph A. Schumpeter, *Capitalism, Socialism, and Democracy,* 3d ed. (New York: Harper & Row, 1962).

25. Robert Dahl and Edward Tufte, *Size and Democracy* (Stanford, Calif.: Stanford University Press, 1973), pp. 4–12; L. Davis, "The Cost of Realism: Contemporary Restatements of Democracy," *Western Political Quarterly* 17 (1964): 38.

26. See Davis, "The Cost of Realism," or Schumpeter, *Capitalism, Socialism, and Democracy.*

27. Carole Pateman, *Participation and Democratic Theory* (Cambridge: Cambridge University Press, 1970), pp. 1–21; Schumpeter, *Capitalism, Socialism, and Democracy.*

28. The populace was, as many scholars have noted, strictly limited in Athens. Slaves, immigrants, and women were not citizens, and were therefore restricted from the forms of political participation we associate with Athenian democracy.

29. Dahl and Tufte, *Size and Democracy.*

30. Pateman, *Participation and Democratic Theory.*

31. Davis, "The Cost of Realism," p. 41.

32. Ibid. Also see David Held, *Models of Democracy* (Stanford, Calif.: Stanford University Press, 1987); H. Mayo, *An Introduction to Democratic Theory* (New York: Oxford University Press, 1960).

33. Alexis de Tocqueville, *Democracy in America,* ed. J. P. Mayer (New York: Anchor, 1969).

34. Schumpeter, *Capitalism, Socialism, and Democracy.*

35. Pateman, *Participation and Democratic Theory,* pp. 17–21.

36. See Merkle, "The Effects of Opinion Poll Results on Public Opinion," for a review of empirical studies of the bandwagon effect. Also see S. J. Ceci and E. Kain, "Jumping on the Bandwagon with the Underdog: The Impact of Attitude Polls on Polling Behavior," *Public Opinion Quar-*

terly 26 (1982): 228–42; L. Epstein and G. Strom, "Election Night Projections and West Coast Turnout," *American Politics Quarterly* 9 (1981): 479–91; and R. Henshel and W. Johnston, "The Emergence of Bandwagon Effects: A Theory," *Sociology Quarterly* 28 (1987): 493–511.

37. Paul Lazarsfeld and Robert Merton made a similar argument decades ago about the debilitating effects of mass media. They believed that media discussions of politics make citizens feel smug—as though they are well informed. Yet being well informed does not prompt one to act. As the authors put it, "The interested and informed citizen can congratulate himself on his lofty state of interest and information and neglect to see that he has abstained from decision and action. In short, he takes his secondary contact with the world of political reality, his reading and listening and thinking, as a vicarious performance. He comes to mistake *knowing* about problems of the day for *doing* something about them." See Lazarsfeld and Merton's classic article, "Mass Communication, Popular Taste and Organized Social Action," in Lyman Bryson, ed., *The Communication of Ideas* (New York: Harper and Brothers, 1948), p. 106.

On the importance of conversation in the formation of the public sphere, see *Gabriel Tarde: On Communication and Social Influence*, ed. T. Clarke (Chicago: University of Chicago Press, 1969), and Jürgen Habermas, *The Structural Transformation of the Public Sphere* (Cambridge, Mass.: M.I.T. Press, 1989). For an insightful discussion of the relationship between Weber's theory of rationalization and Habermas's work, see Douglas Kellner, "Critical Theory, Max Weber, and the Dialectics of Domination," in Robert Antonio and Ronald Glassman, eds., *A Weber-Marx Dialogue* (Lawrence: University of Kansas Press, 1985).

38. See especially Michael J. Robinson and Margaret Sheehan, *Over the Wire and on TV: CBS and UPI in Campaign '80* (New York: Russell Sage Foundation, 1983); and Charles Atkin and James Gaudino, "The Impact of Polling on the Mass Media," *Annals of the American Academy of Political and Social Science* 472 (1984): 119–28.

39. See Barber, *Strong Democracy*, or Mansbridge, *Beyond Adversary Democracy*.

40. See Samuel Popkin's recent book on communication patterns during presidential primaries, *The Reasoning Voter: Communication and Persuasion in Presidential Campaigns* (Chicago: University of Chicago Press, 1991).

41. Benjamin Page and Robert Shapiro, *The Rational Public: Fifty Years of Trends in Americans' Policy Preferences* (Chicago: University of Chicago Press, 1991).

42. See Arterton, *Teledemocracy*, pp. 138–44.

43. Jean Elstain has offered a similar critique of QUBE. See her "Democracy and the Qube Tube," *The Nation* (August 7–14, 1982): 108–10. Some teledemocracy schemes do encourage more textured, less formalized types of individual political expression. The Cleveland Free Net system, a community-based computer network, is an example. Citizens can access a large amount of information about government activities and services, but also send their own messages to government representatives whenever they like. See Kathleen L. Maciuszko, "A Quiet Revolution: Community Online Systems," *ONLINE* (November 1990): 24–32.

Another interesting attempt to combine unstructured opinion expression with television is political scientist James Fishkin's idea of a National Issues Convention. He developed a plan to randomly select six hundred individuals, poll them on issues of national importance, and fly them to a "people's convention" in Austin, Texas. The Public Broadcasting Service plans to fund and broadcast the deliberations of the convention event (at a cost of $3.5 million) in hopes of "breaking out of the mold that we—both journalists and politicians—have been caught up in." See Walter Shapiro, "Vaulting Over Political Polls," *Time* (July 22, 1991): 27.

44. See, for example, Philip E. Converse, "Changing Conceptions of Public Opinion in the Political Process," *Public Opinion Quarterly* 51 (1987): S12–S24.

45. Herbert Blumer, "Public Opinion and Public Opinion Polling," *American Sociological Review* 13 (1948): 242–49.

46. Focus groups are extremely popular in political consulting circles, and have been used for years by market researchers. As techniques of opinion articulation, they are suspended somewhere between rationalized and nonrationalized forms of opinion expression. On the one hand, participants are free to speak their minds. On the other, they are asked to speak within the framework provided by the focus group leader. This can be a very narrow framework, depending upon the goals of the client. On the uses of focus groups in American politics, see Larry J. Sabato, *The Rise of Political Consultants: New Ways of Winning Elections* (New York: Basic, 1981).

47. On studying political cognition, see Richard Lau and David O. Sears, *Political Cognition: The Nineteenth Annual Carnegie Symposium on Cognition* (Hillsdale, N.J.: Lawrence Erlbaum, 1986); or Doris A. Graber, *Processing the News: How People Tame the Information Tide* (New York: Longman, 1984).

48. See the "polls on polls" citations in chapter 6.

49. Michael B. Salwen, "Credibility of Public Opinion Polls: Sources, Source Intent, and Precision," paper delivered at the annual meeting of the International Communication Association, Montreal, 1987.

50. See David Morley, *The "Nationwide" Audience: Structure and Decoding* (London: British Film Institute, 1980). More recently, see Ellen Seiter, Hans Borchers, Gabrielle Kreutzner, and Maria Warth, *Remote Control: Television, Audiences, and Cultural Power* (London: Routledge, 1991).

51. See Janice Radway, *Reading the Romance: Women, Patriarchy, and Popular Literature* (Chapel Hill: University of North Carolina Press, 1984); and Tamar Liebes and Elihu Katz, *The Export of Meaning: Cross-Cultural Readings of "Dallas"* (New York: Oxford University Press, 1990).

52. As in audience ethnography, one might probe informants about their backgrounds, belief systems, and ideological identities. With this sort of information, researchers can proceed to interview people about public opinion—its forms and its meaning. It is likely that resistance to opinion polling—if it is significant—will emerge in the context of these interviews.

53. Introduction to "My 'Public-Opinion Baths,'" in Mario Cuomo and Harold Holzer, eds., *Lincoln on Democracy* (New York: Harper Collins, 1990), pp. 284–85.

54. Ibid., p. 285.

BIBLIOGRAPHY

Abramson, Paul. 1983. *Political Attitudes in America: Formation and Change.* San Francisco, Calif.: W. H. Freeman.

Abramson, Paul, John Aldrich, and David Rohde. 1990. *Change and Continuity in the 1988 Elections.* Washington, D.C.: Congressional Quarterly Press.

Albrow, Martin. 1987. The Application of the Weberian Concept of Rationalization to Contemporary Conditions. In *Max Weber, Rationality, and Modernity,* ed. S. Lash and S. Whimster. London: Allen & Unwin.

Allard, Winston. 1941. Congressional Attitudes toward Public Opinion Polls. *Journalism Quarterly* 18:47–50.

Allen, Robert. 1987. Reader-Oriented Criticism and Television. In *Channels of Discourse: Television and Contemporary Criticism,* ed. R. Allen. Chapel Hill: University of North Carolina Press.

Alonso, William, and Paul Starr. 1987. *The Politics of Numbers.* New York: Russell Sage.

Altschuler, Bruce E. 1986. Lyndon Johnson and the Public Polls. *Public Opinion Quarterly* 50:285–99.

Aristotle. 1962. *The Politics.* Edited and translated by T. A. Sinclair. Baltimore: Penguin Books.

Arterton, F. Christopher. 1987. *Teledemocracy: Can Technology Protect Democracy?* Newbury Park, Calif.: Sage.

Asher, Herbert. 1988. *Polling and the Public: What Every Citizen Should Know.* Washington, D.C.: Congressional Quarterly Press.

Back, Kurt. 1988. Metaphors for Public Opinion in Literature. *Public Opinion Quarterly* 52:278–88.

Backstrom, Charles, and Gerald Hursh-Cesar. 1981. *Survey Research.* New York: J. Wiley.

Baker, Keith. 1987. Politics and Public Opinion under the Old Regime. In *Press and Politics in Pre-Revolutionary France,* ed. J. Censer and J. Popkin. Berkeley: University of California Press.

Bakhtin, Mikhail. 1981. Discourse in the Novel. In *The Dialogic Imagination.* Edited and translated by Caryl Emerson and Michael Holquist. Austin, Tex: University of Texas Press.

Barber, Benjamin. 1984. *Strong Democracy: Participatory Politics for a New Age.* Berkeley: University of California Press.

Bauer, Wilhelm. 1930. Public Opinion. In *Encyclopaedia of the Social Sciences,* ed. E. Seligman. New York: Macmillan.

Bender, T. 1978. *Community and Social Change in America.* New Brunswick, N.J.: Rutgers University Press.

Bendix, Reinhard. 1962. *Max Weber: An Intellectual Portrait.* Garden City, N.Y.: Anchor.

Beniger, James R. 1983. The Popular Symbolic Repertoire and Mass Communication. *Public Opinion Quarterly* 47:483.

————. 1986. *The Control Revolution: Technological and Economic Origins of the Information Society.* Cambridge, Mass.: Harvard University Press.

Beniger, James R., and Robert Giuffra. 1987. Public Opinion Polling: Command and Control in Presidential Campaigns. In *Presidential Selection,* ed. A. Heard and M. Nelson. Durham, N.C.: Duke University Press.

Berger, Peter, and Thomas Luckmann. 1967. *The Social Construction of Reality: A Treatise in the Sociology of Knowledge.* Garden City, N.Y.: Anchor Books.

Binkley, W. E., and M. C. Moos. 1958. *A Grammar of American Politics.* New York: Knopf.

Blumer, Herbert. 1948. Public Opinion and Public Opinion Polling. *American Sociological Review* 13:242–49.

Bogart, Leo. 1988. *Polls and the Awareness of Public Opinion.* New Brunswick, N.J.: Transaction.

Bourdieu, Pierre. 1979. Public Opinion Does Not Exist. In *Communication and Class Struggle,* ed. A. Mattelart and S. Siegelaub. New York: International General.

Brody, Richard, and Benjamin Page. 1975. The Impact of Events on Presidential Popularity: The Johnson and Nixon Administrations. In *Perspectives on the Presidency,* ed. A. Wildavsky. Boston: Little, Brown.

Brubaker, Rogers. 1984. *The Limits of Rationality: An Essay on the Social and Moral Thought of Max Weber.* London: George Allen & Unwin.

Bryce, James. 1891. *The American Commonwealth.* New York: Macmillan.

Bulmer, Martin, Kevin Bales, and Kathryn Kish Sklar. 1991. *The Social Survey in Historical Perspective 1880–1940.* Cambridge: Cambridge University Press.

Burke, Kenneth. 1989. *On Symbols and Society.* Chicago: University of Chicago Press.

Calhoun, Craig, ed. 1992. *Habermas and the Public Sphere.* Cambridge, Mass.: M.I.T. Press.

Cantrell, Paul. 1989. Political Polling in America: A Study of Institutional Structures and Processes. Ph.D. diss., The New School for Social Research.

Cantril, Albert. 1991. *The Opinion Connection: Polling, Politics, and the Press.* Washington, D.C.: Congressional Quarterly Press.

Cavalli, Luciano. 1987. Charisma and Twentieth-Century Politics. In *Max Weber, Rationality, and Modernity,* ed. S. Lash and S. Whimster. London: Allen & Unwin.

Ceci, S. J., and E. Kain. 1982. Jumping on the Bandwagon with the Underdog: The Impact of Attitude Polls on Polling Behavior. *Public Opinion Quarterly* 26:228–42.

Childs, Harwood. 1965. *Public Opinion: Nature, Formation, and Role.* Princeton, N.J.: D. Van Nostrand.

Clergue, Helen. 1971. *The Salon: A Study of French Society and Personalities in the Eighteenth Century.* New York: Burt Franklin.

Cohen, Jean. 1972. Max Weber and the Dynamics of Rationalized Domination. *Telos* 14:63–86.

Cohen, Patricia Cline. 1982. *A Calculating People: The Spread of Numeracy in Early America.* Chicago: University of Chicago Press.

Converse, Jean. 1987. *Survey Research in the United States: Roots and Emergence, 1890–1960.* Berkeley: University of California Press.

Converse, Philip E. 1987. Changing Conceptions of Public Opinion in the Political Process. *Public Opinion Quarterly* 51:S12–S24.

Cooper, Lynn. 1974. *Policing America.* Englewood Cliffs, N.J.: Prentice-Hall.

Coser, Lewis. 1970. *Men of Ideas.* New York: Free Press.

Crespi, Irving. 1987. Surveys as Legal Evidence. *Public Opinion Quarterly* 51:84–91.

———. 1988. *Pre-Election Polling: Sources of Accuracy and Error.* New York: Russell Sage.

———. 1989. *Public Opinion, Polls, and Democracy.* Boulder, Colo.: Westview.

Dahl, Robert, and Edward Tufte. 1973. *Size and Democracy.* Stanford, Calif.: Stanford University Press.

Darnton, Robert. 1985. *The Great Cat Massacre and Other Episodes in French Cultural History.* New York: Vintage.

Davis, L. 1964. The Cost of Realism: Contemporary Restatements of Democracy. *Western Political Quarterly* 17:38.

Dicken-Garcia, Hazel. 1989. *Journalistic Standards in Nineteenth-Century America.* Madison: University of Wisconsin Press.

Dinkin, Robert. 1989. *Campaigning in America: A History of Election Practices.* Westport, Conn.: Greenwood Press.

Dreyfus, Hubert L., and Paul Rabinow. 1983. *Michel Foucault: Beyond Structuralism and Hermeneutics.* Chicago: University of Chicago Press.

DuBois, Ellen Carol. 1978. *Feminism and Suffrage: The Emergence of an Independent Women's Movement in America, 1848–1869.* Ithaca, N.Y.: Cornell University Press.

Durkheim, Émile. 1915. *The Elementary Forms of the Religious Life: A Study in Religious Sociology.* Translated by Joseph Swain. London: George Allen & Unwin.

Dutka, Solomon. 1989. Misuses of Statistics in Marketing and Media Research: What Will Happen to Research Quality in the '90s? Transcript of Proceedings of the ARF seventh annual Research Quality Workshop. New York: Advertising Research Foundation.

Easton, D. 1965. *A Systems Analysis of Political Life.* New York: Wiley.

Easton, D., and Dennis, J. 1969. *Children in the Political System: Origins of Political Legitimacy.* New York: McGraw-Hill.

Edelman, Murray. 1985. *The Symbolic Uses of Politics.* Urbana: University of Illinois Press.

Eisenstein, Elizabeth. 1979. *The Printing Press as an Agent of Change: Communications and Cultural Transformations in Early-Modern Europe.* Cambridge: Cambridge University Press.

Ellul, Jacques. 1964. *The Technological Society.* Translated by John Wilkinson. New York: Alfred A. Knopf.

Elstain, Jean. 1982. Democracy and the Qube Tube. *The Nation* (August 7–14): 108–19.

Emden, C. S. 1956. *The People and the Constitution.* London: Oxford University Press.

Emery, E., and M. Emery. 1984. *The Press and America: An Interpretive History of the Mass Media.* Englewood Cliffs, N.J.: Prentice-Hall.

Entman, Robert. 1989. *Democracy without Citizens: Media and the Decay of American Politics*. New York: Oxford University Press.

Epstein, L., and G. Strom. 1981. Election Night Projections and West Coast Turnout. *American Politics Quarterly* 9:479–91.

Evans, Sara M. 1989. *Born for Liberty: A History of Women in America*. New York: Free Press.

Firth, Raymond. 1973. *Symbols: Public and Private*. London: George Allen & Unwin.

Fite, Gilbert. 1971. Election of 1896. In *History of American Presidential Elections, 1789–1968*. ed. Arthur M. Schlesinger, Jr. New York: Chelsea House.

Foucault, Michel. 1973. *Madness and Civilization: A History of Insanity in the Age of Reason*. Translated by Richard Howard. New York: Vintage.

————. 1979. *Discipline and Punish: The Birth of the Prison*. Translated by Alan Sheridan. New York: Vintage.

————. 1980. Two Lectures. In *Power/Knowledge: Selected Interviews and Other Writings, 1972–1977*, ed. Colin Gordon. New York: Pantheon.

————. 1990. *The History of Sexuality* vol. 1. Translated by R. Hurley. New York: Vintage.

Freud, Sigmund. 1972. *A General Introduction to Psychoanalysis*. New York: Simon & Schuster.

Gallup, George, and Saul Rae. 1940. *The Pulse of Democracy: The Public Opinion Poll and How It Works*. New York: Greenwood Press.

Gerth, Hans, and C. Wright Mills. 1953. *Character and Social Structure: The Psychology of Social Institutions*. New York: Harcourt, Brace.

Ginsberg, Benjamin. 1986. *The Captive Public: How Mass Opinion Promotes State Power*. New York: Basic.

Gitlin, Todd. 1980. *The Whole World Is Watching*. Berkeley: University of California Press.

Glynn, Carroll J., and Ronald E. Ostman. 1988. Public Opinion about Public Opinion. *Journalism Quarterly* 65:299–306.

Gollin, Albert E. 1987. Polling and the News Media. *Public Opinion Quarterly* 51:586–94.

Goodman, Dena. 1989. Enlightenment Salons: The Convergence of Female and Philosophic Ambitions. *Eighteenth Century Studies* 22:329–50.

Gordon, Colin. 1987. The Soul of the Citizen: Max Weber and Michel Foucault on Rationality and Government. In *Max Weber, Rationality, and Modernity*, ed. S. Lash and S. Whimster. London: Allen & Unwin.

Gosnell, Harold. 1930. Ballot. In *The Encyclopaedia of the Social Sciences*, vol. 2, ed. E. Seligman. New York: Macmillan.

Gould, Stephen J. 1981. *The Mismeasure of Man*. New York: W. W. Norton.

Gouldner, Alvin. 1976. *The Dialectic of Ideology and Technology: The Origins, Grammar, and Future of Ideology*. New York: Oxford University Press.

Graber, Doris. 1984. *Processing the News: How People Tame the Information Tide*. New York: Longman.

Greenstein, Fred. 1965. *Children and Politics*. New Haven, Conn.: Yale University Press.

Groves, Robert M. 1989. *Survey Costs and Survey Errors*. New York: John Wiley & Sons.

Gusfield, Joseph. 1986. *Symbolic Crusade: Status Politics and the American Temperance Movement*. Urbana: University of Illinois Press.

Habermas, Jürgen. 1974. The Public Sphere: An Encyclopedia Article. *New German Critique* 1:50.

————. 1981. New Social Movements. *Telos* 49:33–37.

————. 1984. *The Theory of Communicative Action*. Translated by Thomas McCarthy. Boston: Beacon Press.

————. 1989. *The Structural Transformation of the Public Sphere: An Inquiry into a Category of Bourgeois Society*. Cambridge, Mass.: M.I.T. Press.

Hardy, Hugh. 1990. *The Politz Papers: Science and Truth in Marketing Research*. Chicago: American Marketing Association.

Hawver, Carl. 1954. The Congressman and His Public Opinion Poll. *Public Opinion Quarterly* 18:123–29.

Hayes, Michael T. 1983. Interest Groups: Pluralism or Mass Society. In *Interest Group Politics*, ed. Allan Cigler and Burdett Loomis. Washington, D.C.: Congressional Quarterly Press.

Held, David. 1987. *Models of Democracy*. Stanford, Calif.: Stanford University Press.

Henshel, R., and W. Johnston. 1987. The Emergence of Bandwagon Effects: A Theory. *Sociology Quarterly* 28:493–511.

Herrnson, Paul. 1988. *Party Campaigning in the 1980s*. Cambridge, Mass.: Harvard University Press.

Hindess, Barry. 1987. Rationality and the Characterization of Modern Society. In *Max Weber, Rationality, and Modernity*, ed. S. Lash and S. Whimster. London: Allen & Unwin.

Holcombe, A. 1925. Round Table on Political Statistics: The Measurement of Public Opinion. *American Political Science Review* 19:123–26.

Honomichl, Jack. 1982. How Much Spent on Research: Follow Me. *Advertising Age*, June 21.

Horkheimer, Max. 1972. *Critical Theory: Selected Essays*. New York: Herder & Herder.

Horkheimer, Max, and Theodor Adorno. 1987. *Dialectic of Enlightenment*. Translated by John Cumming. New York: Continuum.

Hoy, David Couzens. 1986. Power, Repression, Progress: Foucault, Lukes, and the Frankfurt School. In *Foucault: A Critical Reader*, ed. D. Hoy. New York: Basil Blackwell.

Jacobs, Herbert. 1967. To Count a Crowd. *Columbia Journalism Review* (Spring): 37–40.

Jensen, Richard. 1971. *The Winning of the Midwest: Social and Political Conflict, 1888–96*. Chicago: University of Chicago Press.

Käsler, Dirk. 1988. *Max Weber: An Introduction to His Life and Work*. Chicago: University of Chicago Press.

Keller, Morton. 1977. *Affairs of State: Public Life in Late Nineteenth Century America*. Cambridge, Mass.: Harvard University Press.

Kertzer, David I. 1988. *Ritual, Politics, and Power*. New Haven, Conn.: Yale University Press.

Key, V. O. 1961. *Public Opinion and American Democracy*. New York: Alfred A. Knopf.

Kish, Leslie. 1967. *Survey Sampling*. New York: J. Wiley.

Kornhauser, William. 1959. *The Politics of Mass Society*. New York: Free Press.

Lakoff, George. 1987. *Women, Fire, and Dangerous Things: What Categories Reveal about the Mind*. Chicago: University of Chicago Press.

Landes, Joan. 1988. *Women and the Public Sphere in the Age of the French Revolution*. Ithaca, N.Y.: Cornell University Press.

Lasch, Christopher. 1976. The Family as a Haven in a Heartless World. *Salmagundi* 35:42–55.

Lau, Richard, and David O. Sears. 1986. *Political Cognition: The Nine-*

teenth Annual Carnegie Symposium on Cognition. Hillsdale, N.J.: Lawrence Erlbaum.

Le Bon, Gustave. 1977. *The Crowd: A Study of the Popular Mind*. New York: Penguin.

Lécuyer, B., and A. Oberschall. 1968. The Early History of Social Research. In *The International Encyclopedia of the Social Sciences*, ed. David Sills. New York: Macmillan.

Levine, Donald N. 1981. Rationality and Freedom: Weber and Beyond. *Social Inquiry* 51:5–25.

Liebes, Tamar, and Elihu Katz. 1990. *The Export of Meaning: Cross-Cultural Readings of "Dallas"*. New York: Oxford University Press.

Lippmann, Walter. 1925. *The Phantom Public*. New York: Harcourt, Brace.

———. 1965. *Public Opinion*. New York: Free Press.

Locke, John. 1894. *An Essay Concerning Human Understanding*. ed. Alexander Campbell Fraser. Oxford: Clarendon Press.

Lougee, Carolyn. 1976. *La Paradis des Femmes: Women, Salons, and Stratification in Seventeenth Century France*. Princeton, N.J.: Princeton University Press.

Lukács, Georg. 1971. *History and Class Consciousness*. Translated by Rodney Livingstone. Cambridge, Mass.: M.I.T. Press.

Machiavelli, Niccolò. 1986. *The Prince*. Translated by N. H. Thompson. Buffalo, N.Y.: Prometheus.

Mackenzie, W. J. M. 1968. The Function of Elections. In *The Encyclopedia of the Social Sciences*, vol. 5, ed. D. Sills. New York: Macmillan.

Mann, Leon. 1974. Counting the Crowd: Effects of Editorial Policy on Estimates. *Journalism Quarterly* 51:278–85.

Mansbridge, Jane. 1983. *Beyond Adversary Democracy*. Chicago: University of Chicago Press.

Marcuse, Herbert. 1972. Industrialization and Capitalism. In *Max Weber and Sociology Today*, ed. Otto Stammer. New York: Harper & Row.

———. 1981. *Reason and Revolution: Hegel and the Rise of Social Theory*. New York: Oxford University Press.

———. 1982. Some Social Implications of Modern Technology. In *The Essential Frankfurt School Reader*, ed. Andrew Arato and Eike Gebhardt. New York: Continuum.

Martin, Kingsley. 1954. *The Rise of French Liberal Thought: A Study of Political Ideas from Bayle to Condorcet*. New York: New York University Press.

Mayer, J. P. 1943. *Max Weber and German Politics*. London: Faber & Faber.

Mayhew, David. 1974. *Congress: The Electoral Connection*. New Haven, Conn.: Yale University Press.

Mayo, H. 1960. *An Introduction to Democratic Theory*. New York: Oxford University Press.

McClelland, J. S. 1989. *The Crowd and the Mob: From Plato to Canetti*. London: Unwin Hyman.

McGerr, Michael. 1986. *The Decline of Popular Politics: The American North, 1865–1928*. New York: Oxford University Press.

Mead, George Herbert. 1962. *Mind, Self, and Society: From the Standpoint of a Social Behaviorist*. Chicago: University of Chicago Press.

Meadow, Robert G. 1983. Televised Campaign Debates as Whistle-Stop Speeches. In *Television Coverage of the 1980 Presidential Campaign*, ed. William C. Adams. Norwood, N.J.: Ablex.

Meier, Norman, and Harold Saunders. 1949. *The Polls and Public Opinion*. New York: Henry Holt.

Merkle, Daniel M. 1991a. The Effects of Opinion Poll Results on Public Opinion: A Review and Synthesis of Bandwagon and Underdog Research. Paper delivered at the forty-first annual conference of the International Communication Association, Chicago.

———. 1991b. The Impact of Prior Belief and Disclosure of Methods on Perceptions of Poll Data Quality and Methodological Discounting. Paper presented at the annual meeting of the Association of Education in Journalism and Mass Communication, Boston.

Meyer, Philip. 1973. *Precision Journalism: A Reporter's Introduction to Social Science Methods*. Bloomington: Indiana University Press.

Miller, Mark Crispin. 1988. *Boxed In: The Culture of TV*. Evanston: Northwestern University Press.

Miller, Peter V. 1985. The Folklore of Audience Measurement. Paper presented at the annual meeting of the Midwest Association for Public Opinion Research, Chicago.

———. 1991. Which Side Are You On? The 1990 Nicaraguan Poll "debacle." *Public Opinion Quarterly* 55: 281–302.

Miller, Peter, Daniel M. Merkle, and Paul Wang. 1991. Journalism with Footnotes: Reporting the "Technical Details" of Polls. In *Polling and Presidential Election Coverage*, ed. Paul J. Lavrakas and Jack K. Holley. Newbury Park, Calif.: Sage Publications.

Mills, C. Wright. 1961. *The Sociological Imagination.* New York: Grove Press.

Minar, David. 1960. Public Opinion in the Perspective of Political Theory. *Western Political Quarterly* 13:31–44.

Monkkonen, Eric H. 1981. *Police in Urban America, 1860–1920.* Cambridge: Cambridge University Press.

Morley, David. 1980. *The "Nationwide" Audience: Structure and Decoding.* London: British Film Institute.

Mosteller, Frederick. 1949. *The Pre-Election Polls of 1948: Report to the Committee on Analysis of Pre-Election Polls and Forecasts.* New York: Social Science Research Council.

Mott, Frank. 1968. *American Journalism, A History: 1690–1960.* New York: Macmillan.

Nathans, Benjamin. 1990. Habermas's "Public Sphere" in the Era of the French Revolution. *French Historical Studies* 16:620–44.

Noelle-Neumann, Elisabeth. 1984. *The Spiral of Silence: Public Opinion—Our Social Skin.* Chicago: University of Chicago Press.

Ozouf, Mona. 1988. "Public Opinion" at the End of the Old Regime. *Journal of Modern History* 60:S1–S21.

Page, Benjamin, and Robert Shapiro. 1991. *The Rational Public: Fifty Years of Trends in Americans' Policy Preferences.* Chicago: University of Chicago Press.

Paletz, David L., et al. 1980. Polls in the Media: Content, Credibility, and Consequences. *Public Opinion Quarterly* 44:495–513.

Palmer, Paul. 1964. The Concept of Public Opinion in Political Theory. In *Essays in History and Political Theory in Honor of Charles Howard McIlwain,* ed. C. Wittke. New York: Russell & Russell.

Papajohn, George. 1991. Numbers Serve to Prove You Can't Quantify Life. *Chicago Tribune,* 1 May, p. 18.

Parsons, Talcott. 1964. Introduction to *The Sociology of Religion,* by Max Weber. Translated by Ephraim Fischoff. Boston: Beacon Press.

Pateman, Carole. 1970. *Participation and Democratic Theory.* Cambridge: Cambridge University Press.

Pennock, J. Roland. 1979. *Democratic Political Theory.* Princeton, N.J.: Princeton University Press.

Piven, Frances Fox, and Richard A. Cloward. 1988. *Why Americans Don't Vote.* New York: Pantheon.

Platt, Anthony. 1974. *Policing America.* Englewood Cliffs, N.J.: Prentice-Hall.

Popkin, Samuel. 1991. *The Reasoning Voter: Communication and Persuasion in Presidential Campaigns.* Chicago: University of Chicago Press.

Porter, Theodore. 1986. *The Rise of Statistical Thinking: 1820–1900.* Princeton, N.J.: Princeton University Press.

Price, Warren. 1953. What Daily News Executives Think of Public Opinion Polls. *Journalism Quarterly* 30:287–99.

Quenell, Peter. 1980. *Affairs of the Mind: The Salon in Europe and America from the Eighteenth to the Twentieth Century.* Washington, D.C.: New Republic Books.

Radway, Janice. 1984. *Reading the Romance: Women, Patriarchy, and Popular Literature.* Chapel Hill: University of North Carolina Press.

Robinson, Claude. 1932. *Straw Votes: A Study of Political Prediction.* New York: Columbia University Press.

Robinson, John P., and Robert Meadow. 1982. *Polls Apart.* New York: Seven Locks Press.

Rogers, Lindsay. 1949. *The Pollsters: Public Opinion, Politics, and Democratic Leadership.* New York: Knopf.

Roper, Burns W. 1983. Some Things That Concern Me. *Public Opinion Quarterly* 47:303–9.

Ross, Dorothy. 1991. *The Origins of American Social Science.* Cambridge: Cambridge University Press.

Roth, Guenther. 1987. Rationalization in Max Weber's Developmental History. In *Max Weber, Rationality, and Modernity,* ed. S. Lash and S. Whimster. London: Allen & Unwin.

Rothenbuhler, Eric. 1985. Media Events, Civil Religion, and Social Solidarity: The Living Room Celebration of the Olympic Games. Ph.D. diss., University of Southern California.

Rousseau, Jean-Jacques. 1950. *The Social Contract and the Discourses.* Translated and edited by G. D. Cole. New York: E. P. Dutton.

Roustan, M. 1926. *The Pioneers of the French Revolution.* Boston: Little, Brown.

Routh, Harold. 1932. Steele and Addison. In *The Cambridge History of English Literature,* vol.9, ed. A. Ward and A. R. Waller. Cambridge: Cambridge University Press.

Rudé, George. 1959. *The Crowd in the French Revolution.* London: Oxford University Press.

————. 1981. *The Crowd in History: A Study of Popular Disturbances in France and England, 1730–1848.* London: Lawrence and Wishart.

Ryan, Mary. 1981. *Cradle of the Middle Class: The Family in Oneida County, New York, 1790–1865.* New York: Cambridge University Press.

————. 1990. *Women in Public: Between Banners and Ballots, 1825–1880.* Baltimore: Johns Hopkins University Press.

Sabato, Larry J. 1981. *The Rise of Political Consultants: New Ways of Winning Elections.* New York: Basic.

Salwen, Michael B. 1987. Credibility of Public Opinion Polls: Sources, Source Intent, and Precision. Paper presented at the annual meeting of the International Communication Association, Montreal.

Sapir, Edward. 1934. Symbolism. In *Encyclopaedia of the Social Sciences,* vol. 14, ed. E. Seligman. New York: Macmillan.

Schumpeter, Joseph A. 1962. *Capitalism, Socialism and Democracy,* 3d ed. New York: Harper & Row.

Seiter, Ellen, Hans Borchers, Gabrielle Kreutzner, and Maria Warth. 1991. *Remote Control: Television, Audiences, and Cultural Power.* London: Routledge.

Sennett, Richard. 1970. *Families Against the City: Middle Class Homes of Industrial Chicago, 1872–1890.* Cambridge, Mass.: Harvard University Press.

Sinclair, John. 1798. *The Statistical Account of Scotland.* Edinburgh: William Creech.

Stigler, Stephen M. 1986. *The History of Statistics: The Measurement of Uncertainty before 1900.* Cambridge, Mass.: Harvard University Press.

Smart, Barry. 1985a. *Foucault, Marxism, and Critique.* London: Routledge & Kegan Paul.

————. 1985b. *Michel Foucault.* London: Tavistock.

Smith, Tom. 1990. The First Straw? A Study of the Origins of Election Polls. *Public Opinion Quarterly* 54:21–36.

Sudman, Seymour. 1978. *Applied Sampling.* New York: Academic Press.

Sudman, Seymour, and Norman Bradburn. 1987. The Organizational Growth of Public Opinion Research in the United States. *Public Opinion Quarterly* 51:567–78.

Schudson, Michael. 1978. *Discovering the News: A Social History of American Newspapers.* New York: Basic.

Sussman, Barry. 1988. *What Americans Really Think and Why Our Politicians Pay No Attention.* New York: Pantheon.

Sussmann, Leila. 1963. *Dear FDR: A Study of Political Letter Writing.* Totowa, N.J.: Bedminster.

Taft, William H. 1986. *Encyclopedia of Twentieth-Century Journalists.* New York: Garland.

Thompson, E. P. 1971. The Moral Economy of the English Crowd in the Eighteenth Century. *Past and Present* 50:76–136.

Tilly, Charles. 1984. Speaking Your Mind without Elections, Surveys, or Social Movements. *Public Opinion Quarterly* 47:465.

Tinker, Chauncey Brewster. 1915. *The Salon and English Letters.* New York: Macmillan.

Tocqueville, Alexis de. 1969. *Democracy in America,* ed. J. P. Mayer. New York: Anchor.

Wattenberg, Martin P. 1986. *The Decline of American Political Parties, 1952–1984.* Cambridge, Mass.: Harvard University Press.

Weber, Max. 1946. Science as a Vocation. In *From Max Weber: Essays in Sociology.* Translated and edited by H. H. Gerth and C. Wright Mills. New York: Oxford.

————. 1958. *The Protestant Ethic and the Spirit of Capitalism.* Translated by Talcott Parsons. New York: Charles Scribner's Sons.

————. 1978. *Economy and Society: An Outline of Interpretive Sociology,* ed. Guenther Roth and Claus Wittich. Berkeley: University of California Press.

Wellman, Walter. 1908. The Management of the Taft Campaign. *Review of Reviews* 38:432–38.

Winner, Langdon. 1983. *Autonomous Technology: Technics-Out-of-Control as a Theme in Political Thought.* Cambridge, Mass.: M.I.T. Press.

Wheeler, Michael. 1976. *Lies, Damn Lies, and Statistics: The Manipulation of Public Opinion in America.* New York: Liveright.

Zelinsky, Wilbur. 1988. *Nation into State: The Shifting Symbolic Foundations of American Nationalism.* Chapel Hill, N.C.: University of North Carolina Press.

INDEX

Page numbers in italics refer to illustrations.

Eisenstein, Elizabeth, 51
Elites, 44, 46, 127, 168, 171
Ellul, Jacques, 47
Épinay, Madame de', 53, *54*
Essay Concerning Human Understanding, An (Locke), 45
Essay on Man, An (Cassirer), 29
Everybody's magazine, 73
Expression, 67–68, 75–76; in coffeehouses, 55–57, *58*; rationalization and, 155–57; in salons, 53–55; sample surveys and, 65–67; techniques of, 51–52. *See also* Opinion techniques; Straw polls

Federalist Papers, The, 59
Fields, James, 128
Firth, Raymond, 33–34
Flag: symbolism of, 33, 35–36, 37
Focus groups, 121, 126
Foreign trade, 9
Formal rationality. *See* Instrumental rationality
Fortune magazine, 110
Foucault, Michel, 3, 4, 8, 40, 158; *Discipline and Punish*, 20–21; *The History of Sexuality*, 22–23; *Madness and Civilization*, 22; Max Weber and, 19–20; on power, 20–24, 25; on rationalization, 20–24, 25, 180n.58
Frankfurt School, 19
French Revolution, 55
Freud, Sigmund, 30–31; "Symbolism in Dreams," 31

Gallup, George, 69–70, 83, 89, 141, 198n.22; *The Pulse of Democracy*, 45, 160–61
Gallup polls, 12, 110, 117, 127, 128, 160

General elections, 47, 57, 60, 62
General Social Survey (GSS), 123, 130
Gerth, Hans, 35, 36
Ginsberg, Benjamin, 38, 47, 62, 86, 148, 159; *The Captive Public*, 26
Gitlin, Todd, 36
Glynn, Carroll, 128–29
Gollin, Albert, 12
Great Plague, 9
Groves, Robert, 124
Guardian, The, 57

Habermas, Jürgen, 19, 46, 55, 67, 166, 184n.8
Halpine, Charles, 173
Hanna, Mark, 140
Harrisburg Pennsylvanian, 70
Harris polls, 12, 160
Hart, Peter, 121
Hawver, Carl, 91
Hayes, Carlton, 35–36
Herrnson, Paul, 120
Heteroglossia, 22, 180n.52
History of Sexuality, The (Foucault), 22–23
Horse-race, 116; polls and, 117
Hotline, 116
Hughes, Charles E., 142

Ideology: polling and, 157, 160, 199n.5; polls and, 172, 204n.52; rationalization and, 154–58
Idiosyncratic methods, 107–8
Image management, 50
Inaugural addresses, 174
Instrumental rationality, 12, 14, 18, 19, 24, 153; crowd estimation and, 148–49; polls and, 158–60; quantification and, 3, 4, 29, 30, 39–41, 107–8, 170;